Advance Praise for *When Bad Things Happen to Other People*

"*Schadenfreude* is a fascinating emotion, much neglected but obviously of great importance for practical ethics and moral psychology. Portmann's book cuts across the intersection of current emotion theory, psychology, and ethics, and invites philosophical interaction with some classic literature on some of the nastier emotions. The author is obviously well read and has a rich store of literary and philosophical examples."
—Robert C. Solomon, author of *The Joy of Philosophy*

"John Portmann has directed our attention, in a most interesting and helpful way, to the neglected emotion of *Schadenfreude*. Whether the reader accepts or rejects Portmann's conclusions, the journey through his discussion provides wonderful insights. Not only is his book instructive on its own terms, but it will also help to open the door to further reflection on this and other neglected emotions."
—James F. Childress, co-author of *Principles of Biomedical Ethics*

"That we should have had to wait this long for a book-length study of *Schadenfreude* — the 'purest joy,' as a dubious German saying would have it — shows how difficult we find it to take an honest look at ourselves. . . . Portmann's readable study of an all-too-common phenomenon casts new light on the morality of our emotions, challenging some of our most deeply entrenched preconceptions."
—Karsten Harries, author of *The Ethical Function of Architecture*

"When we laugh at slapstick comedy or delight in others' getting their painful just deserts, we are feeling *Schadenfreude*. Given the cultural premium placed on compassion and the love commandment, what are we to think morally of ourselves when we experience this all-too-human guilty pleasure? In this original and wide-ranging book, Portmann challenges philosophical and theological condemnations of *Schadenfreude* and offers intriguing and sometimes unsettling reflections on suffering, divine and earthly punishment, compassion, and liberal tolerance."
—Cheshire Calhoun, co-editor of *What is an Emotion?*

When Bad Things
Happen to Other People

John Portmann

Routledge
New York and London

Published in 2000 by
Routledge
29 West 35th Street
New York, NY 10001

Published in Great Britain by
Routledge
11 New Fetter Lane
London EC4P 4EE

Frontispiece: Georges de La Tour, *The Fortune Teller* (17th century, France). Courtesy of The Metropolitan Museum of Art, Rogers Fund, XXXX 1960. (60.30) Photograph © 1982 The Metropolitan Museum of Art

Library of Congress Cataloging-in-Publication Data

Portmann, John.
    When bad things happen to other people / John Portmann.
      p. cm.
    Includes bibliographical references.
    ISBN 0-415-92334-4 (alk. paper).
     1. Suffering—Moral and ethical aspects. 2. Pleasure—Moral and ethical aspects. 3. Sympathy—Moral and ethical aspects.
    I. Title
    BJ1409.P67 1999
    248.4—dc21
                                                 99-26106
                                                        CIP

What a wee little part of a person's life are his acts
and his words! His real life is led in his head,
and is known to none but himself.

—Mark Twain

Contents

Acknowledgments

GAYATRI PATNAIK AND BILL GERMANO WARMLY WELCOMED ME TO Routledge. Their judicious suggestions and unswerving enthusiasm propelled me through the final round of revisions. Finding them at the end of two years of reflection on suffering brought me joy.

Many of our most penetrating thinkers in the West have pondered the central themes in this book — pleasure, malice, justice, punishment, compassion — and my debt to them is very great. Knowing when to footnote requires good judgment, and I hope I have done justice to those now dead.

Some of my scholarly debts are to the living. Exploring our emotional reactions to the bad things that happen to other people led me to Aaron Ben-Ze'ev and Jerome Neu, two philosophers who graciously shared with me their rich insights into the morality of the emotions. Their various objections to and reservations about an earlier draft shaped the scope of this work.

I appreciate the goodwill and useful comments of friends who took the time to read through the manuscript. Paul Barolsky, James Childress, Elizabeth A. Clark, Matthew Crosby, Jessica Feldman, Eugene Rogers, Richard Rorty, Robert Scharlemann, Patricia Meyer Spacks, and Daniel Westberg have my gratitude. Emma Cobb suggested the title just before I finished writing and urged me to leave behind my own, which she found drab. Andrew Solomon, the pride of our Yale class, carried the unbound tome with him through Africa and offered copious improvements. David Cartwright read the chapter on Nietzsche, Brian Hebblethwaite the chapter on God, and Virginia Germino went over every word with loving solicitude. Diane Gibbons copyedited the manuscript with great skill. Each of these readers has disagreed with me in some way, and I value the challenges they have set before me.

Cynthia Read breathed life into this project. Her measured criticism of earlier drafts encouraged me along the way.

More than anyone else, Daniel Ortiz inspired and supported me throughout my research. To express fully my gratitude to him would require more space than I have here. Dedicating this book to him will have to suffice.

The Sometimes Sweet Suffering of Others

WE SUFFER. IN VARIOUS WAYS AND TO VARYING DEGREES, WE SUFFER.
Do we deserve to suffer? If not, then why do we suffer? And what, if anything, does our suffering mean?

Though answers to these perennial questions elude us, we have not stopped wondering if we are to blame for our hardships. For many centuries very different kinds of people have believed that God, or some all-knowing cosmic force, causes us to suffer after we sin. Not long ago Rabbi Harold Kushner tried to assure us that God does not operate like this: it is not because we are bad people that we suffer, for bad things can happen even to good people. Much suffering happens randomly, Kushner urged us to accept, and has nothing to do with cosmic justice. Kushner's message, by no means an original one in the late twentieth century, landed his book *When Bad Things Happen to Good People* on the best-seller lists.

What about the bad things that happen to *other* people? The doubts we have about our own goodness pale in comparison to the doubts we entertain about the goodness of others. Especially when we think about others with whom we have nothing in common, skeptical thoughts colonize our minds. We are more likely to view the misfortunes of others as deserved than we are our own. Even when we do not genuinely believe that someone else deserves his suffering, we may try to convince ourselves he does.

This book concerns how we *feel* about the bad things that happen to other people, not what we *do* about them. As such, this book concerns character, not conduct. Curiously, some moral philosophers have insisted that a person's character and emotions don't merit much attention. Kant and his many followers tend to see conduct as all-important. It's not how we feel about other people that matters, it's how we *treat* other people. I disagree. With Aristotle, Schopenhauer, and Nietzsche, I view a person's character and emotions as compelling subjects of moral study.

Our emotional responses to the misfortunes of others can tell us much about our characters. Some of our most revered moralists have insisted that virtually everyone feels sympathy when bad things happen to other people, for being human means being sympathetic to others. This cheery position seems to *require* us to feel sympathy for people who suffer, which I see as a problem. For nothing undermines sympathy more than the requirement to feel it. (The indiscriminate yearning to feel sympathy, a form of sentimentality, comes in a close second.) Sympathy either comes to us uninvited or not at all.

Other, less cheery thinkers have roundly rejected the idea that to be human is to feel sympathy for others. This crucial discrepancy signals trouble ahead: if we cannot agree about whether people naturally sympathize with others, we will not be able to acknowledge, much less evaluate, people who celebrate the bad things that happen to others.

We are surrounded by people who take pleasure in our misfortunes. Nietzsche and Freud agreed on this and constructed philosophical arguments around what they took to be the frequently selfish motives of people caught up in moral deliberations. Although I am less cynical than they, I believe Nietzsche, Freud, and others who agree with them describe our emotional lives much better than anyone else. I also believe that the fears of our moralists have much to teach us about how to get along well with others.

We do well to appear sympathetic generally. This may be difficult when we feel indifferent to the bad things that happen to others. In indifference we do not engage with those who suffer in any way. We simply do not care about their setbacks, or cannot be bothered by their misfortunes. We may feel that we have to save our limited sympathy for someone who merits it more, or we may feel that time constraints prevent us from thinking much about the suffering of another.

Sometimes we pretend to sympathize with others when we don't, because we are taking out a sort of insurance policy to cover our own needs when disaster strikes us. Pretending to be sorry remains a permanent possibility for all of us, which complicates human relations. It seems in our best interest to appear benevolent toward those around us: doing so increases the likelihood that others will help us get what we want, or at least decreases the chances that others will disrupt our plans. Faking our feelings comes at a cost, though: we wonder whether others might be doing it too when they comfort us.

It can be difficult indeed to *make* ourselves feel as we think we ought to feel. Saying "I'm sorry" is easier than feeling sorry, even though many people consider "sorry" the hardest word to say. Nonetheless, sorrow may at times seem simply impossible, for it can feel wonderful to learn that something bad has happened to someone else. Even Kant, who believes we are all inclined to feel sympathy toward others, admits this much, writing in the *Critique of Practical Reason*:

> When, however, someone who delights in annoying and vexing peace-loving folk receives at last a right good beating, it is certainly an ill, but everyone approves of it and considers it as good in itself even if nothing further results from it; nay, even he who gets the beating must acknowledge, in his reason, that justice has been done to him, because he sees the proportion between welfare and well-doing, which reason inevitably holds before him, here put into practice.[1]

Kant does not state in this passage that *all* people deserve to suffer, but even the claim that *some* people deserve to suffer can set us to arguing. It might be thought that a stiff Protestant moralist such as Kant would advocate tirelessly forgiving everyone, even annoying neighbors (this is what Jesus exhorts his followers to do). However, even Kant's patience has its limits.

Kant's thinking in this passage raises a vexing question: does permission to "approve" of the suffering of other people amount to permission to *celebrate* it? Not exactly. Kant's moral psychology resembles that of Augustine, St. Thomas Aquinas, and some modern moral philosophers: love the sinner, hate the sin. It is not the suffering of others that brings us joy, but rather the evidence of justice triumphing before our eyes. Through this crucial difference Kant can think of himself not as a malicious person, but a virtuous one.

Michelangelo depicted this pleasure in *The Last Judgment*, perhaps the most famous painting in the West. As we raise our eyes above the sinners suffering horribly in hell, we see a joyful group of angels. Looking beneath them at the damned, the angels blow trumpets in jubilation. One of the angels brandishes the tablets of the law as if to say to the damned, "See, you're getting what you deserve." Another artistic depiction of Kant's pleasure can be found in an arresting and highly unusual painting of the Crucifixion by the Norwegian painter Edvard Munch. *Golgotha*, which contains autobiographical elements, includes a couple of prominent onlookers who smile with delight. One of them looks directly at us. It is surprisingly rare in paintings of the Crucifixion for a witness in the crowd to engage us so openly in his approval of Christ's suffering, even though we know that plenty of onlookers that day believed Jesus received exactly what he deserved. These are presumably some of the same people whose misery the angels celebrate in Michelangelo's masterpiece, the spiritual core of the Sistine Chapel.

We often believe, as Kant seems to in this passage, that bad people cause trouble for themselves. We may view misfortunes as the appropriate consequences of imprudence, stupidity, incompetence, bad judgment, or evil. Good people love justice; loving justice is a virtue. When bad things happen to bad people, the world seems to be working fine.

When *we* suffer, we may fear that others think we deserve to suffer. The harsh judgment of others only increases our suffering. And so, we may cringe when we read of Kant's confidence that a man who suffers will agree with others that he deserves to suffer (Anna Freud was later to classify such feelings as a neurosis, "identifying with the aggressor"). As we grow older and get to know suffering better, we may find that we have to overcome something slightly dreadful when we resolve to hold someone else guilty for his or her suffering. Reassuring ourselves that we are good even when we approve of the suffering of others may lead us to tell ourselves a story such as Kant tells himself.

Disagreement about suffering — what it is, who deserves it, and how much — divides us deeply. Schopenhauer asserts that mental afflictions hurt much worse than physical ones — he even suggests that we slap, burn, or puncture our bodies when mental afflictions beset us. The resulting physical pain, he counsels, will serve as a good distraction from the horror of mental suffering. We might argue at length over whether mental suffering hurts more than physical pain, but we will all agree that suffering deserves our attention. Surprisingly, Schopenhauer was the first Western philosopher since the ancient Greeks to ponder suffering at length. Following Schopenhauer, I focus here on mental or spiritual tribulations and neglect torture and sadism.

Schopenhauer and Kant both understand that what other people think of us can make us suffer or increase our suffering. A black slave in the novel *Beloved*, by the American writer Toni Morrison, silently endures decades of cruelty at the hands of white people, only to announce shortly before her death what she had at last learned from sixty years as a slave and ten years as a free woman: there is no such thing as bad luck in the world, only white people. She restates Sartre's famous line from the play *Huis clos* "Hell is other people" (*"L'enfer, c'est les autres"*). Baby Suggs, Morrison's fictional slave, does not believe that she has deserved the bad things that have happened to her. More to the point, she affirms that *people are a part of the bad things that happen to others*. Deliberately excluding natural catastophes such as hurricanes, I will argue that we are ourselves the bad things that happen to other people — living in community virtually requires us to be so. All of us share responsibility for the social world we constitute; we share reponsibility for many of the bad things that happen to other people. We do well to regret that we are a part of the bad things that happen to other people, but not to deny it.

Character drives judgments of whether other people deserve to suffer. That we may disagree with the moral viewpoints of people who suffer leads to the question of how sensitive we should be to other moral viewpoints. Two centuries after Kant, there is something deeply dissatisfying about the *Zeitgeist* according to which we ought to embrace different moral stances as wonderful, if exasperating, examples of cultural diversity. This *Zeitgeist* is a subset of the notion that we owe everyone compassion. It is easy to prescribe compassion for every tear another sheds, so easy that our own displays of compassion may strike us as perfunctory and hollow. Those who demonize taking pleasure in others' misfortunes find in the cultivation of an ideal of compassion a defense against the idea that we cause others to suffer by pursuing our own private goals and projects.

That we can have mistaken and pernicious beliefs is no objection to the claim that we take what we believe to be true. The world remains full of people who believe that Jews, gays, and blacks, for example, deserve persecution, physical assault, or segregation. By discerning and clarifying beliefs about what people deserve, we gain better access to a culture's general idea of what kinds of suffering deserve sympathy and, accordingly, of what a good person's character should include or exclude. The ways people think about the suffering of others in any given era contain fascinating glimpses of important cultural forces we cannot plainly see or perfectly control.

In our own time, there would be few court battles or wars if those who suffered simply accepted their plights as deserved. Nietzsche showed how easily we persuade ourselves that anyone who competes with us for a good job, an attractive mate, or a comfortable home is a bad person in some real sense. Nietzsche thought lofty ideas about social justice were just thinly disguised rationalizations for revenge. This cynicism undermines belief in our moral goodness as civilized people. Our insistence that some people really do deserve their misfortunes presents a real problem, in part because the rules and conventions that determine who deserves what change over time and, moreover, regularly provoke disagreements within a society and across nations.

However imperfectly, we distinguish between trivial and serious misfortunes. In comedy, for example, we laugh at what we take to be the trivial misfortunes of others. In tragedy, however, we could scarcely conceive of laughing. What we think about justice guides our emotional responses. Just as people disagree about justice, so do they disagree over separating the trivial from the profound.

Most of us will allow ourselves in good conscience to laugh at the minor embarrassments of others. Consider banana peels. Someone slips on a banana peel and an audience erupts in laughter. Cartoonists have deployed this familiar image of an unsuspecting person flailing and falling to great comical effect. And yet Schopenhauer and other moralists have insisted on the immorality of taking pleasure in *any* misfortune another person suffers. This very serious view makes some sense, for the pleasure of comedy frequently arises from the defects, failures, or absurdity of another person or of other groups of people. *The Name of the Rose,* by the Italian semiotician and novelist Umberto Eco, played off of and dramatized the vague apprehension of evil in all laughter. Not just Roman

Catholic monks of the Middle Ages in Eco's novel, but a variety of other thinkers as well have detected shades of the diabolic in comedy. Not surprisingly, some of our own laughter may lead us to question the robustness of our compassion for others.

The laughter cartoonists elicit through slips and falls turns on a belief in the triviality of some misfortunes. If there were such a thing as trivial misfortune, then taking pleasure in it might be an aesthetic matter akin to worries over taste, manners, and modes of self-presentation. Those who laugh might defend themselves by saying that morality does not or should not descend into triviality. Triviality certainly does suggest limits to the reasonableness of moral inquiry. Laughter at even the harmless slips and falls of others, however, raises important questions about both the starting-point and the structure of justice, guilt, blame, responsibility, and benevolence.

We still struggle to cope with suffering — our own or anyone else's. Although he died over a century ago, I take Schopenhauer to represent a powerful, conservative moral current in the contemporary West. He vehemently denies that there is such thing as a trivial misfortune. He warns us in *The World as Will and Representation* that we should expel from our communities anyone ever caught taking pleasure in the injury of others. He asks us how, if we take morality seriously, can we both love our neighbor and laugh when he falls? A profoundly difficult question finds a simple answer: play it safe, treat all suffering as though it were a sickness unto death. Surely Schopenhauer's solution must be wrong-headed, even though it is impossible to draw a clean line between trivial and non-trivial suffering. His position tempts us to a quick and easy resolution, for his denial of triviality in the realm of suffering circumvents the pressing need for a way to distinguish minor from significant misfortunes.

Schopenhauer carefully insists that the only pleasure we may take in the bad things that happen to other people is in the triumph of justice. Religious thinkers and moral philosophers have thought that the object of our pleasure — someone else's suffering or justice — makes all the difference to moral evaluation of our emotions. Indeed, we are all expected to love justice. Think here of the first Psalm in the Hebrew Bible, where we read, "Happy are those who do not follow the advice of the wicked . . . *their delight is in the law of the Lord, and on his law they meditate day and night*" (my emphasis). Change the "law of the Lord" to "the law of morality" and Schopenhauer the atheist agrees enthusiastically.

The justice people sought in biblical disputes and early courts took as their model the justice God metes out for mortals. Various creeds have endorsed an ideal of justice according to which God punishes the sinful. Religious believers aim to imitate God when they make decisions about the appropriateness of suffering. Can such an undertaking ever succeed? It is difficult to say. According to a negative view of human motivation (for example, Hobbes, Nietzsche, and Freud), beliefs about justice serve the interests of the person who holds them. According to a positive view (for example, Kant and Schopenhauer), people hold beliefs without regard to personal benefits. (It is of course possible that disinterested justice and self-interest may sometimes coincide.) We can assure ourselves that we are good people if the pleasure we take in others' misfortunes has nothing to do with ourselves and everything to do with God. Religious believers can circumvent the same apprehension of evil many thinkers have located in laughter by attributing their pleasure to the recognition of divine justice, not to the ugly enjoyment of another human being's suffering.

In most of the modern world, beliefs and principles are more prevalent forms of aggression toward others than physical attacks. In the subtlety of these beliefs and principles lies a conviction that many of the bad things which happen to others are appropriate and that at least some of our pleasure in that suffering is moral. The principles and beliefs by which we organize our lives and make sense of the world lead us into frequently invisible conflict with people who do not share our principles and beliefs. Aversion to sexual promiscuity or sex between men, for example, may lead us to think of someone bearing the visible scars of syphilis or AIDS, "He deserves that." Cancer is an even better test of how we work out the "game" of who deserves what. Other people know that our views about appropriate suffering may someday affect them personally; not surprisingly, other people may try to dissuade us of our belief that their suffering, or the kind of suffering they are likely to experience, is appropriate.

A troublesome notion of moral appropriateness emerges as both the solution and the problem here. The Cambridge philosopher C.D. Broad asserted, "It is inappropriate to cognize what one takes to be a fellow man *in undeserved pain or distress* with *satisfaction* or with *amusement* [his emphases]."[2] He found this matter "plainly of the utmost importance to ethics and to esthetics," and lamented that it still awaited an adequate analysis. Several years later the Berkeley sociologist Arlie Russell Hochschild issued a similar call: "We need to ask how different sexes, classes, and ethnic and religious groups differ in the sense of what one 'ought to' or 'has the right to' feel in a situation."[3] And ten years after her advice, Richard Rorty concluded a study of human suffering by asserting that "detailed descriptions of particular varieties of pain and humiliation," rather than philosophical or religious treatises, are "the modern intellectual's principal contributions to moral progress."[4] Moral progress comes down to clarifying and testing our notions of the appropriateness of suffering.

Moral philosophers invoke a standard of appropriateness frequently and with varying success, as in discussions of sexuality, just war, or capital punishment. This tendency extends far into the past, certainly back to Plato's *Republic,* in which descriptions of the good life hinge on proportionality. Judgments about both appropriate and trivial suffering depend on judgments about proportionality. No one has managed yet to produce an algorithm for deciding just what suffering is appropriate and what is not.

A decision in the abstract could hardly be of much use; we must attend to the nature of the relationship between the sufferer and the judger. The same is true in comedy, where a joke's success depends on appropriateness: it would be unwise to tell Polish jokes to Polish people, or "dumb blond" jokes to a blond person. Were a blond person to tell the "dumb blond" joke, however, the humor might well seem appropriate. We notice the attitude of the person who tells the joke and take that into consideration before reacting to the joke. We laugh *with* people when we include ourselves among those being laughed at. Determining whether we laugh with others or at them requires self-awareness. And so our sense of where we fit into the world surfaces when we react emotionally to the bad things that happen to other people.

A person who detests Polish people might fail to make us laugh at a hilarious joke about someone Polish. By the same token, we might react with revulsion to a judge who invites a murder victim's father to pull the switch on the murderer. Justice affects our emotions, despite the reluctance of philosophers to admit as much. The emotions, many philosophers have insisted, should have nothing to do with justice. But they do.

In the course of defending some of the pleasure that comes from others' suffering, I want to question whether modern justice differs from primitive revenge. If our ideal of justice is not itself entirely moral, then neither is our pleasure that justice has been served when bad things happen to other people.

What if this distinction between justice and revenge were just a fantasy? Or bad faith? Then it would be impossible to find a moral defense for taking pleasure in the misfortunes of others. I don't think there is much difference between enjoying that someone suffers and enjoying that justice is being served (through his suffering), and yet I allow that there is *some* difference. Ultimately, it is a vital difference, one that keeps our justice system in business. This difference — or the possibility of difference — makes pleasure in the misfortunes of others morally acceptable. My own sense, which could hardly be proven in empirical terms, is that most pleasure in the misfortunes of others includes *both* objects — knowledge that another suffers deservedly *and* the suffering itself. For this reason my defense of pleasure in others' misfortunes is an ambivalent one.

My examination of pain and humiliation contributes to moral progress by straining and clarifying conventional standards of the appropriateness of suffering. The point of this inquiry is not to extend the range of permissible hatred by legitimizing emotional cruelty around transgressions of divine law and grave offenses against the state. Rather, the point is to show that those who feel joy when bad things happen to other people can claim they do not feel hatred at all, but rather love for justice. If Kant could speak to us, he would surely tell us that the passage quoted above testifies to his revulsion to injustice, not to any kind of malice.

The distinction between taking pleasure in the suffering of another and taking pleasure in the execution of justice will lead to a discussion of how societies make sense of prisons and institutional punishment. Justifications for penal codes help explain how we can think ourselves high-minded advocates of justice rather than vengeful primitives when we take pleasure in the execution of, say, a serial killer. The distinction relies on finding a moral difference between pleasure which derives from our own well-being and pleasure which stems from the well-being of others.

My exploration of demonized pleasure has been motivated in part by a desire to understand the sensibility of people who routinely seek out stories of tragedy or betrayal among public figures. If there is no such thing as morally acceptable pleasure in others' misfortunes, then we should feel guilty when we relish the sudden reversals of good fortune we hear about on television or read about in the newspapers. We stand guilty of malice, because any pleasure in the misfortune of another is immoral.

Our culture both encourages and thwarts pleasure in the misfortunes of others. These mixed messages can generate terrible anxiety, some of which I aim to dispel.

Key to Abbreviations

Sigmund Freud	CD	*Civilization and Its Discontents*
	FI	*The Future of an Illusion*
	JR	*Jokes and Their Relation to the Unconscious*
Immanuel Kant	MM	*The Metaphysics of Morals*
	LE	*Lectures on Ethics*
	OFBS	*Observations on the Feeling of the Beautiful and the Sublime*
Friedrich Nietzsche	A	*The Anti-Christ*
	BGE	*Beyond Good and Evil*
	EH	*Ecce, Homo*
	GM	*On the Genealogy of Morals*
	HH	*Human, All Too Human*
	WP	*The Will to Power*
	Z	*Thus Spake Zarathustra*
Arthur Schopenhauer	OBM	*On the Basis of Morality*
	WWR	*The World as Will and Representation*

I

When Pretty Bad Things
Happen to Other People

THESE CHAPTERS CONSIDER THE MORALITY OF TAKING pleasure in others' misfortunes. The main point I try to establish is that this emotional response stands on social standards of moral appropriateness. When it does not rise from convictions about social justice, the pleasure is not necessarily malicious: low self-esteem, for example, should slow us from a hasty condemnation of those who inappropriately celebrate the woes of other people.

Beyond that, comedy complicates our intentions to treat other people well. Appreciation for the comical may signal a willingness to work out moral ambiguity by playing; in comedy we try out attitudes to other people without really knowing where those attitudes will lead. Comedy deserves moral tolerance, for an explorer's attitude differs from an assailant's.

Finally, we disguise this demonized pleasure for reasons that raise questions both about our sincerity and about the sophistication of the communities we inhabit.

One

Much Ado about Nothing?

THE GERMANS HAVE COINED A WORD FOR PLEASURE IN THE MISFORTUNES of other people: *Schadenfreude*. The idea of such pleasure horrified R.C. Trench, whom the *Oxford English Dictionary* identifies as the first person to use the word *Schadenfreude* in English. Trench, an English archbishop, concluded in 1852 that the very availability of a word for "the joy of another's injury" would taint all of a culture that relied on that language. It was as though all German speakers carried an infection, just by virtue of their linguistic resources. Trench worried that the infection might spread to English speakers.

Trench succeeded in persuading at least one editor for the *Oxford English Dictionary*. Unlike the *Oxford English Dictionary*, most American and German lexicons do not associate *Schadenfreude* with malice. Because English already included the word "malice" at the time of Trench's writing, *Schadenfreude* stood for something even worse.

The *Oxford English Dictionary* also runs together *Schadenfreude* and cruelty. According to the *OED*, cruelty is "the quality of being cruel; disposition to inflict suffering; delight in or indifference to the pain or misery of others; mercilessness, hardheartedness: *esp.* as exhibited in action." On this point C.D. Broad demonstrated a much deeper understanding of cruelty than the *OED*, for he left moral evaluation of pleasure in others' misfortunes open to the notion of appropriateness — both with respect to the just deserts of the sufferer and the degree of suffering involved.

Since Trench, scholars have disagreed about how to translate *Schadenfreude* into English. In a footnote to his translation of Nietzsche's *On the Genealogy of Morals*,[1] Walter Kaufmann claims that Arthur Danto's *Nietzsche as Philosopher*[2] features numerous mistranslations. Kaufmann asserts that there is no English equivalent for *Schadenfreude* and that Danto errs in rendering it as either "the wicked pleasure in the beholding of suffering" (p. 181) or "in the sheer spectacle of suffering: in fights, executions, . . . bullbaiting, cockfights, and the like" (p. 174). Against Danto, Kaufmann insists, "In such contexts the word is utterly out of place; it signifies the petty, mischievous delight felt in the discomfiture of another human being." I agree with Kaufmann that English has no equivalent for *Schadenfreude*. Though Kaufmann does well to eliminate the notion of wickedness from *Schadenfreude*, he fails to make room for the notion of desert, or deservedness, at the heart of *Schadenfreude*. True, *Schadenfreude* does signify petty mischievousness at the shallow end of the spectrum; toward the deeper end, though, *Schadenfreude* can center on quite significant misfortunes (or so I will argue in Part Two).

Danto considers this pleasure wicked; Kaufmann does not. How should we regard the moral status of *Schadenfreude*? To the extent that *Schadenfreude* signifies love of justice or repugnance to injustice, this emotion is a virtue. Aristotle tells us that every virtue is in the middle between two vices; the virtue represents a "golden mean." But for Aristotle, not every vice is a matter of degree. For example, all adultery and all assault are wrong, even once in a while. Envy and spite are wrong emotions, no matter when you feel them. The very words "adultery" and "spite" indicate that they are wrong, unlike "sex" and "anger," which are in many circumstances perfectly acceptable *(Nichomachean Ethics* 1107a8–27). Likewise, pleasure in the misfortunes of others in various circumstances is morally acceptable. Only we ourselves can know whether we have hit the mean, that is to say, whether we feel *Schadenfreude*, as opposed to envy or malicious glee. "*Schadenfreude*," unlike "spite" or "adultery," is morally acceptable. It lies between the vices of envy and cruelty and easily unsettles us by its proximity to both.

Naming pleasure in the misfortunes or suffering of others underscores the extent to which language is conventional. Conventions do not undermine meaning by making it arbitrary; instead, conventions give life to meaning. This is to say that I am not arbitrarily choosing an idiosyncratic definition of *Schadenfreude* in order to validate my defense of it: *Schadenfreude* is not a word I have coined. Different kinds of English speakers already believe that *Schadenfreude* rides on the coat-tails of justice and that this is much as it should be. The account of *Schadenfreude* I develop here may surprise native German speakers, but what I seek to provide is not an etymological sketch but a moral evaluation of the emotion.

Given that the word *Schadenfreude* is German, one might well ask at the outset whether Germans hold that what it names is evil. Even though a simple glance at German dictionaries should readily confirm that they do not usually associate the emotion with the diabolical, caution is in order. There is the real danger that we will simply misunderstand the Germans or be led to think of them as far too much or far too little like us, because the ways we think about them may function to confirm our personal prejudices. I know of no German study of the moral status of *Schadenfreude*, and it is entirely possible that a scholarly German might say that I have pressed too hard on the word, particularly in insisting on a crucial notion of desert at the heart of the emotion. If nothing else, we can use the German word to challenge and rethink our own ambivalence about the misfortunes of others.

I rely principally on Schopenhauer, Nietzsche, Freud, and the moral theologian Bernard Häring to think through *Schadenfreude*. Native German speakers all, they individually take human suffering as the organizing focus of their work (this is not to say that I will provide an elaborate analysis of any of these thinkers; throughout this project I focus on the relevant claims of various philosophers, rather than attempting to do full justice to any single thinker). An unabating curiosity about suffering drives Schopenhauer's contention that philosophical reflection derives from "the sight of the *evil and wickedness* in the world. Not merely that the world exists, but still more that it is such a miserable and melancholy world is the tormenting problem of metaphysics."[3] Schopenhauer faults his predecessors for distancing themselves from the prevalence and urgency of human suffering. Nietzsche, who initially thought of himself as a successor to Schopenhauer, similarly works to stomp out the raging fire of human suffering. An absorbing preoccupation with human suffering unifies the vast work of Freud, who famously claims in the early *Studies on Hysteria* (1895) that his therapeutic goal is to replace hysterical suffering with common unhappiness. Häring, a Catholic priest who played an important role in the Second Vatican Council (1962–1965), strove to eliminate the suffering caused by opposing religious groups.

There is good reason to enlist the help of a religious believer to think through *Schadenfreude*, as religious writers have devoted much more energy to exploring human suffering than have philosophical ones. Only the Roman Catholic Church and Calvinism profess a belief in (their own respective) divinely ordained priesthood, and so caution is in order here. It would doubtless be a mistake to take what Häring has to say about either suffering or *Schadenfreude* as broadly representative of religious thinkers. Häring's is just one view, albeit an influential one. Häring is useful in part because he would have united Schopenhauer, Nietzsche, and Freud in contempt for himself.

People everywhere suffer in a myriad of different ways and for many different reasons. Everyone suffers at least occasionally and usually welcomes solace from suffering. *Schadenfreude* represents one form of solace in a pain-filled existence. Although it is conceivable that a person might enjoy his or her own suffering (as in grief, remorse, masochism, and guilt), I focus on extrinsic suffering (that is, the suffering of others) and the corresponding solace it offers.

I will turn now to an autobiographical confession of *Schadenfreude*. Through it, I hope to illustrate what I consider trivial misfortune.

Kafka's Examination of Conscience

Franz Kafka, a writer whose emotional acuity justifies the exemplification of his use of German, delights in the embarrassment of his sister in the autobiographical *Brief an den Vater* (*Letter to Father*). Writing it at the age of 36, with only five more years to live as a result of tuberculosis, Kafka struggles eloquently to come to terms with his oppressive father. Here Kafka describes his father's mistreatment of a sister:

> . . . for example Elli, at whom I was angry for years. I enjoyed a feast of malice and *Schadenfreude* when it was said of her at almost every meal, "She has to sit ten meters away from the table, the fat girl" and when you, maliciously sitting on your chair without the slightest trace of being a friend, a bitter enemy, would exaggeratedly imitate the way she sat, which you found utterly loathsome.[4]

Shortly thereafter, Kafka remarks that his father's expenditure of anger and malice did not fit its object. The judgment of inappropriateness ultimately supports the blame Kafka levels at his father.

We can safely follow Kafka in thinking of Elli's suffering as fairly trivial, despite the troubling image of "a bitter enemy" on the battlefield. Part of the great value of Kafka's examination of conscience is that it illustrates by its ambiguity the difficulty of analyzing *Schadenfreude*. Pivotal issues that Kafka's passage raises but does not definitively resolve include 1) the idea that *Schadenfreude* is just another word for malice; 2) the idea that, though different from malice, *Schadenfreude* presupposes it; 3) the importance of what others think we deserve; 4) the moral import of the kind of suffering that gives rise to *Schadenfreude*; and 5) the relationship of *Schadenfreude* to cruelty. I will turn to these points now and conclude that Kafka does not reveal himself to be malicious or evil.

1. The identification of *Schadenfreude* with malice

First of all, Kafka does not define *Schadenfreude*. But he juxtaposes *Bösheit* (which can be translated as either "anger" or, more appropriately, "malice," given his purposeful recourse to *Zorn* ["anger"] to emphasize that he means malice) with *Schadenfreude* in a way that distinguishes between them. Malice, generally speaking, is (a) a disposition to injure others and/or (b) to wish that injury occurs to them. Note that malice includes both an active (a) and a passive (b) element. Malice, which I will examine in closer detail shortly, may or may not involve a determination of what others deserve.

The *"und"* of *"Bösheit und Schadenfreude"* (in the original German) unites the two terms but also emphasizes that they are distinct. Some writers, particularly those of poetic bents, might use synonyms in a way that other writers, particularly those of philosophical bents, might construe as unnecessarily repetitive. For example, we might read of somone's "fear and trembling" or of her "sorrow and misery." Kafka's writing throughout the letter suggests a careful articulation of charges against his father. Recounting his father's sins, Kafka strives more to define experience than to embellish it.

Of course, *Schadenfreude* could be a subset of malice, in which case Kafka's avowal would be somewhat tautologous, in the way that the statement "Elisabeth is a woman and a mother" is. Because all mothers are by definition women, it is unnecessary to specify the sex of a mother, which is built into its concept. Analogously, it would be unnecessary to include mention of malice in a reference to *Schadenfreude* if all *Schadenfreude* were malice.

Kafka does not identify *Schadenfreude* with malice. The best way to make sense of his careful use of *Schadenfreude* in this passage is to understand him as referring to his own pleasure in the trivial suffering of his sister Elli. Kafka may take part in his sister's trivial suffering, but he does not exactly *cause* it — Herr Kafka does that (his father is the malicious one, Kafka seems to say). Here we run up against the question of whether those who do not cause another to suffer but take pleasure in that suffering deserve as much blame as those who cause the suffering they celebrate. Thinkers are divided on this question, as I will show in time. For now, suffice it to say that two different approaches prevent us from having to answer that question, or at least from having to answer it here. If we agreed that Elli's suffering was trivial, we wouldn't much care about the answer. If we believed that Elli deserved her comeuppance, then we might say that distinguishing between Kafka and his father here only distracts from Elli's faults. Either one of these justifications for taking pleasure in the injury of another may seem unfeeling or harsh. And yet few of us will deny that we rely from time to time on these same justifications in a non-malicious way.

Even someone who agrees that *Schadenfreude* and malice are not identical may object that *Schadenfreude* presupposes malice. Let's see what can be inferred from Kafka.

2. A presupposition of malice

In her 1996 translation of Kant's *The Metaphysics of Morals*, Mary Gregor consistently renders the German *"Schadenfreude"* as "malice." Though this must be considered an important error, Gregor might reasonably try to defend herself by maintaining that Kant himself seems to view *Schadenfreude*, like the envy and ingratitude with which he associates it, as presupposing malice. A discrepancy between Kant and Kafka emerges here.

Briefly put, malice signifies the intention to harm another person or the wish that another person suffer harm. Kafka's implicit belief that his own blameworthiness (for *Schadenfreude*) was of a different kind than his father's blameworthiness (for malice) only makes sense if *Schadenfreude* does not presuppose malice. The text gives no more reason to conclude that Kafka understands *Schadenfreude* to presuppose malice than to conclude that he sees no interesting difference between acting and watching. For Kafka, seeing suffering and simultaneously approving of it does not clearly indicate a moral failing.

Kafka views his father's transgression as more significant than his own. Why should we agree with Kafka here? Because *Schadenfreude* arises from a judgment of appropriate instances of suffering, *Schadenfreude* does not clearly involve a disposition to take pleasure in all the bad things that may happen to other people. Although *Schadenfreude* may include malice, it needn't presuppose malice.

The pleasure of *Schadenfreude* springs from a person's beliefs about the appropriateness of suffering. Our views of appropriateness can change from situation to situation. To insist that *Schadenfreude* presupposes malice is to insist our views of appropriateness do not change.

Beyond that, it is hardly difficult to imagine other reasons for Kafka's *Schadenfreude* which do not presuppose malice. Kafka may well have believed that Elli "had it coming to her." Alternatively, the injury his father had inflicted on the boy's self-esteem left him with a feeling of inferiority, and insults to Elli may well have allowed him to feel superior to *someone*, if only for a moment.

I will leave off with Kafka in what remains of this subsection in order to fill out this point. Other usages would seem to bear out the claim that *Schadenfreude* can be an episodic emotional response that does not presuppose malice. In *Paradise News*, by the British novelist and literary critic David Lodge, we read:

> We were not encouraged by our episcopal masters to disturb the faith of the ever-dwindling number of recruits to the priesthood by exposing them to the full, cold blast of modern radical theology. The Anglicans were making all the running in that direction, and we derived a certain *Schadenfreude* from contemplating the rows and threatened schisms in the Church of England provoked by

bishops and priests who denied the doctrine of the Virgin Birth, the Resurrection, and even the divinity of Christ.[5]

This usage depicts *Schadenfreude* as a function of mischief or playfulness, not malevolence. The careful reference "a certain *Schadenfreude*" suggests that Lodge understands how much confusion surrounds the moral appraisal of this pleasure.

It is certainly true, however, that for many thinkers *Schadenfreude* does presuppose something morally objectionable, if not outright malice. H. Richard Niebuhr, an eloquent proponent of agape, or love of neighbor, would not condone the professions of Kafka and David Lodge. Playful spontaneity holds little appeal for many moralists, including Niebuhr. Their seriousness may well stem from reservations about what underlies much mischief, namely using others to amuse ourselves. Niebuhr exhorts us to focus on the welfare of others and forget our own needs:

> Love is rejoicing over the existence of the beloved one; it is the desire that he be rather than not be; it is longing for his presence when he is absent; it is happiness in the thought of him; it is profound satisfaction over everything that makes him great and glorious.[6]

Other people around us are not simply neighbors for Niebuhr, but "beloved" ones. Here and in other works, Niebuhr sets out with force a theme that cascades through Christian ethics: we ought to commit ourselves fully to a neighbor's well-being. Implied in this excerpt from Niebuhr is the view that *Schadenfreude* undermines neighbor-love and therefore signals a sin in the person who feels it.

This position does not strike me as persuasive. Though we generally require some kind of goodwill from those people about whom we care (if not from strangers), the forms we expect such goodwill to take do not necessarily exclude *Schadenfreude*. Even our closest friends may disagree with some aspect of our lives and subsequently take our misfortunes as proof of our perceived failings. But because some people assume that benevolence must aim at the *full* good of another, they assume that *Schadenfreude* must presuppose malice.

Consider the matter of competition, an inevitable consequence of living in communities. As Gore Vidal once confessed, "Whenever a friend succeeds, a little something in me dies." A century earlier Mark Twain observed in *Following the Equator*, "It takes your enemy and your friend, working together, to hurt you to the heart; the one to slander you and the other to get the news to you." To be sure, such statements play off of fashionable coquetry. Raconteurs occasionally act merely in order to do justice to maxims, but the maxims no doubt contain a certain grain of truth.

Competition pits us against one another. Wholeheartedness, which lies at the heart of integrity, might seem to rule out our ever taking pleasure in the misfortunes of friends. A focus on integrity, though, runs the risk of oversimplifying our interactions with other people. When friends are competitors, wholehearted devotion to our friends might seem to prevent us from achieving our own potential. How we treat one another in sports may resemble malice, but does not equal it. The same is true of *Schadenfreude*.

3. The importance of what people think we deserve

How can beliefs shape emotions? This question underlies any number of emotional responses. Where indignation amounts to sadness at the good fortune of others who do not deserve it, *Schadenfreude* amounts to happiness at the ill fortune of others who *do* deserve it. In both cases an evaluation of appropriateness dictates an emotional response. Kafka states that he had been angry with Elli for years, which suggests he may have believed she *deserved* to suffer because of some wrong she had done.

Some notion of desert, or what people deserve, underlies judgments about moral appropriateness. This is an illuminating insight, but one of limited usefulness insofar as people tend to judge others more severely than they judge themselves. Assessing ourselves, too, will more likely distort our judgment than assessing others. A judgment about the just deserts of another person often enough involves a conflict — avowed or disavowed — between selfish desire and genuine scruples.

Take for example the advice a widely quoted literary theorist offered to American graduate students studying to become university professors. In the course of a polemical essay on the state of doctoral education in the humanities, the American intellectual Camille Paglia railed against the unfairness of the American system, which allegedly favors superficial self-promoters over highly original thinkers. (Paglia struggled for years to find employment as a professor.) Paglia assured advanced students:

> If you keep the faith, the gods may give you, at midlife, the sweet pleasure of seeing the hotshots who were so fast out of the gate begin to flag and sink, just as your studies are reaching their point of maturation.[7]

Paglia makes it easy for us to understand that she believes many professors deserve to "flag and sink." Although she does not say so explicitly, we can infer that she would take pleasure in a "hotshot" professor's failure to receive academic tenure (which is a permanent contract of employment that may follow six years of hard work as a junior faculty member and at least as many years as a graduate student). It is safe to conclude on the basis of this lengthy essay that Paglia takes a harsh view of what "hotshot" professors deserve.

Anger or jealousy can lead to self-deception and complicate the work of assessing what others deserve. Self-interest generates self-deception remarkably well. Jealousy is especially likely to generate false beliefs about its objects and, consequently, to provide motives for concluding that the suffering of another is condign (such rationalizations abound in war). *Schadenfreude*, like admiration, pride, and shame, is an emotion properly thought of in terms of the apportioning of credit and debt. The most slippery component of *Schadenfreude* is the value judgment regarding the suffering of another person. *Schadenfreude*'s moral status will not be solved simply by reference to desert, for questionable values shape what people think we deserve.

4. The import of the object of *Schadenfreude*

Unlike pain, emotions have objects; we are afraid *of* something, angry *with* someone, ashamed *that* we have acted improperly. We can always point to *some* instance of suffering or misfortune as the source of *Schadenfreude*. Reflecting on the just deserts of someone who supposedly needed to "learn a lesson," we try to classify the kind of suffering that has beset him — not just the extent to which he suffers, but the way in which he suffers. Suffering because we failed to make the Olympic team differs from suffering because a parent has been murdered.

The psychological portrait he offers us of himself in *Brief an den Vater* allows us to infer that Kafka's pleasure at Elli's suffering would have turned to pain at the moment he judged that suffering excessive or inappropriate. His *Schadenfreude* is a reaction to what he considers minor suffering. Though any attempt to distinguish terrible from minor suffering definitively would doubtless be futile, we may reasonably expect consensus about some particular instances of suffering. An understanding of *Schadenfreude* which fails to take into account the variability of suffering will only confuse moral discourse.

A sense of lesser and greater pervades our moral deliberations. The particular belief which evaluates this greater or lesser is conceptually necessary, that is to say constitutive of, the resultant emotion. At the same time, it is construed as causally effective in the production of the emotion itself. Moral evaluation should compel us to look not only to the disposition of the person who delights in the suffering of another but also to the kind of suffering he enjoys.

The disposition of Kafka's father, if Kafka is to be trusted here, merits blame. That said, it can hardly be denied that a good deal of comedy deserves just as much blame. Twenty years after his influential work *Jokes and Their Relation to the Unconscious* (1905) appeared, Freud published a short essay entitled "Humor" (1927), in which he differentiated jokes from humor. The aim of jokes, he argued, was sheer gratification, a kind of mental victory. In jokes the mind manages to find or appreciate the hidden similarity among dissimilar things. The aim of humor, on the other hand, was to evade or lessen suffering. The Kafka family suffered from a lack of harmony, to put it nicely. Elli the scapegoat brought them closer together, albeit against her will. Humor in the Kafka family came at too high a price. That is not to say that all humor does, though.

We can tell a lot about a person from what he or she finds funny. Kafka did not try to hide his laughter; on the contrary, he feasted on it. Father and son alike punished Elli with their laughter. We can infer that neither father nor son was fat; had they been, it is unlikely their laughter would have been so easily, openly mean. If they had also been fat, Kafka and his father would have laughed *with* her, rather than *at* her.

We do not hear the voice of Kafka's sister or father. It is not too hard to imagine how Kafka's father may have defended himself: exasperated, he may have felt that the only option left to him was sarcasm. He may have believed that some laughter at Elli's expense within the privacy of their home would have goaded her to improve her physical appearance and so meet with greater happiness in the world.

If not exactly cruel, Herr Kafka's manner was far from kind. Cruelty properly attaches to suffering, which exceeds mere teasing. We speak of "the cruelty of children" (as in teasing) from time to time, but such "cruelty" usually amounts to curiosity and lacks the destructive intentions of (adult) cruelty.

5. *Schadenfreude* and cruelty

Though a cruel person will invariably celebrate the misfortunes of others, it is by no means obvious that someone who celebrates another's misfortune is cruel. Finding pleasure in the misfortune of another amounts to cruelty whenever such pleasure follows from a lack of respect for the sufferer as another human being.

To be sure, failing to recognize evil when we see it poses a real danger. Is unwillingness to condemn pleasure in the setbacks of other people out of hand an apology for cruelty? Does defending *Schadenfreude* amount to advocating a self-serving morality? No.

Because arguments about what people deserve in the way of suffering may appeal to their actions (as persons to be respected), it can be quite difficult to distinguish *Schadenfreude* from cruelty. Was pleasure taken from the suffering of gay men in the throes of the AIDS crisis in the 1980s or in the suffering of Jews under German National Socialism in the 1930s a function of cruelty or justice? Such pleasure was arguably more cruel than righteous, given the well-known struggle of Jews or gay people to earn social respect for their *personhood*. The Nazis knew well that widespread cruelty requires a legitimating ontology, one which supports the claim that the victims of cruelty are not persons.

Many societies perceive outsiders, enemies, and criminals as beyond the "social contract." Convinced that outsiders need not be treated with the respect due to insiders, those who delight in harm suffered by outsiders may then throw ordinary moral reflection to the wind. In the United States, belief that Jews, Catholics, Muslims, and feminists secretly obey Satan has in certain eras made the most uncivil behavior toward them a badge of piety and religious devotion. Such repugnance can spread easily, due to the insidious way in which such social biases are both reinforced and cultivated. As C. Fred Alford has astutely observed,

> It will do no good to implore people not to demonize others. People demonize the other not out of ignorance or intolerance but to protect their own threatened goodness. Demonization of the other is a defense against doom. That the doom is self-inflicted, the aura of one's own aggression, makes their defense more poignant but no less destructive.[8]

Mentally separating good from evil represents on some level a very healthy love for the self, a commitment to one's own sanity. While we do well to urge others like us to keep the faith, we must be careful not to allow such expressions of support to humiliate or oppress others.

Moral argument and inquiry can sometimes resolve serious moral conflicts. In the United States slavery and civil rights legislation furnish good examples of successful resolutions of moral disagreement. When we agree to disagree morally with other people, we may see ourselves entering a kind of competition with them. This competition can lead to *Schadenfreude*. When bad things happen to other people whose moral beliefs differ from our own, we sometimes take our own good fortune as evidence for the superiority of our beliefs. This, I will argue in Part Two, is a mistake.

We cannot avoid choosing between intrinsically conflicting beliefs and principles. Because moral disagreements concern questions of value, not of fact, *Schadenfreude* implicates itself broadly in our lives. As the emotional manifestation of beliefs about justice, *Schadenfreude* will persist because of differing moral beliefs. Although I want to talk about justice in the context of non-trivial suffering, our anxiety about how much another person is suffering requires mention of justice and cruelty here.

The distinction between commission and omission illuminates the difference between cruelty and *Schadenfreude*. Unlike cruelty, which can be active or passive, *Schadenfreude* is passive, because it evolves in situations we do not create. Certainly it can be cruel to observe the terrible suffering of a person without attempting to help. But bearing in mind that cruelty almost invariably aims at disproportionality, one can see that Kafka experiences another *kind* of pleasure from that of a satisfied rapist or vengeful murderer. The Kafka, Lodge, and Paglia passages support a morally relevant difference of kind between the delight which results from two different sources of suffering: that which we have ourselves inflicted or in some part caused, and that in which we have had no hand.

Disagreement on this point abounds. Colin McGinn would doubtlessly argue that my argument fails, given his view that

> The evil person can be either agent or spectator of the suffering he relishes. He need not always go to the trouble of bringing it about himself; he might be quite content if someone else, or just nature, does the harm. What matters is the state that pain produces in him, not necessarily his agency in producing it. Thus we might distinguish between active and passive evil, depending upon the agent's own intentional involvement.[9]

This is indeed a harsh line, making Kafka and Lodge both evil. In fact, McGinn's view makes all of us evil if *Schadenfreude* is universal. Moral philosophy needs to be more psychologically realistic. McGinn's view begs important, substantive questions about the mitigating effect of desert and the role, if any, of triviality in moral evaluation.

Agency and passivity deserve greater moral priority than McGinn allows. Jon Elster articulates what must be the case for most people: "Many who find a titillating pleasure in a friend's misfortune would be horrified at the thought of going out of their way to provoke it. Doing so by omission or abstention might be easier."[10] Elster believes that we generally see an important difference between celebrating mishaps we have caused and those we have not. McGinn conceptually obviates this difference, misconstruing the moral gravity of comedy and beliefs about trivial suffering.

Whether we ourselves caused the suffering of another matters to moral analysis in roughly the same way that the degree of suffering involved does. In the *Genealogy of Morals* Nietzsche stopped just short of calling trivial that pleasure in suffering we have not ourselves caused: "To behold suffering gives pleasure, but to cause another to suffer affords an even greater pleasure. This statement expresses an old, powerful, human, all too human sentiment . . . " (*GM* II, Section 6). Nietzsche and Elster disagree on this point. Elster may well have come closer to capturing what goes on in our hearts than Nietzsche. In any event, both Nietzsche and Elster oppose McGinn and together suggest that if there weren't a word for *Schadenfreude*, we would need to invent one, in order to maintain the force of our concepts of sadism and cruelty. *Schadenfreude* is at worst a passively *cruel response* (in the eyes of other people, it must be made clear). It does not involve pleasure *in cruelty*.

Far too simplistically, some thinkers have classified pleasure in the misfortunes of others as sadism. Sadism implies cruelty, which delights perpetrators of sadism precisely because they view sadistic pain as intrinsically inappropriate. *Schadenfreude*, by contrast, turns on a belief in moral appropriateness. Strictly speaking, sadism refers to sexuality and violence; however, it is widely used to refer to aggressiveness toward others. In short: The sadist is someone who cannot bear to experience a lack of control over his or her own suffering. The sadist therefore causes another person to suffer, thereby projecting outward that abhorrence of pain and controlling its occurrence and administration in another. The sadist derives pleasure from another person "standing in" for his or her own pain.

This simple, causal distinction indicates the shortcomings of the familiar epigram "misery loves company," which is entirely ambiguous as to the cause of the misery in question (here again a German word — *Miß-gunst* — can be helpful). The French adage, "*Le malheur des uns, c'est le bonheur des autres*" ("The unhappiness of some is the happiness of others"), an aphoristic equivalent of *Schadenfreude*, similarly falls short. If extended a bit further to include another difference, that between the misfortunes of others which we expect and those which we do not, this causal distinction also demonstrates the inadequacy of a word like "gloating," which applies to anticipated pleasure ("I told you so").[11]

In conclusion, the case against cruelty and evil is too well known to need anyone's assent. But when we turn from enjoying examples of cruelty such as murder and rape to pleasure in trivial instances of suffering, there is and should be no unanimity of condemnation of *Schadenfreude* as simply diabolical. Defending *Schadenfreude* against charges that it is simply evil by another name is not a disguised attempt to allow us to feel whatever we like with a clear conscience. Rather, such a defense urges attention to the complexity of our emotional reactions to other people.

I have started out my study by considering what people mean when they claim to feel *Schadenfreude* or to detect it in others. I will continue to do so in subsequent chapters. I have hung my defense of Kafka and Lodge on a distinction between trivial and terrible suffering. The impossibility of definitively marking off trivial from significant suffering, like the impossibility of consistently reaching consensus on matters involving justice or desert, brings into focus a conflict of principles — a conflict that might not have been immediately apparent. The questions provoked by the conflict drive our moral evaluation of Kafka and Lodge — and of ourselves as well.

Mistaking *Schadenfreude* for Something Else

How can *Schadenfreude* be distinguished from envy or other emotions with which it has historically been confused or unreflectively identified? In *The Anatomy of Melancholy*, a widely influential work written in 1628, Robert Burton maintains: "envy is naught else but sorrow for other men's good, be it present, past, or to come: & joy at their harms, opposite to mercy" (part one, section two). In his *Ethics* (III.24) Spinoza follows this lead. And in *Works of Love* Kierkegaard classifies envy with *Schadenfreude*, even though the latter is the "even more hideous cousin" of envy. Though envy stands as a ready explanation for one person's celebration of another's misfortune, little analysis is required to show that the two are distinct. Envy is not a reaction to suffering, and *Schadenfreude* is not a wish for satisfaction. Envy *is* suffering, and *Schadenfreude is* satisfaction. Where envy involves pain caused by the good fortune of others, *Schadenfreude* entails pleasure caused by the ill fortune of others.

The impulse to sort out how we're faring in the world frequently leads to comparisons with others; an unflattering comparison with another may be the most basic source of envy of all. The enduringly relevant sixteenth-century French philosopher Montaigne believed that such comparisons harm us:

Whatever it is, whether art or nature, that imprints in us this disposition to live with reference to others, it does us much more harm than good. We defraud ourselves of our won advantages to make appearances conform with public opinion. We do not care so much what we are in ourselves and in reality as what we are in the public mind.[12]

It is because we live in society that we harm ourselves through these comparisons. If not controlled, impulses to compare ourselves to others can lead us to pretend we are the sort of people we want to be. We debase ourselves by trying to become the sort of person the rest of the world will admire. Montaigne insists that we can avoid such comparisons by focusing on ourselves, by celebrating ourselves. For him, envy signals weakness.

I have said that envy centers upon the good fortune of another (as does indignation, which is anger at the *undeserved* good fortune of others). We may envy others both for what they have (i.e., education, beauty, wealth) and for what they are (nobility, athletic champions, intellectuals). Although differences among individuals may result from accidental contingencies (as opposed to social injustice), the fact of living in a competitive social milieu makes envy a wide-ranging phenomenon. Gossip finds particularly fertile soil in competitive social situations. Frequently, those who gossip act out of a strong need for regular evaluation of their own personal and intimate lives. Envy seems to fuel gossip, a behavior useful for tracing and gauging the extent of a painful emotion.

People who do not compare themselves to others must be rare. Pindar (522–470 B.C.), the greatest Greek lyric poet of his period , complained that "envious hopes flutter over the minds of mortals" (*Isthmia*, II). He stands as one of the first thinkers to advance the claim that all humans feel envy. This claim should not seem controversial, nor should the claim that *Schadenfreude* is universal.

The prevalence of envy has invited reflection from many thinkers, particularly those who worry about social solidarity. There are at least three distinct conceptions of envy. Robert Nozick defines an envious person as someone who does not want anyone to have what he or she cannot have,[13] whereas John Rawls understands an envious person to be someone who is willing to give up part of what he or she has if doing so will bring others down to his or her level.[14] The psychoanalyst Melanie Klein considers envy the desire to destroy what is good because one cannot have it or be it. Her view of envy as the root of all evil is the most drastic of the three. She quotes approvingly from Chaucer's "Parson's Tale": "It is certain that envy is the worst sin that is; for all other sins are sins only against one virtue, whereas envy is against all virtue and all goodness."[15] *Schadenfreude* is compatible with Nozick's understanding of envy, but not with Rawls's or Klein's thicker conceptions. Part of the joy of *Schadenfreude* is that a problematic person has been brought back into line. Nonetheless, it seems unlikely that many people would willingly sacrifice even a part of their own well-being in order to see another receive his or her comeuppance. The point to be taken here is that differences in beauty, wealth, and social status are likely to arouse both envy and *Schadenfreude*.

Because of what it can pointedly reveal about the conceptual construction of suffering, *Schadenfreude* must not be equated with envy, nor with the feeling of relief. The pleasure which Lucretius famously articulates in *De Rerum Natura*, then, is not *Schadenfreude*:

> How sweet it is, when whirlwinds roil great ocean,
> To watch, from land, the danger of another,
> Not that to see some other person suffer
> Brings great enjoyment, but the sweetness lies
> In watching evils you yourself are free from.[16]

Lucretius's pleasure is one of *not* suffering, at his freedom from it. It is a self-regarding emotion, unlike *Schadenfreude*. Kant defends such a distinction in his *Lectures on Ethics* of 1779: ". . . we may enjoy in stormy weather, when comfortably seated in our warm, cosy parlour, speaking of those at sea, for it heightens our own feeling of comfort and happiness . . ."[17] The relief derived from not suffering has given rise in the modern world to much of the popularity of the television and news media, which regularly broadcast details of sad events. People who demonstrate a taste for stories of disaster or who show morbid curiosity about the misfortunes of others should not be considered *schadenfroh* (this is the adjective form of the German noun) too quickly, for it is entirely possible that the pleasure they find is a self-regarding one. News-watchers may find pleasure in learning of problems they don't have.

Consider another example of self-regarding pleasure, taken from *The Black Prince*, a novel by the British writer-philosopher Iris Murdoch:

We naturally take in the catastrophes of our friends a pleasure which genuinely does not preclude friendship. This is partly but not entirely because we enjoy being empowered as helpers. The unexpected or inappropriate catastrophe is especially piquant . . .[18]

This is not *Schadenfreude*. The pleasure in question has nothing to do with either comedy or justice. Further, the speaker describes a kind of emotional neediness that could just as easily be satisfied in a number of other ways: being taken into confidence, asked for important advice, honored at a party. This pleasure is not in the suffering of another person, but in the idea that another person needs us.

Before leaving off with the contrast between self- and other-regarding emotions, it bears remarking that relief bespeaks luck. Lucretius and Kant both point to the contingency and vulnerability of human life in the same sea metaphor. Individually, they raise the question of whether and how luck (that another suffers, not me) might be said to bear on the moral life. It might be thought that the better our fortune, the easier it is to perfect our characters. If we were beautiful, intelligent, wealthy, and loved by others, we would not find it especially difficult to banish feelings of bitterness, envy, or resentment toward others. We would not encounter these feelings regularly, we might tell ourselves. And yet bookstores offer scores of biographies of wealthy, beautiful people who led miserable lives and whose moral characters no one would consider exemplary. Relief often produces a wonderful spirit of thankfulness for what we have; envy for the apparent luck of people who seem to have an easier time of it than we do, though, often indicates that we don't actually know much about the people we envy.

The tediousness of boredom, to continue with a list of cognate emotional experiences, may invite interruption of any sort, but *Schadenfreude* is certainly not boredom. In Charles Dickens's *Great Expectations* the protagonist Pip, who has just been saved from certain death at the hands of a villain, says of one of his unknowing rescuers:

For the present, under the circumstances, we deemed it prudent to make rather light of the matter to Trabb's boy; who I am convinced would have been much affected by disappointment, if he had known that his intervention saved me from the limekiln. Not that Trabb's boy was of a malignant nature, but that he had too much spare vivacity, and that it was in his constitution to want variety and excitement at anybody's expense.[19]

We learn from Dickens that Trabb's boy may well have felt a kind of joy upon hearing of Pip's torture, but this joy would have been an antidote to the weariness of boredom — not pleasure in the fact of Pip's suffering. The kind of thrill Dickens points to in this example of Trabb's boy is also a kind of relief, then, not *Schadenfreude*. This passage illustrates a nexus between boredom and pleasure. The passage is also valuable in that it raises the question of what it is to find pleasure at someone else's expense.

Pleasure which comes at the expense of others can help to distinguish *Schadenfreude* from sadism, revenge, and malice, which share an active intention or desire to harm another and each of which requires personal expenditure of energy and time. How might *Schadenfreude* be confused with revenge and malice? When, to their mutual horror, Mr. Lammle and his new wife, Sophronia, realize in Dickens's *Our Mutual Friend* that each has married the other for a fortune that does not in fact exist, the newly-weds vow to avenge themselves on the world. Says Mr. Lammle: ". . . we owe all other people the grudge of wishing them to be taken in, as we ourselves have been taken in."[20] This particular brand of malice, well captured by the German *Mißgunst*, is only one of several; *Schadenfreude* differs from malice in its passivity. Any glee yielded by the fruition of the Lammles' hope (and activity) is malicious pleasure. *Schadenfreude* should not be considered malicious pleasure, for the reason that it usually does not involve expectation, much less agency.

Intentions differ from hopes, desires, and expectations. Various philosophers have remarked on the utter randomness of expectations and wants compared with the selectivity of intentions. To intend something is not at all the same as to hope for something. This fact is important for moral evaluation, for it is primarily by a person's intentions that we judge his moral disposition. That someone has done something unintentionally bears on our estimate of his virtue. Intentions also hinge on timing. We judge more harshly lies that are crafted in advance than those which are told without forethought.

Annette Baier and others who analyze integrity have shown that expected or desired states of affairs differ from intended states of affairs in that the former are not necessarily linked to states of *my* affairs. I can want and expect my friend Andrew to make the Olympic swimming team without thereby wanting or expecting anything for myself. My intentions, by contrast, generally involve my own future. If I begin to work toward Andrew's success, I *intend* something about Andrew. And if I intend to help Andrew, he will bear upon my future in some way. Even intentions for others imply intentions for oneself.

Schadenfreude could be considered intentional only if it amounted to the resolve to be happy about another's misfortune. We might, for example, say of an arrogant person, "I'll be glad when Camille gets her due." This attitude is not malicious, though, for it does not automatically mean that we expect something for ourselves. We may sincerely believe that the "lesson" in question will benefit Camille, even as it supposedly attests to the invisible hand of justice ("what goes around, comes around"). Our *hoping*, properly speaking, that *something* would happen to "teach her a lesson" (who knows what it would take) neither necessitates nor precludes *Schadenfreude* as an eventual response.

Of course, the same might be said of passive cruelty; for this reason, *Schadenfreude* needs to be set firmly apart from cruelty. In *Contingency, Irony, and Solidarity* Richard Rorty embraced Judith Shklar's definition of cruelty as "the worst thing we do."[21] In *Ordinary Vices* Shklar understands as cruelty "the willful infliction of physical pain on a weaker being in order to cause anguish and fear."[22] It is a wrong done entirely to *another creature*. A parent who physically reprimands his or her son only ambiguously qualifies as cruel, and a German who refused to aid a Jew under National Socialism does not appear to qualify at all. So there is a problem with Shklar's active definition of cruelty. Passive cruelty did not figure into her conception of *moral* cruelty either, which she took to be "deliberate and persistent humiliation, so that the victim can eventually trust neither himself nor anyone else" (*Ordinary Vices*, p. 37). Five years later, Shklar filled out her influential account of cruelty by linking it to evil: ". . . evil is cruelty and the fear it inspires, and the very fear of fear itself."[23] Cruelty is intrinsically evil, despite the fact that it can be instrumentally good (as in "One must be cruel to be kind"). Even passive cruelty is intentional. *Schadenfreude* differs from passive cruelty in the role that beliefs about desert play in the different kinds of pleasure.

Spinoza called rejoicing in the loss or misfortune of other people one of the classic symptoms of envy.[24] Spinoza had malicious glee in mind, not *Schadenfreude*. Kafka may have disliked or disrepected his sister, but he didn't envy her. Nonetheless, it remains that Spinoza joins a chorus of thinkers who raise moral doubts about taking pleasure in the misfortunes of others. This is a good time to ask whether there is any point to trying to defend this despised pleasure.

Yes, there is. We will feel better about ourselves if we recognize not only that people everywhere suffer, but also that people everywhere appreciate others' suffering. Human beings may have any number of natural propensities (to envy, to deceit, to aggression) that we do well to change or control. *Schadenfreude* differs importantly from intrinsically bad propensities in its roots in basically harmless comedy (and in justice, which I pursue in Part Two). In comedy we flirt with all sorts of moral transgressions. We either stop short of condoning moral transgressions or challenge the seriousness of them. *Schadenfreude*, like comedy, verges on cruelty but stops short of it. A look at the structure of the emotion illustrates the flirtatiousness underlying some *Schadenfreude* (as in Kaufmann's understanding and in Lodge's example). Flittering between good and evil, *Schadenfreude* tests how playful — and how complicated — we will allow ourselves to be.

Two

Explaining *Schadenfreude*

EMOTIONS LIKE REGRET, DISAPPOINTMENT, AND SHAME CAUSE US PAIN. It might be thought that painful emotions are justified because we are bad people or because we have made a mistake. Wiser people, we may think, manage to avoid grief and shame. An advisor may tell us that we are wrong to dwell on the disappointment of having narrowly missed a spot on the Olympic team; we should instead focus on having become the sort of extraordinary athlete who could reasonably hope to qualify for the Olympic team. We can change our view of things, the advisor may tell us, and enjoy life more.

We can also agree that there are different kinds of pleasure — the kind that comes from winning an Olympic gold medal, the kind that comes from watching a good movie, and the kind that comes from exacting revenge, for example. Agreement on this point might lead naturally to an effort to establish a moral pecking order of pleasures: we might try to argue that some pleasures are morally superior to others, as John Stuart Mill does in *On Liberty*. Then we might try to define a person's moral worth in terms of the pleasure he or she feels. Especially if we believe God plays an active role in our lives, we might think that people who feel morally acceptable pleasure regularly must deserve their happy existences.

Emotions such as fulfillment, success, and pride cause us pleasure. It might be thought that pleasurable emotions are justified because we are good people or because we are living wisely. We want to take pleasurable emotions as evidence of our having done something right. Even when our pleasurable emotions arise from situations over which we have no control, such as a lottery, we rejoice.

No one will deny that we tend to seek pleasure and avoid pain. By the same token, we naturally want to give in to and prolong pleasurable emotions. Why not allow ourselves the holiday *Schadenfreude* proclaims?

Something for Nothing

We value pleasurable emotions differently. To a number of people, the thrill of winning a Nobel prize means more than the thrill of finding a large sum of money, because they have worked very hard for many years in order to be able to win the prize. This does not mean that they will not value the money they happen upon. It also leaves open the possibility that they may take the smaller pleasure (like the larger) as evidence of living wisely, or of being good people.

John Forrester concluded a recent book on the subject of paying for consolation (through psychoanalysis) with this insight: "Perhaps that is what Freud's discovery that infantile wishes are foreign to the logic of money — and the entire logic of debt, exchange, and reciprocity — amounted to: that our deepest wishes are for something that is as gratuitous, as full of grace, as happiness. The gift of something for nothing."[1] *Schadenfreude* is itself a gift of something for nothing. If Forrester's intuition is correct, then the appeal of *Schadenfreude* runs very deep.

Forrester's use of the word "grace" here begs mention of an institutionalized understanding of "something for nothing." In his comprehensive study *Catholicism*, Richard P. McBrien states that the Catholic tradition has always insisted that the grace of God is given to us, not to make up for something lacking to us as human persons, but as a *free gift* that elevates us to a new and *unmerited* level of existence.[2] The Fathers of the Church, from Irenaeus on, understood this participation in the life of God through Christ as a true divinization. The Latin Fathers, especially Augustine and Pope Leo the Great (d. 461), adopted this concept and made it the foundation of the whole theology of grace, as is particularly evident in Thomas Aquinas. Even today the notion of grace lies at the deepest center of Catholic theology.

The appeal of grace resembles the allure of lotteries. Only a few people win a lottery, but grace makes a winner of everyone. Barbara Goodwin has observed that opponents express moral disapproval of financial lotteries because the games let (some) people get something for (almost) nothing, simply by buying a ticket. The lottery is an anti-meritocratic device: as well as undermining the work ethic, it overturns our notions of moral worth. Goodwin has argued persuasively that lottery system writ large would thus undermine the moral basis of society.[3] People deserve rewards if they work hard, it is often thought.

Augustine emphasized that grace is something personal, intrinsic, and above all a *gratuitous* gift of God, for if it were not gratuitous, it would no longer be grace. He viewed grace as something quite extraordinary, for little in life is free. Taking up the subject of grace centuries later, Paul Tournier observed, "the notion that everything has to be paid for is very deep-seated and active within us, as universal as it is unshakeable by logical argument."[4] *Schadenfreude* subverts this notion, just as the Catholic concept of grace does. If we want to give in to pleasurable emotions generally, we may want even more to surrender to a pleasurable emotion which, unlike the thrill of winning an Olympic gold medal, costs nothing.

Why persons should strive for the good if it involves sacrifice remains one of the central problems in moral psychology. Charity and justice concern the welfare of others and what is owed to them. Given that both charity and justice may require the virtuous person to sacrifice self-interest, each may appear a burden to the virtuous person and a benefit to others. Since at least the time of Plato, this perception has generated controversy. Suffice it to say that the traditional answer has been that virtuous behavior is rewarded by happiness. Virtuous people supposedly enjoy life more than do the non-virtuous.

Virtuous people do not hope that people around them will suffer. That we believe another deserves to suffer some injury does not necessarily mean that we hope for or attentively wait for an injury to occur. The pleasure of *Schadenfreude* can cause (or causally sustain) a desire that it simultaneously satisfies. In *Schadenfreude* we receive a delight that we did not desire, if by "desire" we are to understand any motivational factor that may figure in the explanation of intentional action. Something bad happens to someone else, and we suddenly realize that we find the resulting suffering appropriate.

Because we do not desire *Schadenfreude*, we do not work to obtain it: it simply falls into our hands, as a fruit of passivity. In speaking of the passivity of *Schadenfreude* I do not mean to imply that we are victims of our emotions in the sense that emotions seem to toss us about like ships in a storm. I do not claim that either *Schadenfreude* or malicious glee is beyond our control; indeed, because we are not purely passive in the face of feelings and emotions, our efforts to manage our emotions sometimes succeed. We can repudiate, silently, the opportunity to feel pleasure in the injury or suffering of another. Alternatively, we can rationalize our enjoyment of the suffering of another: we can tell ourselves that we take pleasure in the fact that another suffers (as opposed to pleasure in the actual suffering) and that this pleasure results from love of justice. Such mental dodges attest to the rationality of *Schadenfreude*, as well as to our responsibility for it.

That we could stop ourselves from feeling *Schadenfreude* with some willpower, but might choose not to, makes the emotion appear to stand in tension with the religious commandment to love others as ourselves (Mark 12:31), a normative principle that has exercised an incalculable influence on Western culture. How one thinks about and experiences aggression and cruelty determines to some extent the way one views the love commandment, as well as one's own acts of cruelty and betrayal. Explanations of why we are driven toward or tempted by hatred and cruelty tend to fall into two general and sharply divergent categories. According to the tradition at whose heart the love commandment stands, humans are born with original sin and naturally possess hateful and cruel instincts. The baseness of human nature stems from Adam's original, moral freedom to reject a life free of pain and suffering. According to a contrary tradition, over which Freud to some extent presides, we are born innocent, although some of us become hateful and cruel from having suffered deprivation or cruelty. Freud's view of human nature, which resonates with that of the ancient Greeks, seems to hold out more hope for the prospect of human happiness. Likewise did Marx view strife, conflict, and competition among human beings as pathological conditions that admit of solutions. A psychological and sociological axiom of Marxism is that persons are permanently constituted to seek harmony, not discord. Although Jewish, neither Freud nor Marx professed to be religious. It is somewhat ironic, then, that each seemed more optimistic than many Christians about putting into practice the spirit of the love commandment.

Many religious thinkers and various philosophers (Kant and Schopenhauer, for example) have endorsed the moral obligation to feel sympathy for other people. Other people, by the same token, must feel sympathy for us when we suffer. This obligation has nothing to do with reciprocity, for we are expected to feel sympathy even (or especially) for those who feel no sympathy for us.

Love subverts rationality here, for it might seem entirely reasonable to dislike or shun people whose moral views appall us. In *Schadenfreude,* rationality predominates. Consequently, we need to look most searchingly not at pleasure virtually everyone would reject as unconscionable, but at pain or suffering that someone may view as entirely legitimate to enjoy. A defense of such enjoyment, like condemnation of it, requires an account of the rationality of *Schadenfreude.*

The Rationality of *Schadenfreude*

Revulsion to *Schadenfreude* as a sign of the diabolic seems to deny the rationality of *Schadenfreude.* It is easier to censure *Schadenfreude* if we portray it as a knee-jerk, sadistic response. Sometimes emotional reactions (such as fear and simple likes and dislikes) grab us before we have time for deliberate thinking. Other emotional reactions (such as love and reverance for justice) represent emotional sophistication. Accordingly, I want to introduce *Schadenfreude* as a sophistocated emotion, not as a feeling.

What is the difference between emotions and feelings? Simply put, emotions matter more to moral analysis than do feelings. Because feelings lack the complexity, intentional focus, and susceptibility to appraisal often ascribed to emotions, cognitivist theorists of emotions de-emphasize them and focus on emotion, which they analyze chiefly in terms of belief and desire. No doubt feelings and emotions are sometimes confused with one another, in part because of the admittedly nebulous line that separates them. Various philosophers set themselves to distinguishing the various emotions from each other and from feelings in general: for example, Aristotle in the *Rhetoric*, Descartes in *The Passions of the Soul*, Hobbes in the *Leviathan*, Spinoza in his *Ethics*, and Hume in his *A Treatise on Human Nature*. Feelings are never sufficient to identify emotions, which means that emotions are more than just feelings. Feelings are mental states distinguished by their qualitative, phenomenological properties. They are neither beliefs nor desires.

Philosophers take cognitive processes to be somehow essential to emotions, but not to feelings, and generally agree that emotions are subject to normative appraisal though feelings are not. For, depending upon the circumstances, we may judge an emotional response to be justified or unjustified, warranted or unwarranted, reasonable or unreasonable. Unlike feelings, emotions can be admirable, blameworthy, or childish. Love, respect, and grief stand as ready examples of emotions, as do malice and hatred. *Schadenfreude* is an emotion as well, for *Schadenfreude* always has an object (for example, we are happy *that* Camille has failed at something). Though certain feelings (such as hunger) may involve objects as well, they do not entail cognitive analysis.

Knowledge or belief precedes and contributes to *Schadenfreude*. Thus, for example, I am glad that Yale rejected Camille (because I know that her grades did not qualify her for admission or because I believe that she cheated on placement tests). Depression, melancholy, and euphoria are not "about" anything in particular, even if they are supposedly "about" everything (namely, the whole world). But if Camille steals my car, any revenge I seek will be directed specifically at her. And any *Schadenfreude* others consequently feel will center on my loss of a valuable possession. This is not to say that *Schadenfreude* cannot center on a large object: a Dutchman may have felt *schadenfroh* about Germany's total defeat in the Second World War, for instance.

Why should we care at all about the moral status of taking pleasure in the hardships of others if this pleasure doesn't stem from or lead to action? I follow Aristotle and oppose Kant in presupposing that emotions constitute an important part of character. Character deserves as much moral attention as conduct.

Kant viewed the emotions as "brute" forces that lie beyond the will and thwart reason. Subversive of the ideals of autonomy and rationality, the emotions prevent all-important reason from working smoothly. Western philosophers have largely equated (inferior) femininity with the emotions and (superior) masculinity with reason. Kant endorses this bias and weaves it into moral philosophy that exhorts us to banish the emotions from the courtroom. When thinking about what someone else deserves, we are not to allow our emotions to influence our conclusions. But we can hardly keep our emotions at bay, especially when people we love have suffered injustice. The assumption that women cannot properly think through justice now offends us, and yet we still wrestle with fundamental questions about how our emotions might inform judgments about what other people deserve.

A century before Kant, Descartes insisted in his *Meditations on First Philosophy* that emotion is not essential to human nature, although reason is. This position has exercised a profound influence on much philosophical thinking and has come to be associated more closely with Kant, who deepened and rounded out the view. Even today, moral philosophers who follow Kant (and, implicitly, Descartes) focus their attention on action or conduct, as opposed to character. Professional preoccupation with moral *action* explains in part why *Schadenfreude* has received very little philosophical attention in either the English or German traditions. Such preoccupation derives in large part from Kant's emblematic devaluation of emotion.

Kant must be wrong that we know nothing of moral significance about a person just from knowing his or her emotions, for we frequently *do* focus on a person's emotions in judging his or her worth. Our knowledge of the emotions of other people often determines whether we wish to befriend or avoid them. Familiarity with our own emotions precedes the honest examination of conscience through which we determine whether other people deserve their suffering. Without some basic understanding of how our emotions affect our beliefs, we will not be able to identify the sources of *Schadenfreude*. Our deepest and strongest emotions, oblique as they may sometimes seem, reveal the effect others have had on us. Far from an irrational passion, *Schadenfreude* reflects both the moral sensibility of the communities around us and the social notion of where we stand in those communities.

The Genesis of *Schadenfreude*

Beyond the myriad of possible causal antecedents of *Schadenfreude* lie what I consider its principal sources: 1) low self-esteem; 2) loyalty and commitments to justice; 3) the comical; and 4) malice. Each of the four contributes uniquely to an understanding of why people might choose to profit emotionally from the misfortune or suffering of someone else.

We ought to view the first three categories as mitigating factors in the determination of moral guilt and blame. The fourth cause, like its resulting case, must always be condemned. Both the second and the third catalysts are intrinsically questionable from a psychological point of view. This is so because of the ease with which we may rationalize pleasure in the suffering of others as a function of love for justice (with regard to the second category) or the value of a sense of humor (with regard to the third).

Nietzsche and Freud found human aggression lurking behind both religious devotion and laughter. I aim to move beyond this insight. Less convinced of the intersection of religious devotion and aggression than they, I take particular interest in expectations among the pious that sinners will suffer. As for laughter: while I agree that much of the comical does hinge on aggression, enough joy qualifies as what Freud referred to as the "regained lost laughter of childhood" to caution us against a hasty reduction to aggression.

Common to all four categories is a thought about another person. The following self-other contexts set the stage for *Schadenfreude*:

1. Low self-esteem

Injuries to self-esteem often generate suffering. An experience as insignificant as negotiating day-to-day life or as potentially torturous as romantic disappointment can collapse self-confidence and trigger aggressive responses which reverberate through everything else a person does. Self-esteem problems may plague a particular group or even an entire nation. Writing in 1843, the young Karl Marx worried about the self-esteem of his countrymen:

Man's self-esteem, his sense of freedom, must be awakened in the breast of [the German] people. This sense vanished from the world with the Greeks, and with Christianity it took up residence in the blue mists of heaven, but only with its aid can society ever again become a community of men that can fulfill their highest needs, a democratic state.[5]

Marx is by no means the first philosopher to make the point that self-esteem appears necessary to human flourishing. Marx deems self-esteem a political precondition for achievement. Over a century later the state of California followed suit. Republican governor George Deukmejian ratified in September 1986 the creation of the California Task Force to Promote Self-Esteem and Personal and Social Responsibility. The stated purpose of the task force was to promote the well-being of the individual and of society in order to diminish an ever-growing epidemic of casualties resulting from serious social ills.[6]

Although a broad array of groups experience distinctly social problems with self-esteem, I have individuals in mind here. According to Francis Bacon, individuals who have endured temporary setbacks, catastrophes, or deprivations are likely to think that other men's harms redeem their own sufferings (hence the familiar "misery loves company").[7] Perhaps intentionally, Bacon leaves unspecified the role of familiarity in the generation of this pleasure. Familiarity with a sufferer is neither a necessary nor a sufficient condition for *Schadenfreude*.

Philosophers and psychologists dispute what distinguishes self-respect from self-esteem and even whether there is a difference. Such scholarly debates notwithstanding, self-esteem can be understood as the capacity to value oneself despite one's imperfections and limitations. Self-esteem enhances our sense that we are leading good lives; indeed, it is difficult to separate the two. There are two ways to understand the social aspect of self-esteem. Healthy self-esteem dovetails with egalitarianism insofar as self-esteem presupposes that all persons can come to like themselves. The inherent worth of one person does not increase because of superior attributes or talents or decrease because of inferior attributes or talents. Self-esteem does not blind us to interpersonal differences; rather, it prevents us from concluding that the superiority of one person signifies worthlessness or inherent defect in another.

That said, we can understand self-esteem in precisely the opposite way as well. In fact, many people believe that our individual worth, while not static, rises and falls on our attributes and talents. A consumer-driven society conditions us to think of people as goods. It is easy to see how an unreflective person who enjoyed healthy self-esteem might agree with someone who had little self-esteem here: without certain talents or attributes, a winner might think, it would be impossible to like oneself.

According to political philosopher John Rawls, people enjoy self-esteem if they consider their aims and ideals as worthy and, second, believe that they are well suited to pursue them.[8] Low self-esteem, like anxiety over perceived bad luck, brings squarely into the foreground of consciousness the occasionally agonizing interplay of what belongs to us and what belongs to the world, of conquering our world and being conquered by it. Further, low self-esteem causes suffering insofar as it alerts us to the possibilities that our values are shoddy or that we are not capable of attaining what we hope for. Although ethically excusable, the *Schadenfreude* born of low self-esteem manifests weakness of character, even as it illustrates the social merits of proposals for eliminating envy or reducing its effects on human interaction.

Various egalitarian writers have claimed that since envy arises from inequity, the way to reduce the prevalence of envy is simply to reduce the extent to which some people possess more of something good than others. Rawls's theory of justice can be taken to suggest that *Schadenfreude* is an appropriate emotional experience because of social injustice, the condition in which the less fortunate are forcibly reminded of what they lack. He writes in *A Theory of Justice*: "When envy is a reaction to the loss of self-respect in circumstances where it would be unreasonable to expect someone to feel differently, I shall say that it is excusable" (p. 534). Rawls maintains that the principles of justice are reasonable despite the propensities of human beings to envy and jealousy. He is perhaps unique among moral philosophers in acknowledging good excuses for envy. He defines the primary good of self-respect as a person's sense that his or her plan of life is a worthy one and its fulfillment is of value. Rawls's thinking here resonates with some of Marx's central tenets.

Conversely, some anti-egalitarian writers have claimed that egalitarianism is itself a product of envy and therefore deeply suspect: it injures those who have more of something good and thereby appeases the envy of those who have less. When the fortunate suffer sudden reversals of good fortune, their social inferiors may rejoice at seeing them brought back into line with others. Nietzsche equated the doctrine of egalitarianism with *ressentiment*[9] and decay in his analysis of the "order of the rank" in *The Will to Power*. He regarded it as a form of cultural pessimism that opposed the instincts of life and sentenced existence itself to death. The search for plausible arguments for egalitarianism requires analysis of envy itself. I argue that one's self-esteem may be so weak as to make any sort of eminence another person enjoys painful. Such weakness underscores the import of moral education and the value of sympathy. An important link connects self-esteem and resentment. Resentment consists of anger caused by an affront to one's dignity. Those who believe themselves morally enti-tled to certain treatment are disposed to resent what they regard as indig-nities. Just as resentment reflects a healthy self-esteem, *Schadenfreude* indicates a reasonable and defensible pleasure that another has received his comeuppance ("those who live by the sword die by the sword").

To the extent that a feeling of inferiority seems to invite celebration of others' woes, condemning a *schadenfroh* person is a bit like castigating people for not liking themselves more. And to the extent that a feeling of disempowerment seems to invite resentment, condemning a *schadenfroh* person is a bit like blaming him or her for dissatisfaction with an unjust social framework.

2. Justice and loyalty

A commitment to justice or a sense of loyalty may also generate *Schadenfreude*. This brand of *Schadenfreude* reflects a belief that if people violate moral obligations, others may appropriately enjoy the setbacks of the transgressors.

It might seem odd to group together here concerns about justice and loyalty, as Rawls does. Against Rawls, Michael Sandel and others have ar-gued that insisting on justice in intimate relationships corrupts the senti-ments that sustain friendship, love, and family bonds. Sandel claims in *Liberalism and the Limits of Justice* that the qualities of loving relation-ships deserve priority over justice in the pecking order of virtues of social life. For my purposes justice and loyalty serve similar roles in the genera-tion of and justification for *Schadenfreude* because each involves strong commitments to conceptions of morally good states of affairs. Without loyalty to a conception of justice, it would be difficult to view strangers as fellow travelers. Loyalty provides the basis for group cohesion without which a commitment to justice cannot take social root.

Games children learn at school, like athletic competitions, promote the psychological benefits of belonging to a particular group and of valuing that group through opposition to other groups. Athletic competitions, like wars, frequently employ combat metaphors urging the destruction of opponents. Extreme versions of these metaphors portray opponents as less than human, as animals to be abhorred. The modern-day *jihad* and the medieval Crusade both illustrate the relevance of this mentality to morality, or more precisely to the struggle to ensure that one version of morality reigns supreme. The idea of competition among different moralities increases the difficulty of following Augustine's exhortation to hate the sin and love the sinner, for the allegiance to one system (or team, if you will) can justify labeling opponents as "sinners." Competition, whether religious/moral or economic, can pit people against one another; in so doing, competition can diminish trust and dehumanize relationships.

To compete effectively, we must put aside some of our tender feelings. To judge fairly, we must do the same. The way we overcome or ignore compassion in such instances raises far-reaching moral questions. An excerpt from *The Reader,* by the German judge and novelist Bernhard Schlink, sums up the difficulty of loving the sinner but hating the sin. Michael, a young German, loses a lover in the 1940s only to find her again in a German courtroom. Hanna, the lover who suddenly abandoned him without explanation years earlier, stands trial for having worked as a Nazi prison guard. Horrified at the new knowledge of his old lover, Michael struggles to love Hanna while hating her sin:

> I wanted simultaneously to understand Hanna's crime and to condemn it. But it was too terrible for that. When I tried to understand it, I had the feeling I was failing to condemn it as it must be condemned. When I condemned it as it must be condemned, there was no room for understanding. But even as I wanted to understand Hanna, failing to understand her meant betraying her all over again. I could not resolve this. I wanted to pose myself both tasks — understanding and condemnation. But it was impossible to do both.[10]

I do not wish to deny that it is impossible to do both, only to assert that it can be extremely difficult to do so. Michael still loves the woman he believes must have carried out her duties only because she feared death for disobeying. Few among us will hesitate to condemn Nazi atrocities, yet Michael's struggle may, in different contexts, nonetheless resonate with many of us. It can be enormously difficult to forget ourselves, yet judging others seems to require something like that.

Each of us lives within a broad and shifting network of relationships, personal, professional, social, economic, and religious. Loyalty to one person, group, or tenet may impede the benevolence we might otherwise feel to an outsider who has been wronged by someone to whom we feel loyal. Competition can breed visceral feelings of loyalty. We want to protect those to whom we feel loyal; should a wrongdoer try to hurt our friend or group and hurt himself or herself in the process, we may feel justified in celebrating that pain. Even though we expect decision-makers across a broad range of social institutions to put aside their personal loyalties and act impartially, we often question whether they do so. A pessimistic view of human motivation undermines a distinction between loyalty and justice. This is not to express skepticism about the idea of impartiality, but rather to emphasize that impartiality does not come easily.

Most Western models of legal justice aim to transcend personal loyalties. According to Rawls, the sense of justice bespeaks goodwill toward humanity; it is a sentiment of the heart, one that grows out of the natural sentiments of love and friendship (*A Theory of Justice*, pp. 453–512). Even if we accept such a characterization, love for justice may still prompt pleasure in the suffering of others no less than personal loyalties might. This is so because of a sense of personal investment (resulting from self-esteem) which may accompany the endorsement of a moral or political view. Of crucial importance is the question of whether such suffering signifies a means to an end (that is, whether the suffering instructs someone whose worldview seems to require correction) or an end in itself (that is, whether the suffering should come to the sort of person who deserves to suffer). Once again, there is an important difference between enjoying *that* someone suffers and enjoying actual suffering. The former case must be held apart from *Schadenfreude*, for the attendant pleasure is not properly in seeing someone suffer, but in the hope that someone will learn a valuable lesson from having suffered. Thus we take pleasure not in the suffering of another, but in the hope that he or she will correct a mistake (because we may take pleasure in both, this case is not entirely distinct from *Schadenfreude*). The latter case, including as it does a notion of desert, involves *Schadenfreude*. Ultimately, it is the notion of desert that makes justice a more important and a more complicated consideration than loyalty. By "justice" I mean the fairly straightforward notion that people receive their just deserts. As I have said, we generally believe that a talented person who works hard deserves success, that an innocent person harmed by wrongdoers deserves compensation, and, to a lesser extent, that an arrogant person deserves his or her comeuppance. Such outcomes strike us as morally appropriate.

Freud denied the relevance of desert to justice, or at least to one way of understanding justice. He accounted for the egalitarian understanding of the principle, in which justice requires (subject to important qualifications) equality of net welfare for individuals, by attributing it to a psychology of envy.[11] Freud believed that the only reason we strive for social equality is that the disadvantaged envy the advantaged. This is a ponderous claim. Critics have pointed out that Freud's view of justice cannot, however, readily explain why the advantaged as well as the disadvantaged figure among lovers of equality. That persons are motivated by opposing interests, further, does not mean that they are motivated by envy or jealousy.

Religious convictions may decisively shape an understanding of desert or justice. The conceptualization of hell as the paradigm and culmination of suffering almost seems to beg comparisons of temporal suffering with eternal suffering and, consequently, thoughts about day-to-day justice. Contentious examples of religious justice may surprise us by their sheer variety. Some of the best known illustrations involve claims to land, as we find in the former Yugoslavia, Northern Ireland, and the West Bank of Isreal. These examples suggest what is perhaps the most familiar objection to religious ethics, that organized religions breed intolerance and hypocrisy. In considering arguments as to how morality might depend on loyalty to any religion, it is surely prudent to keep in mind at what and whom the arguments are aimed.

In their introduction to the "Symposium on 'God'" recently featured in a 1994 issue of *Critical Inquiry*, Françoise Meltzer and David Tracy remarked that the invocation of God currently seems to work as a point of obstruction, or a limit, in most contemporary critical discourses. As they put it, "the word *God*, in or outside of quotation marks, has become the last taboo in the postmodern era."[12] Certainly, it could be disarming to hear a neighbor invoke scripture to explain our own (i.e., intrinsic) suffering. A good deal of confusion has surrounded the idea of divine retribution, for the same God who famously proclaimed "Vengeance is mine" also avowed: ". . . I take no pleasure in the death of the wicked man, but rather in the wicked man's conversion, that he may live" (Ezekiel 33:11). Nonetheless, the belief in suffering as punishment and as evidence of divine disfavor has often recurred in both Judaism and in Christianity, especially at the level of popular belief. Religious convictions, by virtue of their great explanatory power and reference to justice, can play an integral role in the most contentious kind of *Schadenfreude*.

But Christianity is a missionary religion based on conversion, as Judaism is not. Like Buddhism and Islam, Christianity has aimed at world dissemination in a way Judaism never has. As early as the sixth century B.C., Buddhist missionaries from India sought conversions throughout Asia. Christian and Muslim missionaries later followed suit, traveling throughout the world for centuries with the express purpose of achieving conversions. Jews certainly developed ethical ideas with an eye to universal application of such ideas, but Jews never mounted campaigns to convert non-Jews to their beliefs. This is because Jewishness rests on a shared historical identity in a way that the other three religions do not.

I do not mean to suggest that Jews cannot feel a religiously charged *Schadenfreude*. When they do, the pleasure usually issues from the misfortunes of other Jews. The same religious "will to power" that creates strife between religions can lead to division within them. Think here of Luther. Splits within Christianity highlighted the growing problem of how Christians of various creeds could get along with another. It may well be that people are more likely to feel *Schadenfreude* when their fellow believers land in trouble than when adherents of other creeds suffer, for we often expect more of those who claim to share our loyalties than we do of others.

3. The comical

The comical is the source of *Schadenfreude* perhaps the most resistant to analysis, and, when compared to the previous two components, best evinces the enormous differences within this emotion-type. Philosophical attention to comedy will broaden our cultural conception of what qualities a good moral character must include or exclude (by "character" I mean one's predominant pattern of thought and action, especially with respect to concerns affecting the happiness of others or of oneself). Such attention will simultaneously frustrate efforts to condemn *Schadenfreude*.

Should we hold humor to be fully answerable to ethical considerations? If we do so, life becomes even heavier than it already is. Nonetheless, many moral thinkers have linked humor to evil. In his frequently reprinted essay "*De l'essence du rire*," Baudelaire identifies as "one of the most commonplace examples [of the comic] in life" a man falling on the ice or on the road, or tripping on the edge of a pavement. Baudelaire deplores the comic, which he considers "one of the clearest marks of Satan in man" ("*Le rire est satanique; il est donc profondément humain*").[13] Comic laughter frightens Baudelaire with the thought, "There but for the grace of God go I." Indeed, the enjoyment of comedy would seem to depend on confidence that what afflicts someone else will not, could not, happen to us.

Schadenfreude is, of course, a function of both pleasure and suffering. Socrates tells us in the *Philebus* that all comedy is a mixture of pleasure and pain: "Whether the body be affected apart from the soul, or the soul apart from the body, or both of them together, we constantly come upon the mixture of pleasure with pain."[14] Because the ironies and utter impermanence of life loom larger on the horizon during wars and social crises, comedy flourishes when we might least expect it to. Comedy points to what actually happens, Aristotle tells us in the *Poetics*, in the interests of what may happen. Aristotle worried about comedy, even as a remedy for human suffering. Comedy naturally aims at laughter, and Aristotle believed that laughter masks aggression toward others.

Hobbes's reflections on comedy also turn importantly on aggression. In *Human Nature* (1650) and *Leviathan* (1651) he affirms that selfish motives propel comedy. Laughter, Hobbes says, is the result either of self-satisfaction or the "sudden glory" of the moment in which a person realizes his or her superiority over someone or something. For Hobbes, laughter at the weakness of others reveals a character flaw; it is unfitting for the strong to enjoy a sense of superiority over the weak.

Nietzsche's terse description in *The Gay Science* of laughter as "being *schadenfroh*, but with a good conscience" is indebted to Hobbes, but whereas Hobbes concerns himself specifically with laughter, Nietzsche is more interested in a general attitude toward the world, toward life, and toward oneself. Nietzsche's aphorism places the roots of the comic in feelings of superiority, a link Freud explores at length in *Jokes and Their Relation to the Unconscious*. Freud saw that jokes create problems and then remove them by the act of recognition. "The enjoyment of recognition," Freud explains, "is joy in power, a joy in the overcoming of a difficulty. . . . Recognition is pleasurable in itself, i.e., through relieving psychical expenditure — and the games founded on this pleasure make use of the damming up only in order to increase the amount of such pleasure."[15] The power of the joke is to succor us, to relieve temporarily the pressures of civilized life. This same sense of overcoming obstacles or resistance figures into Nietzsche's understanding of why the satisfactions of making others suffer are so sweet. The ability to make others suffer represents for Nietzsche a uniquely gratifying manifestation of the will to power.

Arguing that the comic is invariably somewhat infantile, Freud criticizes Henri Bergson's influential theory of humor as defective because the underlying comparison involved in humor need not evoke childish pleasures and childish *play*, but simply childish *nature*. In the only passage in that work in which Freud refers to *Schadenfreude* by name, he simply shrugs his shoulders and concludes, "certain motives for pleasure in children seem to be lost to us adults . . ." (*JR*, p. 279).

Laughter serves such good purpose that moralists hesitate to condemn mirth. Toward the end of the *Critique of Pure Reason* Kant praises laughter for helping us withstand the sheer difficulty of living. The same can be said of *Schadenfreude*.

4. Malice

Malice, or ill will, may either be general, directed toward all persons indiscriminately, or specific, focused on certain individuals or institutions. Because malicious persons are quite apt to revel in the suffering of others, it is difficult to dissociate *Schadenfreude* from the diabolical. Though malicious glee and *Schadenfreude* resemble one another in taking pleasure in the misfortunes of others, they are nonetheless distinct. Ill will is not a necessary condition for *Schadenfreude*.

Socrates and Aristotle both associated malice with *Schadenfreude*. In the *Philebus* Socrates declares, "one will find the malicious man pleased at his neighbor's ills" (48 b 7) and that "it is malice that makes us feel pleasure in our friends' misfortunes" (50 a 1). In the *Nichomachean Ethics* (2.7) Aristotle ties pleasure in the misfortune of others to spite (he specifically decries *Schadenfreude*, NE 2.6.18). Aristotle classifies envy with malice and shamelessness as feelings evil in themselves and for which there can be no golden mean (*NE* 2.6.102 and *Rhetoric* 2.9–10.231–43). Here Aristotle neglects the reality that we sometimes approve of and even celebrate the suffering of another for reasons we take to be moral.

Malice frequently causes people to lose a sense of proportion, causing them to hope for or actually to inflict terrible suffering upon another who has committed a fairly trivial offense. Of course, malice need not stem from any offense at all. Malice may subvert any attempt to develop consensus on the appropriateness of suffering in any given context. To make matters worse, cruelty and hatred may erupt indiscriminately, unprovoked by the persons toward whom they are unleashed. This fact further frustrates and impedes efforts to reach agreement on what punishment or suffering any given person may deserve.

The impossibility of reading the minds of others prevents us from knowing whether another feels malicious glee or *Schadenfreude*. The empirical complexity of human needs and interests blurs the distinction between the two. Commentators on *Schadenfreude* have seized on this ambiguity and taken the easy way out by declaring any pleasure in the distress of another morally off limits. This is not so surprising, given that numerous taboos aim to regulate ambiguities which would further complicate morality. *Schadenfreude* frustrates a moralist's desire for simplicity.

Low self-esteem, commitments to justice and loyalty, responses to the comical, and dispositional malice, these four are the principal antecedents of *Schadenfreude*. Only the last unequivocally calls for moral blame. Given the differences among the cognitive components of pleasure we take in the misfortunes of others, it should not seem farfetched to claim that this pleasure takes several forms.

These four sources divide themselves equally between worry and release. With either injuries to self-esteem or commitments to justice, another person (or other persons) threatens the self in some way or triggers a worry about the possibilities for self-realization, self-fulfillment, and happiness. These instances reflect worry about one's personal safety, possessions, status, or self-respect. In the cases of the comic and malice, however, pent-up emotion is released. Some prior attitude toward another person (or other persons) prompts a need for a release of sadness, aggression, or perhaps both.

What objections might be raised to this account of the genesis of *Schadenfreude*? The very idea of cutting *Schadenfreude* up into small pieces might itself seem suspect. For one way of taming a threatening idea would be to dissect the idea into so many harmless elements that nothing remains of the threat (as, for example, when Rawls distinguishes among at least six kinds of envy). The threat is all in our minds, the dissection would demonstrate, not in the idea itself. Of course, the threat *is* all in our minds, but not in the way that Schopenhauer insists. Schopenhauer makes *Schadenfreude* disappear by collapsing it into malice. In so doing, he makes moral monsters of us all. Schopenhauer fortifies a moral tradition that insists that good people always feel compassion when bad things happen to other people. When a moral tradition produces universal guilt and willful ignorance about that guilt, our personal and social stake in transforming common assumptions is quite high.

This section on the genesis of *Schadenfreude* sets up a framework for assessing morally acceptable examples of pleasure in the misfortunes of others. Far from a knee-jerk reaction, *Schadenfreude* evolves from a thought process that leaves us judges of what other people deserve. In *Schadenfreude* we find ourselves winners: experience has presented us with evidence that the world punishes bad people, or people who have managed their affairs badly.

This framework, focusing as it does on how much we like ourselves, will not lead us to find morally acceptable every emotion of people who suffer from low self-esteem. But our new knowledge should prevent us from hastily condemning the *Schadenfreude* of people who possess little self-esteem and help us make sense of our interaction with other people generally. We are less apt than others to consider our own suffering deserved or trivial. We forget that just as we can assure ourselves that we take a morally acceptable pleasure in the suffering of others (because it seems deserved), so also can others justify their pleasure in our miseries. When we realize that so-called justice can just as easily work against us as for us, we should think twice about how hard we will allow ourselves to be on others.

Our way of looking at the world possesses extraordinary power: it can make a heaven of hell, or a hell of heaven. That outlook can make others suffer more than they already do. Or less.

II

When Really Bad Things Happen to Other People

TALKING ABOUT THE BAD THINGS THAT HAPPEN TO OTHER people raises questions about the experience of suffering. Suffering can harm most deeply by eroding cherished beliefs we hold about ourselves or the world around us. Suffering threatens to rob us of control. Few would dispute that there are *degrees* of sadness; I argue as well for a difference *of kind* between trivial and significant misfortunes. Another father-son narrative will prove useful here; this one turns on *Schadenfreude* that arises from significant misfortune.

Further, I ask what it is to take suffering too seriously and what it is to take suffering in stride. I then turn to the matter of interpreting suffering as a sign of God's punishment. The main idea I advance is that interpreting suffering as a message from either God or the invisible hand of justice will almost invariably land us in trouble. We have shown great difficulty in accepting the role of randomness in our lives and in the world.

Injustice similarly confounds our way of thinking about the world. The violation of a law or a social norm angers us so deeply that we feel we must see the violator brought low, as Kant said. Our institutional response to bad people has been to make them suffer (at the hands of judges we have appointed). We do to others what we do not want done to us. In order for justice to be reasonable, we must have well-founded notions both of what is due us and what is due others.

Those whose suffering we celebrate must possess the intelligence necessary to conform to social standards. We ourselves must realize that it is only fair for others to judge us as we have judged them: the same rationale that justifies our taking pleasure in another's suffering today may justify his or her taking pleasure in our suffering tomorrow.

Forgiveness and mercy point to a different way out of our bad feelings. Even when we manage to forgive people who have transgressed, though, we may still insist on punishment in order to demonstrate loyalty to our principles. Proper self-respect, so vital to our flourishing, stands in the way of our forgiving readily people or classes of people who have harmed us. Few have been willing to concede that we often possess morally acceptable reasons for not forgiving others. Although we may morally choose not to forgive others, we forget at our peril an ancient maxim: judge as ye shall be judged.

Three

The Meaning of Suffering

> It is in the response to suffering that many and perhaps all men, individually and in their groups, define themselves, take on character, develop their ethos.
> — H. Richard Niebuhr

"WHAT ARE THE SORROWS OF OTHER MEN TO US, AND WHAT THEIR joy?," Defoe asks in *Robinson Crusoe*. H. Richard Niebuhr, a towering figure in modern theology, never mentions Defoe but supplies the beginning of what must be the best answer to this, the question from which moral philosophy and moral psychology begin. It is in our responses to suffering — both our own and others' — that we prove our moral worth. Of all the slings and arrows of outrageous fortune, few hurt more than watching others take joy in our sorrow. And of all the ties that bind, there can be few greater than sharing sorrow.

As extraordinarily varied as people are, we become in some real sense the same as everyone else when we suffer. This is particularly true in instances of great suffering. The elasticity of *Schadenfreude*, the emotional corollary of justice, can accommodate terrible suffering. The awfulness of suffering I discuss here will set the stage for a parallel with the awfulness of justice (or what others consider to be justice for us). I want to probe whether the pleasure we take in the suffering of another does in fact say more about the sufferer than it does about us.

To insist that the happiness of others affects our own is only to acknowledge a truism, not to account for it. Why should the unhappiness of another produce an opposite state in us? That this happens seems obvious enough, given the extent to which both philosophical and religious ethics oppose the phenomenon. Why this happens requires attention to two questions: What is suffering? And what is it about suffering that might give pleasure to someone else? Answers to these questions will help explain why it is that taking pleasure in others' misfortunes causes moral revulsion.

The idea that it is appropriate to make criminals suffer raises the question of why we should not subsequently take pleasure in that suffering. Our ideas about criminal and social justice inform and shape each other. Underlying them both are difficult questions about central elements of suffering: its causes, its significance, its usefulness. My discussion of suffering will distinguish pain from suffering and show that suffering is not only the absence of pleasure but also a disruption of identity. Although a harmless slip on the ice or on a banana peel might involve such tension (we might pride ourselves on our agility), it is principally in significant suffering that identity disruption occurs. At the heart of *Schadenfreude* lies a celebration that another person may have to re-evaluate his or her self-worth and the principles by which he or she lives. This means that we are unlikely to feel *Schadenfreude* toward people with little or no self-esteem. Only a cruel or malicious person takes pleasure in the injuries of those who do not like themselves.

The suffering of others dominates this discussion, although not to the exclusion of our own suffering. I will examine the idea that we should attribute greater moral significance to others' suffering than to our own. My argument that our own suffering is no less important than the suffering of others begins with the wisdom at the heart of Freud's critique of the love commandment. Proper care of the self throws into question the appropriateness of indiscriminate sympathy and, further, makes *Schadenfreude* a badge of healthy self-esteem.

Separating Suffering from Pain

What is the point of claiming a distinction between suffering and pain? *Schadenfreude* centers on suffering for the most part, not pain. To understand *Schadenfreude*, we must understand its source. To understand this source, we must see how suffering differs from pain.

A toothache exemplifies pain; guilt exemplifies suffering. A toothache has little to do with one's relation to the human community; guilt that one has transgressed a social norm has everything to do with the human community. The distinction between pain and suffering is a moral one. Why is this so?

Moral problems do not precede us in the world: we bring them to life. Moral problems are not like trees — something we can run into if we drop our guard. Moral problems ride on the coattails of our thoughts. Marrying a person of another race or another social class becomes a moral problem in a world that forbids such things. These days such marriages do not cause the social controversy they did in Europe and the United States in the early twentieth century. Having a toothache has always and likely always will cause pain. Pain affects the way we think of ourselves, to be sure, but suffering affects us much more profoundly. Pain is less interesting than suffering because pain lacks the rich social dimension of suffering.

Pain involves damage or likely damage to the body; it emanates from a particular location on or in the body. By contrast, most suffering involves unlocated emotions. Emotional suffering can be either psychological or biological (as with clinical depression, which is linked to chemical imbalances in the brain), although it tends to be the former. Pain can be mild or moderate, acute or chronic. Emotions can be blameworthy or praiseworthy, and can center on large and small objects.

It would be misleading to link pain to the purely physical and suffering to the purely mental. In a widely lauded study, Mark Zborowski has tied ethnicity to how we respond to pain.[1] He found that Jewish-American patients voiced existential, philosophical concern about the pain they experienced and tended to be pessimistic about the course of their pain. Protestant patients, on the other hand, displayed optimism about the course of their illnesses and felt quite confident about the abilities of physicians to help them. Italian-American patients differed from Jewish-Americans in that they did not seem to care much at all about the larger meaning or significance of their pain; Italian-Americans simply wanted quick relief from pain. Pain, like suffering, prompts different responses in different cultures.

Although the common-sense view is that pain entails some degree of awfulness, pain can be separated from our response to it. It is well known that masochists profess to enjoy pain and humiliation and that prizefighters and soldiers will occasionally report that they were totally unaware that they had been severely injured until after the struggle concluded. Because leprosy can destroy the microscopic fibers that carry the sense of pain, someone stricken with leprosy will feel no pain at all if he or she places his or her hand on a burning kitchen stove. These perhaps obscure examples make it hard to say that pain is always or necessarily unpleasant.

As for suffering: do we always want to avoid it? Apparently not, given that people frequently reject relief from grief, remorse, guilt, or unrequited love. This is more serious than simply noting that what distresses others may differ from what distresses us. It won't do simply to declare anyone who enjoys feeling pain or who dislikes himself or herself neurotic and therefore anomalous. Too many characters from books, theater, film, comic strips, and television, whose troubles in love, honor, and fortune have long held us rapt with attention, testify to the appealing underside of some disagreeable emotional trials. The same may be said of guests on many television talk shows or of many a magazine interviewee. If pain and suffering are not always or thoroughly unpleasant, then, how can it be said that we reasonably seek to avoid them? Given that we might simply be mistaken about our presumption of unpleasantness, *Schadenfreude* might appear either an irrational or an unintelligible response to the suffering of another person.

Schadenfreude is neither irrational nor unintelligible. For although it may be that some pains are either pleasant or at least not unpleasant, anyone who objects that pains are not necessarily unpleasant must turn to the marginal cases to prove the point. That so many people seek treatment for or consolation from their physical pain or emotional suffering indicates the reasonableness of the premise that we dislike pain and suffering. That there is a problem both with verifying statements about pain and suffering (we cannot be sure about the accuracy of another's report of pain) and with the idea that pain and suffering are awful (we cannot be sure how bad a person feels) means that it is difficult to agree on what kind or degree of unpleasantness *Schadenfreude* celebrates.

How much can we really know about the pain of another person? Afflicted people will often complain about the difficulty of communicating their anguish. We may find ourselves perplexed even at the sound of another's pain, as Proust did:

. . . one never understands precisely the meaning of an original sound expressive of a sensation which one does not experience oneself. Hearing it from a neighbouring room without being able to see, one may mistake for a chuckle the noise which is forced by pain from a patient being operated on without an anaesthetic; and as for the noise emitted by a mother who has just been told that her child has died, it can seem to us, if we are unaware of its origin, as difficult to translate into human terms as the noise emitted by an animal or by a harp.[2]

Proust seemed to think that even knowing the cause of another's pain may leave us struggling to understand what is happening to him or her; the obstacle to understanding, Proust believed, came down to ". . . the curtain that is forever lowered for other people over what happens in the mysterious intimacy of every human creature."

Wittgenstein saw pain as a curtain that divides us from others. His ruminations on the sensation of pain, especially in *Philosophical Investigations* I, Sections 243–308, have set in place an epistemology of pain.[3] Although it would be absurd to say that no one can ever know whether another is in pain or not, or even conceive what it would be for another to be in pain, Wittgenstein concluded, we cannot readily verify either the presence or the extent of suffering in another. But we can certainly *believe* that he or she suffers (because it makes no sense to argue with sincere people who insist they feel pain). That belief suffices to generate an emotional response to the pain or suffering of another.

I have said that pain emanates from a location on or in a body, but that suffering does not. The presence of pain is neither a necessary nor a sufficient condition for suffering. Pain has a felt quality, a felt intensity. Suffering, on the other hand, is not located in the body. The suffering of grief, envy, and anxiety do not relate to the nervous system, as does the sensation of pain.

Numerous writers concur that only bodies feel pain and that only persons suffer. (Bentham held that animals suffer and so possess moral rights, but I do not consider animals here.) This distinction is useful. For example, it helps to put in context the biomedical ethicist Tristram Engelhardt's approval of the practice of subjecting newborn infants to painful procedures (for example, circumcision) on the grounds that they cannot integrate the experience of pain sufficiently so as to be said actually to suffer.[4] I accept this narrowing of the concept of suffering and accordingly stipulate that pain is neither a necessary nor a sufficient condition for *Schadenfreude*. That pain often includes suffering does not diminish the point of this distinction, for the converse cannot be said to be true.

Unlike pain, suffering always entails a psychological and/or a social component. This component can change suddenly or evolve gradually: in any event, it is not static. The suffering of children forced to work in factories or immigrant families crowded into dirty, unsafe hovels commands a different popular reaction today than it would have a century, or perhaps even a decade, ago. The legal theorist Richard Posner remarks in *Overcoming Law* that, "Slavery just doesn't mesh with our current belief system, which includes a historically recent belief in racial equality that is held as dogmatically (though secretly doubted by many of its holders) as our ancestors held their belief in inequality."[5] This social dimension shapes and refracts the experience of suffering.

Whereas pain calls out for medication or bandages, suffering waits for sympathy. The experience of suffering marginalizes us all by isolating us from other people. The successful articulation of suffering, in poems, novels, and paintings, serves to move us closer to others whose understanding is a primary source of consolation. The closer we move to others, the more we can feel triumphant over suffering. T.S. Eliot once summed up the sense of hell in Dante's *Inferno* as a place "where nothing connects with nothing." Hell is a place where people do not, cannot, console one another. *Schadenfreude* brings to light and reinforces distances between people, however temporarily. All this is to say that the *Schaden* (literally "injury" or "harm") of *Schadenfreude* focuses on suffering, on the relation in which we stand to others.

Suffering Great and Small

Satisfaction in witnessing the execution of a murderer differs in several important ways from laughing at the sight of someone slipping on a banana peel, but *Schadenfreude* can accurately describe both instances of pleasure.

Kafka's sister Elli has no voice in *Brief an den Vater*; we know her only as someone who suffers. (And, later on, as someone who leaves home and establishes herself successfully as a wife and mother, Kakfa triumphantly tells his father.) Can we quantify her suffering, and if so, why would we want to do so? In Sophocles's *Oedipus Rex* and *Oedipus at Colonus*, Oedipus informs the chorus that his suffering exceeds theirs. ("I know you are all sick, yet there is not one of you are, who is as sick as I myself.") A hero and king, Oedipus believes his capacity for suffering to be deeper than that of his people. Just before Jocasta's suicide, the line "the greatest suffering is that one brings on oneself" suggests the accuracy of Oedipus's early statement to the chorus. Later Oedipus's devastated daughters wonder aloud if it would be better never to have lived at all; they claim to envy the dead, because the dead, which now include their father, do not suffer. It seems unlikely that Kafka's sister found herself envying the dead in the course of enduring her father's mimicking, yet she might well have told us that she felt united to Oedipus's daughters through what she endured.

Suffering is awful. It might seem that only enemies of some sort would take pleasure in each other's suffering. This pleasure in the suffering of another must be more pervasive than that, though. La Rochefoucauld famously claimed, "In the adversities of our best friends we always find something which is not displeasing to us" (*Réflexions morales*, number 99). La Rochefoucauld does not delimit the idea of "adversities" in this maxim, an unsettling omission. Dostoyevsky carries the ball a bit farther. In *Crime and Punishment* he expands the category of misfortunes capable of generating *Schadenfreude*:

> . . . that strange feeling of inner satisfaction which always can be observed, even in those who are near and dear, when a sudden disaster befalls their neighbor, and which is to be found in all men, without exception, however sincere their feelings of sympathy and commiseration.[6]

The word "disaster" signifies something beyond trivial suffering. Dostoyevsky, albeit an insightful moral psychologist, probably overstates the frequency of pleasure in the disasters of others. Learning that our quiet, law-abiding neighbor has just been diagnosed with cirrhosis of the liver or made a victim of ethnic cleaning would provide few of us with unfettered delight. Underneath the overstatement, if we want to call it that, we can glimpse Dostoyevsky's sympathy with the claim that good people may enjoy even the very bad things that happen to others.

Dostoyevsky's alarming claim in a sense ignites and begins this study, for great suffering makes *Schadenfreude* a much more unsettling and important topic than comedy. Hamlet doesn't spend his energy trying to make sense of *bad* fortune, but rather of the slings and arrows of *outrageous* fortune. *Schadenfreude* can accommodate great suffering because the notion of desert that lies at the heart of much *Schadenfreude* can expand infinitely. Note that Dostoyevsky does not state or imply that people feel pleasure in the face of their friends' disasters out of a sense that justice has been done; like La Rochefoucauld, he acknowledges the phenomenon of pleasure over the great suffering of others but does not account for it. Without a sincere appeal to justice, Dostoyevsky's pleasure amounts to perversity, cruelty, or both.

Another father-son interchange will make this point more concrete. Like Kafka's example, this one also comes from an autobiography. In *My German Question* Peter Gay confesses to the great joy he took in the defeat of the German women's relay team in the track and field portion of the 1936 Olympics in Berlin. The eminent Yale professor, perhaps the greatest living social historian of our day, bore the name Peter Fröhlich in 1936. His Jewish family, most of which eventually managed to escape to the United States, was suffering Nazi persecution throughout the 1930s.

Gay writes in his autobiography of his "unqualified idealization of the United States" as a boy. In view of Hitler, Gay sat with his father in the stadium and cheered wildly the victory of every American at the Berlin games. "Unfortunately, many German athletes also did well enough to win an array of gold medals," he remembers. "I took them all as virtually personal insults." We should not quickly dismiss Gay as merely malicious here, for we generally believe that the wicked do not deserve to flourish.

The success of Nazi athletes in the 1936 Olympics was not complete, however. The German women's relay team failed and here is how Gay reacted to their defeat:

As long as I live I shall hear my father's voice as he leaped to his feet, one of the first to see what had happened: *Die Mädchen haben den Stab verloren!* he shouted, "The girls have dropped the baton!" As Helen Stevens loped to the tape to give the Americans yet another gold medal, the unbeatable models of Nazi womanhood cried their German hearts out. A number of years ago, in a brief reminiscence, I wrote that seeing this calamity "remains one of the great moments in my life."[7]

There is an element of ugliness in Gay's profession here, the same ugliness we sometimes find in others who resolutely hold us accountable for our wrongdoing. Anything that comes at the cost of human suffering may repel us, even justice. That said, I certainly do not wish to incriminate Gay here.

Gay, a native German speaker, makes room for great suffering in his understanding of *Schadenfreude*. As was the case with Kafka, *Schadenfreude* unites a father and a son in this passage. Note that Gay tells us he does not regret or condemn his *Schadenfreude*; instead, he relishes it.

If it is true that "Pleasure not known beforehand is half-wasted: to anticipate it is to double it,"[8] then *Schadenfreude* should present itself as a comparatively minor pleasure, smaller than revenge and sadism. I think it is true. Curiously, Gay asserts that *Schadenfreude* "can be one of the great joys of life." How can this be? We love justice so profoundy that we may literally rejoice when we come face to face with it. Gay craved justice and leapt to his feet in jubilation over Nazi humiliation on the race track. In other instances of *Schadenfreude,* we may find satisfied a wish we didn't fully realize we had. *Schadenfreude* can and often does turn on the unexpected.

Before moving on, I ought to explain why I translate *Schadenfreude* as pleasure in the *suffering* of another, as opposed to pleasure in the *misfortune* of another. Aaron Ben-Ze'ev's lucid analysis of the emotion deserves such praise that I hesitate to disagree at all. While noting that *Schadenfreude* is usually translated as the former, he suggests that the latter is in fact more appropriate because of the triviality of the injury (and corresponding suffering) involved in *Schadenfreude*.[9] Ben-Ze'ev's is a more literal translation of the term, one that gives emphasis to the fact of another's misfortune, as opposed to the probable suffering that ensues from it.

Ben-Ze'ev and I agree that suffering varies according to both degree and kind. In contrast to other theorists of suffering, however, Ben-Ze'ev seems to resist the idea that the misery of suffering stems from a disruption of identity. Indeed, he wants to limit *Schadenfreude* to misfortunes that seem neither particularly unpleasant, nor threatening to personal identity. A mishap such as slipping harmlessly on the ice, while technically a misfortune, can only ambiguously be said to involve full-blown suffering. Ben-Ze'ev prefers to restrict pleasure in the misfortunes of others to trivial harm, although he does not straightforwardly disqualify significant injury from the equation. I explicitly allow significant injury.

William Ian Miller has more clearly restricted *Schadenfreude* to the realm of the trivial.[10] Miller's objection to my characterization of *Schadenfreude* implies discrepancy over the structure of the emotion. For, unlike Ben-Ze'ev and myself, Miller refers to *Schadenfreude* as a kind of malice (even though he puts "malice" between quotation marks). This view is consonant with one he expressed in an earlier work: "For just as our humiliations provide others with the basis for their *Schadenfreude*, so do their humiliations provide us ours. Such a nice gift, we believe, could hardly do without an equally nice return."[11] Like Ben-Ze'ev, Miller seems to view *Schadenfreude* as akin to white lies, as an inconsequential moral failing. In this spirit and in the name of inevitability, Miller suggests that we are foolish not to accept the pleasure offered us by the misfortunes of others. Miller has a point here, namely the wisdom underlying the exhortation *Carpe diem*.

Miller's use of the word "humiliation" stands at odds with his insistence that *Schadenfreude* includes only insignificant instances of suffering; nonetheless, he specifically states in his later work *The Anatomy of Disgust*, "Pleasure in another's *major* misfortune is truly malicious and hateful" (my emphasis). Miller shuts the door to the possibility that we might believe a corrupt political leader deserves impeachment or exile. In this respect his view differs from Ben-Ze'ev's and mine. Holding that *Schadenfreude* is morally acceptable as an emotional corollary to beliefs about justice opens the door to serious suffering. *Schadenfreude* does not restrict its object to the trivial. The objection to linking serious suffering with *Schadenfreude*, centering on a cut-off point beyond which *Schadenfreude* is no longer felt, is simply another way of putting the question of the appropriateness of suffering — not a way of circumventing that question.

Although I insist that all suffering (even that involved in comedy) is in some real sense awful, I acknowledge the importance of Ben-Ze'ev's assertion that persons are more prone to enjoy what they believe to be the minor suffering of others than they are to enjoy the more serious examples of suffering. The greater the misfortune involved, the more likely *Schadenfreude* is to center principally or exclusively on some principle of justice. Outside of the theater, envy and jealousy generally cling to the shallow end of human experience. There must be a point beyond which no one would feel morally justified in taking pleasure in the suffering of others — only malicious people could celebrate the suffering of Oedipus's daughters — but this cut-off point cannot be specified definitively. Reluctance to link *Schadenfreude* to significant suffering reflects discomfort with competing moralities. Others disagree, sometimes strenuously, with the values we hold. Reflection on the moral beliefs others espouse sometimes makes it more difficult for us to think of them as friends.

Rationalizing Suffering

Explaining the moral range of acceptable emotional reactions to the setbacks of others requires mention of self-awareness. Fear of suffering — our own or someone else's — may compel us to pretend to ourselves.

The most common mental dodge to *Schadenfreude* must be telling ourselves that we enjoy that another suffers (i.e. that justice prevails), not the actual suffering itself. This rationalization represents a defense in some people, one consciously chosen to ward off guilt and ramp up self-worth. In other people, however, the appeal to justice stems from sincere commitments to a moral order of some sort and should not be considered a rationalization. We might refer to the first group as selfish and to the second as selfless. The second group can astonish us no less than the first with creative struggles to make sense of suffering.

Judith Shklar's insight into the difference between misfortune and injustice nicely illustrates the most obvious path for rationalizing the bad things which happen to other people. In *The Faces of Injustice* she argues that we tend to see misfortune rather than injustice when we are unwilling to act, to respond to a problem.[12] Homeless people wandering the streets of our cities, for example, become the agents of their own misfortunes in this mindset, and we thereby distance ourselves from them. The homeless are to blame for their plight. If we view the homeless as victims of an unjust social system that has somehow caused their plight, however, then we can hardly help feeling responsible for their suffering. We are ourselves part of the problem.

Over a period of twenty years, Melvin Lerner directed a series of psychological experiments and surveys on misfortune.[13] He found that about two-thirds of all his respondents resorted to a perceptual shortcut similar to the one Shklar follows. People who fear the vagaries of life or sudden reversals of good fortune may rely unduly upon a belief in the invisible hand of justice. When such people come across examples of suffering, they tell themselves that the suffering has happened to a person who somehow deserved it. Lerner concluded that the need to believe that sufferers are somehow bad unites many under its banner. According to Lerner, we see justice where we want to or need to. This mental defense comes at a price: when we suffer, we will know that others blame us for our suffering on some level. This knowledge pulls the people around us into our seemingly private suffering, by making them a part of the bad things that happen to us. In those moments of despondency, when we feel utterly disconnected to other human beings, they are there.

What are we to make of the moral judgments of other people, judgments which often magnify our suffering? When others rationalize our suffering, persuading themselves that we deserve to suffer when they do not really believe we do, cruelty raises its head. The familiar moral objections to cruelty apply to rationalizing the undeserved suffering of others.

Why would anyone rationalize in this way? To survive, we have to make some sense of our world. Dividing people into categories of "us" and "them" facilitates an easy but untenable conclusion about appropriateness: they suffer because they and their kind are bad. I and people like me will not suffer, because we are good. Beyond that, we might rationalize the suffering of people like us because our emotional attachment to or investment in them might not be whole-hearted. Self-interest can divide us even from people we like. If Freud succeeded in any way, it was in illuminating the fundamental ambivalence of our psychic lives.

We ought not to dismiss the mental defense of seeing justice where we choose to before acknowledging its merits. In *The Wisdom of the Ego* Harvard psychiatrist George Vaillant draws a compelling analogy between the body's immune system and the mind's defenses. Far from condemning the emotional and intellectual dishonesty underlying these defenses of the mind, Vaillant praises them as "healthy" and "creative" means of coping with life's misery. Milton writes in *Paradise Lost*: "The mind is its own place, and in itself / Can make a heav'n of hell, a hell of heav'n." Vaillant holds out Milton's insight as perhaps our best defense for coping with events which would otherwise overwhelm us. Vaillant emphasizes the survival value of such defenses. It would be all too easy to maintain a moral hard line and, against Vaillant, to condemn such mental defenses as weaknesses. Rallying behind this moral hard line, we hide from the fierceness of suffering. To continue with our lives sanely, we sometimes feel entitled to tell ourselves stories imaginatively.

We need to remember that two opposing perspectives are at work here: that of a person suffering and that of another person, who may or may not be suffering. It might seem preposterous to maintain that we can deceive ourselves about whether suffering is deserved. Can we really make ourselves believe something when we know it is not true? Yes, from either a first-person or a third-person point of view. Self-loathing happens, particularly among the disenfranchised. To make sense of the world, we may come to identify with our aggressors. By the same token, we may persuade ourselves that a particular person or an entire class of persons must surely deserve the bad things that happen to them. Our motivation for persuading ourselves might be either fear of the idea of random suffering or fear of standing apart from the community that has taught us certain beliefs about appropriate suffering.

We can learn something from reflecting on the kinds of people whose sufferings bring us pleasure. We rarely celebrate the bad things that happen to the poor, the crippled, the powerless, unless we have identified them in some other way that we may find objectionable (Larry Flynt or George Wallace, say). We celebrate the bad things that happen to people who compete with us in some way or to people who have what we want (beauty, wealth, fame, talent, social position). Our *Schadenfreude* reveals what really matters to us. And rationalization of *Schadenfreude* indicates our emotional investment in what we care about.

The Meaning of Suffering

Many people think suffering happens for a reason: it does not, could not, befall us randomly. A belief about the presumed meaning of our suffering may increase or decrease its intensity. Just as we do, others are likely to adopt a belief about the meaning of our suffering. If suffering has no meaning, what I call *Schadenfreude* could not arise (because *Schadenfreude* relies on the belief that someone else deserves to suffer). If people did not think that *Schadenfreude* involves beliefs about justice, then no one could defend *Schadenfreude* as morally acceptable. In a sense, my defense perpetuates the problem of *Schadenfreude*, even enacts it. If the randomness of suffering could be proven once and for all, then no one could affirm the rationality of *Schadenfreude*.

As it is, people in the West are as likely to stop thinking of suffering in terms of cause and effect as they are to abandon belief in a divine authority who administers punishment for wrongdoing. *Schadenfreude*, a social emotion, says something about the milieu in which it circulates. People habitually seek meaning in suffering.

In the final section of *On the Genealogy of Morals* Nietzsche tells us that mankind's curse is not suffering itself but rather the *meaninglessness* of suffering. We believe we could bear a great deal of suffering, provided it served some good purpose. Whether thinking about our own or others' suffering, we grope for some comprehensible purpose for it, such as patriotism, foolishness, or ignorance. The suffering or pain of a soldier wounded in war, for example, is easier to bear — both for him and for his family and friends — than the suffering of the same soldier seriously hurt by an injury during basic training or through foolish behavior.

Ecclesiastical penance, at least in its original form, institutionalized meaningful suffering. The distress incurred and then released by penance atoned for sin. The satisfaction of penance signified extinction of sins and thus made reconciliation possible. Priests tailored penance to fit given sins. This practice triggered considerable anxiety, for it was only a matter of chance whether a precisely equivalent penance was found for any given sin. Believers feared God's wrath more than any earthly penance and thus accepted a penitential system of draconian severity on the theory that the harsher the penance in this world, the smaller would be the punishment in the next. Penance evolved from and enforced a belief that bad people will get what they deserve.

Nietzsche takes issue with the practice of penance, or "ascetic ideals," in *On the Genealogy of Morals*, reasoning that it is pointless to make life worse by voluntarily increasing what persons would otherwise try to avoid. Nietzsche does not miss the difference on which penance turns: meaningless suffering is unendurable, but suffering we inflict upon ourselves comes with a clear meaning on its face, a meaning that can be extended to the rest of life. What is that meaning? That we are the cause of our own suffering:

> Human beings, suffering from themselves in one way or other . . . uncertain why or wherefore, thirsting for reasons — reasons relieve — thirsting, too for remedies and narcotics, at last take counsel with one who knows hidden things, too — and behold! they receive a hint, they receive from their sorcerer, the ascetic priest, the first hint as to the "cause" of their suffering; they must seek it in themselves, in some guilt, in a piece of the past, they must understand their suffering as punishment. (*GM* III, Section 20)

The ascetic priests cannot eliminate suffering, but they can explain why it is inevitable. The suffering they prescribe gives adherents a sense of control over the rest of life's suffering. In *The Varieties of Religious Experience* William James articulated from a quite different perspective the great attraction of a sense of control over suffering: "There are saints who have literally fed on . . . humiliation and privation, and the thought of suffering and death — their souls growing in happiness just in proportion as their outward state grew more intolerable. No other emotion than religious emotion can bring a man to this peculiar pass."[14] James and Nietzsche both view asceticism as a function of religious devotion. Nietzsche thought the love of ascetic ideals masked a pathological fear of happiness and beauty. For him asceticism was akin to cruelty, insofar as it entailed taking satisfaction in the creation of suffering. Because Nietzsche deplored all suffering, self-imposed suffering seemed to him perverse. Nietzsche further opposed attributing the cause of suffering to divine justice. He affirmed that religious believers preferred feeling guilty to feeling helpless.

Despite the enormous differences among various examples of suffering, one aspect remains constant: he who suffers believes that he has to some extent lost control of his world. Even suffering out of sympathy for another person or cause can cause us to lose grip of our self-identity. Suffering signals that the rules we live by are somehow inadequate or no longer valid. Suffering challenges the vision and the assumptions upon which identity is based.[15] The suffering of a mean-spirited or hypocritical person might be considered good, insofar as the rules by which he or she lives seem unfair or uncharitable. The suffering of an ostensibly kind-hearted person is another matter entirely. What is immediately at issue is how we judge a person's moral worth, which in turn colors our ideas of what a person might deserve.

Nietzsche offers us a final, crucial insight into the meaning of suffering. Emotional identification with the alleged perpetrator of the suffering of others can explain why the injury of another person would afford us any satisfaction at all. Because of the competition between belief systems, we identify with the force we imagine to have caused another's suffering. This force may be God, reason, or the invisible hand of natural justice. Whatever we perceive this force to be, we identify with it and celebrate its strength. This emotional identification that Nietzsche nods to in various writings would seem to reveal justice and not suffering as the object of *Schadenfreude*; however, Nietzsche is careful to leave room for both objects in the experience of *Schadenfreude*. In fact, he says explicitly that to observe suffering causes pleasure, but to cause it delivers an even greater pleasure.

Schadenfreude, an emotional corollary of justice, offers us something for nothing, as does the Roman Catholic notion of grace. Like grace, *Schadenfreude* testifies to a higher power. Nietzsche does not need a higher power than himself; not surprisingly, he also has no need of grace. In *Beyond Good and Evil* he tells us: "The concept 'grace' has no meaning or good odor *inter pares*; there may be a sublime way of letting presents from above happen to one, as it were, and to drink them up thirstily like drops — but for this art and gesture the noble soul has not aptitude" (Section 265). Our investment in a system of belief may be so strong that the desire to find meaning in suffering drives us to conclusions that surprise and infuriate others. At this level of social interaction, *Schadenfreude* thrives. Although Nietzsche wants to say that he is above this, he cannot really be, for he espouses a system of belief about desert as well, albeit one that he takes to have created himself.

Religious thinkers have remarked on Nietzsche's idolatry; their skepticism produces *Schadenfreude*. Of course, one need not be religious to experience *Schadenfreude*: utilitarians, vegetarians, and humanitarians may well search for the kind of external justification for their beliefs that *Schadenfreude* represents. Nietzsche's response to anyone who would include him in the cycle of this kind of *Schadenfreude* pierces to the heart of the matter. In one of his most famous passages Nietzsche says:

> For just as the popular mind separates the lightning from its flash, and takes the latter for an action, for the operation of a subject called lightning, so popular morality also separates strength from expressions of strength, as if there were a neutral substratum behind the strong man, which was free to express strength or not to do so. But there is no such substratum: there is no "being" behind doing, effecting, becoming; "the doer" is merely a fiction added to the deed — the deed is everything. The popular mind in fact doubles the deed; when it sees the lightning flash, it is the deed of a deed: it posts the same event first as cause and then a second time as its effect. (*GM* I, Section 13)

Here Nietzsche cuts off at the knees the whole enterprise of seeing suffering in terms of cause and effect. The urge to find meaning in suffering amounts to superstitiousness. The bad things that happen to other people are not the sign of the invisible hand of justice: these bad things have no supernatural or hidden meaning. For better or for worse, he also undermines confidence in our ability to make sense of the world. The things that we see happen around us do not reach out to us with a message; we simply impute meaning to them. Here Nietzsche exposes *Schadenfreude* as basically irrational. *Schadenfreude* continues to be rational, however, insofar as we disagree with Nietzsche that effects have no causes.

Nietzsche's final insight seems to undermine the distinction I have sought to establish between pleasure in the suffering of another and pleasure in justice. Because Nietzsche considers justice a fantasy, a flamboyant projection of our own interests, for him there is no substantive difference between pleasure in another's suffering and pleasure in the spectacle of justice. I differ from Nietzsche in that I have greater (although far from complete) faith in the idea of objective justice.

Just as we assess what other people deserve, so we assess whether they *really* suffer. Elisabeth Young-Bruehl begins an insightful study of prejudice with a sensitive and serious discussion of the suffering her Asian-American college students endured in the shower room after a wrestling match, while other competitors joked about the allegedly modest genital endowments of Asian men.[16] Anyone who might counter that these young men did not in fact suffer, Young-Bruehl contends, demonstrates not only emotional obtuseness but also a fundamental ignorance of the profoundly personal nature of suffering. Determining whether another person really suffers, Young-Bruehl advises us, must not become a function of what we ourselves deem awful, as opposed to, say, unpleasant. But it remains that we *do* make judgments about not only the degree but also the kind of suffering that confronts us. We insist on an important difference between the suffering of a soldier who returns home from the war impotent and the suffering of Young-Bruehl's students. We want to dismiss her description of the emotional experience of the wrestlers as unimportant or even silly.

At other times we may dismiss some descriptions of suffering as sentimental. The Bloomsbury Group members were frequently falling in love with one another and just as frequently expressing themselves on that subject. The unrest which Vita Sackville-West expresses in a love letter to Virginia Woolf might not seem large enough to qualify as suffering at all:

> Like a little warm coal in my heart burns your saying that you miss me. I miss you oh so much. How much you'll never believe or know. At every moment of the day. It is painful but also rather pleasant, if you know what I mean. I mean, that it is good to have so keen and persistent a feeling about somebody. It is a sign of vitality.[17]

Of course, Sackville-West is talking about her own suffering here, not someone else's. It may be tempting to dismiss Sackville-West's pangs as merely sentimental, but we should not, for they return us to the importance of how we think about the suffering of others. Sackville-West enjoys *that she is distressed*, which is different from *the enjoyment of her distress*. The word "suffering" implies the presence of distress, and it is logically impossible to enjoy suffering. Marginal examples aside, no one likes to suffer. Can it be that no one likes *others* to suffer either? Surely not.

When we take pleasure in the suffering of another, we celebrate a misfortune we ourselves hope to avoid. To say that suffering is aversive, however, is not to say that it is pointless. Nietzsche appreciated just how much persons strive to attach meaning to suffering, both their own and others'. We can sometimes discern *value* in suffering as well, precisely by calling into question what we take to be problematic values or beliefs. Adjustments to a coherent personal identity, then, need not be considered entirely baleful. Education and imagination can similarly initiate or accelerate moral growth. We may naturally hope that our moral growth, or that of those persons about whom we care, will result principally from education or imagination, rather than suffering. Attention to the suffering of others — its genesis, longevity, and demise — is itself an education of sorts.

Although I argue that we don't need to worry about *Schadenfreude* as a threat to social coherence, I nonetheless acknowledge that it can be unpleasant to realize that one's own suffering has made someone else happy. A crisis of identity or self-esteem is made only more painful by the knowledge that someone else views this crisis with approval and perhaps even joy (approval and joy, as I have said, differ significantly). Apprehension of the indignation of others may bring on this same crisis; we may perceive that others believe we do not deserve our good fortune (which may amount to a belief that we deserve to suffer, even though we do not). Learning of the disapproval of others can compel us to revisit values and ambitions, examine their usefulness, and question whether those values or ambitions may threaten or oppress others. *Schadenfreude* reminds us that others may suffer just by virtue of our having convictions. The possibility of inspiring *Schadenfreude* can collapse only when our own beliefs and principles do, for beliefs and principles are forms of aggression. Especially in the context of moral and social disagreements, others are likely to interpret our misfortunes as a leveling action wrought by the invisible hand of justice.

Suffering beneath Rules

With the exception of the Sackville-West passage, we have largely looked at extrinsic suffering to this point, that is, at the suffering of others. I have argued for the inherent unpleasantness of suffering and have suggested that persons regularly take pleasure in the suffering of others, principally through seeing that suffering as somehow condign.

I have suggested that suffering may result from any number of different causes, in any number of different contexts. I have focused on the notion of identity disruption as the key to understanding suffering. Specific persons or groups of persons are often responsible for challenges to our own identities. Michel Foucault tells us in "The Subject and Power," "Generally, it can be said that there are three types of struggles: either against forms of domination (ethnic, social and religious): against forms of exploitation which separate individuals from what they produce: or against that which ties the individual himself and submits him to others in this way (struggles against subjection, against forms of subjectivity and submission)."[18] What interests me is this first form of struggle, one that binds the individual to the moral judgment of others.

We do not choose the moral standards of the communities into which we are born. Communal moral standards resemble various systems of domination. It is not difficult to understand how someone might suffer underneath the weight of social or moral rules. To the extent that we can be said to live in a heterosexual society, for example, gay people must wrestle with the moral judgment of non-gay people. Similarly, women must make their way in a man's world, despite there being more women than men in the world. Non-Christians must accommodate what they think a Christian society expects. A non-Christian in particular may suffer as a result of the distance between what Christianity expects of good persons and how he or she sees him- or herself. And we cannot take as a given that white, hetrosexual, Christian men who have followed all the rules of society into which they were born do not suffer beneath the weight of these rules. So many societal pressures are always in effect, and social experiences vary widely.

Freud insisted that the progress of civilization in general and that Christianity in particular comes at a high cost to individuals. He investigated unconscious consequences of attempting to follow traditional principles or rules, and his conclusions bear importantly on ethical inquiry. For Freud, aggression is innate. The aggression that was circumscribed by the increasing number of laws and social codes in various civilizations had to be displaced somewhere. Humans instinctively began to repress aggression as they organized themselves into communities; this repression enabled humans to get along with one another more easily but caused their greater unhappiness. This aspect of Freud's legacy — the notion that the development of civilization has violated our behavioral instincts — surfaces regularly in psychological literature.

Freud demonstrated that striving to follow the love commandment may prove exceptionally costly in terms of the moral principle of noninjury to self or others. Religious commentators have noted that while Freud illuminated pathological forms of religiosity — moral masochism, a cruel conscience, blind obedience to coercive religious leaders, and unquestioning submissiveness to church authority — these pathologies distort proper religious devotion and faith. Still, Freud remains one of the most trenchant of all commentators on the social consequences of religious practice. The suffering rules can cause disturbed Freud.

Exactly how can rules make us suffer? The love commandment requires us to love others.[19] Freud argued that forcing oneself to feel sympathy entails a psychic cost. In *The Future of an Illusion* (1927) Freud portrayed religion as demanding from mankind unnecessary sacrifices of happiness in service of irrational beliefs. Religious rules and laws cause human suffering, Freud warned, to which we must attend if we are to ease existence.

Consider that one of the most famous of all rules in the West, the love commandment, aims to reduce suffering in the world by compelling us to love others, to treat them as we ourselves wish to be treated. Perhaps the most penetrating critique of the love commandment emerges in *Civilization and Its Discontents*. It can be painful for anyone to believe or even to fear that he or she is not living up to the ideal set in place by the love commandment, Freud shows us. This fear can induce severe and unrelenting reproaches of conscience.

A committed Christian, Kant had maintained over a century before Freud that we have a duty to share in the suffering of others. Kant urges us to view as our neighbors all persons, not just family, friends, or those living in proximity to us. The idea that it is morally objectionable to favor our family and friends over others has bothered many philosophers. Carol Gilligan, for example, claimed to hear in women's "different voice" the capacity for affiliation, not a generic love of humanity.[20] Freud objected as much to the idea that we should regard every person as our neighbor as he did to the idea that we should (or could) love strangers and even enemies. A rule that commands us to love might instead impel us to resent, or even hate.

Ernest Wallwork has clarified the strengths and weaknesses of Freud's exposition of the psychological and psychoanalytic problems posed by the love commandment.[21] What interests me particularly is the sense of shame that underlies the failure to live up to its standard. Although mainstream Christian theology has always stressed the sinfulness of human nature, the love commandment can cause suffering through inducing shame in those who cannot or do not meet its requirements. The suffering (to us) caused by the love commandment has not been considered as morally important as the suffering (of others) it seeks to eradicate by exhorting universal love.

Guilt calls for punishment, whereas shame, being a condition of dishonor or disgrace, invites ridicule and opprobrium. Regarded as subjective states, guilt is an emotion one feels over disobeying a rule or command whose authority one accepts, whereas shame is an emotion one feels over falling short of a standard of worth or excellence with which one identifies. More succinctly, guilt is felt over wrongdoing, shame over shortcomings. Freud's five lines of criticism of the love commandment in *Civilization and Its Discontents* concern both guilt and shame (any departure from the love commandment is an occasion for the intensification of guilt feelings, even when the departure is merely a thought or wish), but I shall focus on shame.

As Wallwork explains, Freud's criticisms of the love commandment are often misread, in part because Freud is thought to be impugning all forms of other-regarding behavior. In fact, however, Freud discusses only selected versions of the love commandment. The excessive scope attributed to Freud's argument derives in part from the ambiguity of his purpose in critiquing the morality of "civilized society." It is easy to misinterpret his aim as a desire to attack the psychological foundations of morality as such, that is, on our very capacity to care about other people at all, given our underlying narcissism. But Freud's real target is not our ability to be moral. Rather, he takes aim at what he deems excessively demanding moral requirements, such as the Christian view that agape requires both thoroughgoing selflessness and equality of love for all persons alike, including enemies (Matthew 5:44; Luke 6:27–28). Freud questions whether strangers are as worthy of love as family and friends.

According to Freud, inability to love strangers as much as favored familiars constitutes a valid reason for bestowing our sympathies on others as we see fit. The sheer impracticability of the love commandment justifies disobedience. As Wallwork makes clear, however, much of what Freud says about the impracticability of the commandment is compatible with orthodox Christian doctrine, which has long held that the highest ideals of the love commandment (e.g., selflessness and love of enemies) cannot be fulfilled (at least by fallen creatures, without divine assistance of some sort). The chief difference between orthodox theologians and Freud is that the former hold that an impracticable commandment has a valid theological and ethical function, as a way of convicting persons of sin and as a spur to higher ethical achievements. Freud holds to the contrary that an "ought" is unreasonable unless it is psychologically possible to comply with it. Many Christian theologians maintain that human beings are responsible in some sense for failing to reach moral perfection, whereas for Freud, the fault lies with the commandment, not with human beings. Because we cannot be reasonably blamed for failing to do what cannot be done, he finds feelings of sin and guilt deplorable. Freud also points to the unexpected, often unconscious, ways in which the inevitable feelings of guilt brought about by unrealizable moral standards damage both the self and others. It follows that the cure for Freud is not repentance combined with additional moral effort, but a foreshortening of the moral horizon.

Wallwork suggests that Freud's strict interpretation of the love commandment and incautious use of language in *Civilization and Its Discontents* is partly a product of his animus against Christianity, an animus triggered in this context by Christianity's claim to cultural superiority over Judaism on the basis of its universal reading of the neighbor as every person in the commandment to "love your neighbor as yourself." Freud is determined to puncture this grandiose assertion of the superiority of

Christianity. "Reciprocity," in the sense set out in the Hebrew Bible, is the key to Freud's ethic, not universal love. The centrality of reciprocity explains why Freud finds it unfair to disregard special obligations to family and friends by treating strangers on a par with them. In this ethic, too, reciprocity determines responsibilities to strangers, but it is significantly qualified by non-maleficence (that is, the duty to avoid harming), as well as by principles like promise-keeping.

Wallwork argues that Freud stops considerably short of declaring the psychological impossibility of other-regarding behavior, and indeed commends it as an essential ingredient of mature affection. Far from repudiating the love commandment in all its variations, as some passages seem to imply, Freud ends by interpreting it along lines that resonate with the ethics of Judaism (at least in its covenantal aspects) more than with those of Christianity. The middle position between the extremes of self-sacrifice and self-absorption is a form of reciprocity or mutuality that is the key to a healthy relationship. This is the gist of Freud's suggestions for improving the Christian model.

Because we live in a Christian milieu, the discovery within ourselves of the "defect" Wallwork describes better than Freud himself can increase the likelihood of self-contempt, an inherently miserable mindset. If the world tells us long enough that we deserve contempt, we may break down and agree with the world. We may, in Anna Freud's words, identify with the aggressor. In our endeavors to make and present ourselves, shame's power is great indeed. Freud's critique sensitizes us to the way in which a rule designed to decrease the total sum of suffering in the world can increase the total suffering of a particular individual. Freud's thought poses the question of the moral worth of intrinsic suffering relative to extrinsic suffering. Freud views the focus on others that underlies the Golden Rule as deleterious, to the extent that it can be seen to slight the interest we have in ourselves and in our own welfare. If pleasure and pain, respect and disrespect, are what matter morally, then consistency demands that love of self have moral weight equal to that of love of others.

Various writers have emphasized that premodern societies differ from modern societies in the amount of attention accorded to individuals' emotions. When the individual was not as important as the community, individuals' emotions were not very important. In complex societies, by contrast, the individual's "psychic life" is freer to develop on its own, separate from the "collective personality." Not only do social actors develop inner, psychic lives, they also deem these inner lives important and valuable. Others now tend to think more highly of us if we take deliberate steps toward maintaining our well-being. Accordingly, we try to follow healthy diets, exercise regularly, and lessen stress in our lives. Foucault, Christopher Lasch (in *The Culture of Narcissism*), and others, have noticed that the care of the self has become a distinctly moral matter in the modern West. Care of the self extends to managing our emotions. Appropriate emotions will produce appropriate lives.

Against Kant, numerous philosophers, psychologists, and sociologists have argued that a person's emotions will often motivate behavior and should do so — people cannot help but pay attention to their emotions and should (to some degree) heed them. Thus we believe people should pursue happiness, marry for love, and under some circumstances express their justified anger. A growing number of psychologists, sociologists, and philosophers tell us that the more important a society considers emotions, the more it expects us to govern our emotions wisely. Behavior at funerals, inaugurations, weddings, and at the office entails conforming to some important extent to what is expected of us emotionally. Even in our most private thoughts, we can see evidence of social structures. A neverending stream of books and films center on characters who suffer mightily from social pressures.

Freud's critique would carry little force if emotion were generally unresponsive to deliberate attempts to suppress or evoke it. In several different places the sociologist Erving Goffman demonstrates that social and religious rules affect emotions as well as behavior. He concludes,

> We find that participants hold in check certain psychological states and attitudes, for after all, the very general rule that one enter into the prevailing mood in the encounter carries the understanding that contradictory feelings will be in abeyance . . . so generally, in fact, does one suppress unsuitable affect, that we need to look at offenses to this rule to be reminded of its usual operation.[22]

The love commandment and failures to live up to it form a good case in point here. We try to conform inwardly as well as outwardly. Belonging to a particular group affects not only the way we appear to others, but also the way we appear to ourselves. We can control to some extent these appearances. Following Goffman, Arlie Hochschild aims to demonstrate how profoundly social we are by arguing that we frequently endeavor to pay tribute to reigning conceptions of appropriateness with our emotions.[23] Within a social system of mutual dependence, it can be self-destructive to ignore or oppose the opinions and judgments of those on whom we depend. Taking a moral stance against our neighbors or our government carries risks.

To study why and under what conditions persons hold in check certain psychological states, one must begin with the premise that persons are capable of assessing when an emotion is appropriate. If people were not socially conditioned to feel the inappropriateness of not following the Golden Rule, the sort of suffering I take Freud to articulate would make no sense. With Freud, I agree that the Golden Rule compels us to manage not only outward appearances but also inward sentiments.

Our own suffering should morally trouble us as much as the suffering of others. To be sure, there is something dangerous lurking beneath the claim that love of ourselves matters more than love of others. Racists, for example, may argue that they simply cannot bring themselves to care for members of other races, and that asking them to do so requires an unreasonable sacrifice of their own self-interest. Certainly this is an important objection to the sort of argument Freud advances in *Civilization and Its Discontents*, and it is one that had occurred to Freud. Freud argues for a moral justification not for hating others, but for loving some people more than others. By urging us to treat ourselves in the way that we strive to treat others, Freud wants to ensure that we maintain adequate psychological resources to pursue and honor those commitments that make our lives seem worth living. Freud discovered existing structures; he did not invent new ideals.

Freud's critique of the love commandment reaches farther and strikes harder than the quip of Oscar Wilde, who three decades earlier in the essay "The Soul of Man Under Socialism" had sarcastically prayed for a society that, by an equitable distribution of duties and pleasures, would emancipate humankind from "that sordid necessity of living for others which, in the present condition of things, presses so hardly upon almost everybody." Wilde's weak sigh passed largely unnoticed by the world around him, but Freud managed to elevate the same concern to a position of urgent prominence. That those who cannot bring themselves to love strangers or enemies like friends or family members might risk important psychological harm draws into question the goals of compassion. Freud's attention to the sacrifice involved in rule-following contributes to and expands our understanding of suffering through its insistence that the happiness of any one individual is as important as the happiness of any other.

Four

Wicked Feelings

SCHOPENHAUER PROFESSES TO BELIEVE THAT PEOPLE ARE ALL BASICALLY the same (although, as we will see, his adulation of genius undermines this profession). This monolithic view leads to another: Schopenhauer believes that all suffering is essentially the same. In this second belief Schopenhauer typifies much reflection on evil and suffering. He stands in the way of coming to accept the rationality of *Schadenfreude*.

Schopenhauer's profound appreciation of the awfulness of human suffering leads him to sanctify suffering and to equate *Schadenfreude* with evil. His somewhat unreflective reverence for suffering culminates in a full-blown condemnation of *Schadenfreude*. Revulsion to *Schadenfreude*, specifically, refusal to view the emotion as an object of rational assessment, suggests confusion about suffering. The question to be answered is precisely what is so evil about *Schadenfreude*?

Schopenhauer, who thought that Germans use unusually long words in order to give themselves more time to think, claims that *Schadenfreude* is "diabolical" and "the infallible sign of an entirely bad heart":

> In some respects the opposite of envy is the *malicious joy at the misfortunes of others* [this is Payne's translation of *Schadenfreude*]. Yet to feel envy is human; but to indulge in such malicious joy is fiendish and diabolical. There is no more infallible sign of a thoroughly bad heart and profound moral worthlessness than an inclination to a sheer and undisguised malignant joy of this kind.[1]

In contrast to many other philosophers who link envy to happiness in the misfortunes of others, Schopenhauer conceptually separates the two and regards *Schadenfreude* as essentially the opposite of envy (*Neid*). So far, so good. But Schopenhauer then proceeds to defend envy as human and universal, only to admonish that the man in whom *Schadenfreude* is observed should be "forever shunned."

Schopenhauer's is an extreme position, to be sure. In our own century, after numerous psychological and sociological studies of human motivation have cast light on the question of why some people act morally while others seem driven to commit evil, educated persons are loath to think that any given human being could be either completely good or completely evil. Coincidentally, just as Schopenhauer's censure of *Schadenfreude* has lost much of its invective power, so too has popular fear of Satan.

Schopenhauer's censure of *Schadenfreude* is directly indebted to Kant, though Kant links it with envy and ingratitude as the three devilish vices and explicitly specifies that they become *teuflisch* only "when they reach their full degree." Because Kant leaves to us to determine the contours of this "full degree," Schopenhauer's somewhat less ambiguous statement might serve as a helpful starting-point. The question-begging qualifications "*reiner*" (sheer) and "*herzlicher*" (undisguised) serve not so much to mitigate the scope of his condemnation as to persuade his readers of his having ruminated over this question at reassuring length. However intimately enmeshed Schopenhauer's personality is in the spirit of this condemnation, the charge of simple hyperbole at the expense of its psychological shrewdness slights Schopenhauer's talent for transforming raw insights and buried fears into forceful moral judgments. Nietzsche and Wittgenstein alike were impressed by that ability.

The most charitable reading of Schopenhauer would attribute to him the view that any pleasure from another's misfortune is always the sign of a bad heart, period. Every instance of that pleasure exhibits the same vice. The amount and kind of suffering are likewise irrelevant; it is the disposition, that is to say character, that matters in every case, for "in *morality*, the will, the disposition, is the object of consideration and the only real thing" (*WWR* I, p. 344). Even if it were true that character deserved greater moral attention than conduct, some problems remain with Schopenhauer's judgment.

Various objections can be raised to Schopenhauer's interpretation of this moral experience. He takes a remarkably narrow view of good character. He leaves crucially underspecified the description of a "bad heart," which consequently leaves him open to the charge of circularity. His formulation seems to make sense only if we grant the view, curiously consonant with Christianity, that evil results from, is constituted by, finding pleasure in the (unqualified) misfortunes of others. But we should not grant Schopenhauer that view because he offers no real argument for it. He simply appeals to the sentiments of his readers as if those sentiments represented a body of unquestioned and unquestionable fact. His reasoning is circular: *Schadenfreude* is diabolical, therefore only diabolical people feel *Schadenfreude*.

Whether or not a bad character or simply a bad attitude is necessary in order for *Schadenfreude* to arise obscures the underlying question of prediction. The problem with correlating responses to attitudes is that emotional reactions can rarely be predicted, irrespective of what we know of the attendant attitude. We are often at a loss to explain even to ourselves why one particular misfortune will affect us so deeply or, possibly, so little. Not surprisingly, philosophers of the emotions remain divided over the question of whether our emotional attitude toward someone *entails* a certain way of thinking about that person, or that our thinking that way about that person *causes* our emotional attitude toward him or her.

If only someone with a bad character would cause others to suffer, how can a society justify a prison? Schopenhauer does not oppose punishment, the deliberate infliction of suffering on other people. He justifies punishment in a familiar way: through a distinction between enjoying another's suffering and enjoying justice. This is the conceptual difference between retributivist and utilitarian (or deterrent) theories of punishment.

Schopenhauer refuses to acknowledge distinctions between various *kinds* of suffering. Differences of kind figure into moral deliberation in many ways. Utilitarians, for instance, often cite white lies as a particular *kind* of deception in order to justify them. Again and again Schopenhauer demonstrates a distaste for such differences of kind. He tells us, "Intentional mutilation or mere injury of the body of another, indeed every blow, is to be regarded essentially as of the same nature as murder, and as differing therefrom only in *degree*" (I, p. 335, emphasis added). This is a strong claim indeed, one with which our legal system is at odds. Witness that one receives quite a different punishment for assault than for homicide. Further, there are a great many different kinds of homicide, some of which are even considered lawful (e.g., killing in self-defense or in a "just war"). In order to understand homicide or *Schadenfreude*, one must attend to the specific circumstance behind it. This entails a discussion of kind.

Not only does Schopenhauer ignore specifics, he fails to indicate what does and does not qualify as pain (*Schmerz*) or suffering (*Leiden*) in the first place. Regrettably, Schopenhauer uses these two terms interchangeably and neglects to argue for his assertion that mental pain is plainly more important than physical pain (*WWB* I, p. 299).[2] He notes with approval that in cases of intense mental suffering, the self-infliction of physical pain serves as a useful diversion (the contrast here with Elaine Scarry's discussion throughout *The Body in Pain* of "the annihilating power of pain" to "utterly nullify the claims of the world" suggests that Schopenhauer does not take seriously enough the formidable potential of physical pain). The premise that physical pain is unworthy of much attention, as academic and implausible as it may seem, might intuitively emerge as a good reason to show leniency toward the brand of pleasure which results from observing a harmless slip on a banana peel. Schopenhauer, however, does not open this door.

Consider once more Baudelaire's view of comedy. Baudelaire agrees with his contemporary Schopenhauer about *Schadenfreude* and explains at greater detail why we should condemn the emotion. Claiming that "human laughter is intimately linked with the accident of an ancient fall" in "the orthodox mind,"[3] Baudelaire concludes that "the comic is a damnable element, and one of diabolic origins" (note that *teuflisch* is generally translated as "diabolic"). He asks:

> I said that laughter contained a symptom of failing . . . and [was] prompted by the sight of someone else's misfortune. . . . This misfortune is almost always a *mental* failing. And can you imagine a phenomenon more deplorable than one failing taking delight in another? (p. 138)

For Baudelaire all laughter signifies *Schadenfreude*. Baudelaire holds that bad though it may be to take pleasure when someone else has misunderstood something or failed to grasp it altogether, it is even worse for the "orthodox mind" to take pleasure in, for example, the sight of a man falling on the ice or in the street.

It is interesting to note that the examples Baudelaire chooses do not involve suffering such as would result from mutilations or rapes, but rather slipping on the ice or coming up with incorrect answers to mathematical problems. The concept of suffering is perplexing and analytically inadequate, and in assessing the moral status of human reactions to it, close attention must be paid to whatever detail is provided to qualify it. A single parenthetical clause of Baudelaire's is of crucial importance here. Of pain which evokes delight, he claims: "*ce malheur est presque toujours une faiblesse d'esprit*" (p. 530). This clause goes far toward answering such impossibly difficult questions as "What is the dividing line between trivial and important pain?" and "At what point does celebration of suffering become cruelty?" Baudelaire circumvents these questions by expanding upon the logic we find ambiguously expressed by Schopenhauer.

What Baudelaire is trying to do is extend the boundaries of moral condemnation, which would naturally include pleasure in others' relatively serious (mental) suffering, to pleasure in their relatively minor (mental) suffering as well. In this Baudelaire and Schopenhauer would seem to share a common goal. Baudelaire, however, is clearer in his exposition. It might seem reasonable to conclude with Baudelaire that only a hardened, cruel person could take pleasure from the *physical* pain of others: even if it does, it is more difficult to condemn those who take pleasure in the mental failings of others in the same terms.

Because the extent of a person's contribution to an act has always been a standard touchstone of moral evaluation, the examples upon which each thinker fastens are illuminating. Whereas Baudelaire's two examples of suffering (slipping on ice, erring in arithmetic) both involve activity, Schopenhauer's do not. The examples of "permanent evils" which Schopenhauer offers concern for the most part circumstances into which we are born, not episodic failings (having a "bad heart" stands as an obvious exception). The former category of examples excludes the happiness of anticipation, the latter category does not.

Certainly, Schopenhauer abhors the pleasure of anticipation that precedes evil acts; it is curious that his examples of great suffering do not leave room for it. It makes no sense to say that we cannot wait for someone to live a life of poverty or to be born lame. Baudelaire's more robust exposition captures worrisome designs. Waiting eagerly for another to fall on his face, or setting a trap in order to make him fall on his face, bothers us more than simply noticing with approval that someone has fallen. The question of agency will prove pivotal in the course of isolating *Schadenfreude* as a particular emotional response, for we generally hold people morally responsible for a state of affairs insofar as they have brought about that state of affairs (the implication being that those who happily anticipate some suffering are more likely to contribute to or otherwise encourage suffering).

Schopenhauer's disregard for distinctions of kind leads him to view suffering as essentially monolithic. Schopenhauer ennobles and sanctifies suffering, all suffering. In *The World as Will and Representation* Schopenhauer depicts human existence as early Buddhist literature does: a state of inextinguishable suffering. Like Buddha, Schopenhauer sees in the insatiable will the cause of all suffering. Schopenhauer holds that there is no important difference between various instances of suffering (I, p. 309). We should notice at once that the transient feeling of wounded vanity appears on a par with the spectacle of the brutal murder of someone we care about:

> The ceaseless efforts to banish suffering achieve nothing more than a change in its form. This is essentially want, lack, care for the maintenance of life. If, which is very difficult, we have succeeded in removing pain in this form, it at once appears on the scene in a thousand others, varying according to age and circumstance, such as sexual impulse, passionate love, jealousy, envy, hatred, anxiety, ambition, avarice, sickness, and so on. Finally, if it cannot find entry in any other shape, it comes in the sad, grey garment of weariness, satiety, and boredom, against which many different attempts are made. Even if we ultimately succeed in driving these away, it will hardly be done without letting pain in again in one of the previous forms, and thus starting the dance once more at the beginning. (*WWR* I, p. 315)

Depressing as all this sounds, it is also quite disappointing to realize that a thinker compelled to pose such distinctly interesting questions could come up with such a dissatisfying answer to them. Without referring to Schopenhauer, Freud (whose admiration for Schopenhauer is well known) remarks in *Civilization and Its Discontents*: "If we cannot remove all suffering, we can remove some, and we can mitigate some: the experience of many thousands of years has convinced us of that."[4] Schopenhauer's pessimistic resignation to suffering calls for self-destruction. Although suicide can be taken as a manifestation of frustrated vitality, still it remains that the onset of a desire for self-destruction signifies, or ought to signify, something alarming about that vitality. If to care genuinely about another person is to encourage escape from the unrelenting suffering of the world through self-destruction, then the sort of reverence for suffering Schopenhauer exhorts is deeply problematic. The approval of suicidal fantasies or desires might thinly veil his own desire for self-destruction. Misery loves company, but does it prefer destruction? Schopenhauer's own avoidance of suicide suggests ambivalence on this point.

Schopenhauer's view of suffering as monolithic lives on. In his work *What Evil Means to Us*, C. Fred Alford declares:

> Deep down in the mind (or maybe not even so deep down) there is no difference between the desire to squash someone's hand and the desire to murder millions. Desires like this, primitive, destructive, malicious desires are by their very nature unmodulated. (p. 142)

People who tell nasty jokes, Alford would have us believe, are people on the verge of crimes against humanity. This statement comes in the midst of a book deeply sensitive to human evil. Consider how sharply Alford's view contrasts with the following passage from Freud's *The Future of an Illusion*:

> There are countless civilized people who would shrink from murder or incest but who do not deny themselves the satisfaction of their avarice, their aggressive urges or their sexual lusts, and who do not hesitate to injure other people by lies, fraud and calumny,

so long as they can remain unpunished for it; and this, no doubt, has always been so through many ages of civilization.[5]

Alford, like Schopenhauer, has lost all sense of proportion. He also overlooks or implicitly believes that our penal policies have nothing to do with revenge.

Because he views pain as inevitable, Schopenhauer judges distinctions among various sorts of pain as insignificant or wholly irrelevant (the rudimentary distinction between physical and mental pain being an exception). In contrast to Pascal, who claims in the *Pensées* that most of the troubles and sufferings of the world can be traced to the inability of people to stay contentedly in their rooms, he tells us tersely that *suffering results from the gap between what we demand or expect of life and what actually comes to us* (*WWR* I, p. 88). Countless psychological self-help books have failed to credit Schopenhauer with this most useful insight.[6] He instructs us that if we recognize once and for all our strengths and our weaknesses and resign ourselves to what is for us unattainable, we will escape in the surest way that *"bitterest* of all human sufferings, dissatisfaction with our own individuality"* (*WWR* I, p. 307, emphasis added). And if we avoid entirely those pursuits at which we do not excel, we can manage to circumvent humiliation, "the *greatest* of mental suffering" (*den größten Geistesschmerz*) (*WWR* I, pp. 305–306, emphasis added). Schopenhauer's use of the superlative demonstrates that comparisons of suffering do matter, but only to a point. So the ability to make distinctions, pertinent as it is to an analysis of suffering, is not one entirely lacking in Schopenhauer, but rather one not permitted to run laterally.

This blind spot gives rise to other, related problems. One might, with regard to the substance of these last two remarks, immediately object that humiliation ought to appear lower on the pecking order of mental tribulations than, say, bereavement or unrequited love. Given that the very realization of personal limitations or inadequacies produces "the greatest suffering," one might find confusing Schopenhauer's subsequent assertion that "more fortunate people" simply do not understand the utter indifference with which people may endure "innumerable permanent evils" ("*unzählige bleibende Uebel*") such as "lameness, poverty, humble position, ugliness and unpleasant dwelling place" (I, p. 306).[7] (In *The Metaphysics of Morals* Kant uses *Böse* for moral evil and *Uebel* for what might be termed physical evil or "ills." Schopenhauer follows his lead here.) Apparently the realization of, say, one's lameness initially gives rise to "the greatest of mental suffering," but quickly becomes a matter of indifference or boredom. In an age of rapidly advancing medical technologies, this alleged indifference may be a thing of the past. Even if Schopenhauer were correct here, though, lameness simply couldn't produce what we usually think of as great suffering, for without mitigation or resolution, great suffering will commonly involve longevity (that, together with intensity, is presumably what makes it great). And if it did cause "the greatest suffering," even among the unenlightened, Schopenhauer would simply be wrong to take the eventual numbness engendered by great pain as evidence of pain's impotence.

Another related difficulty with his definition of suffering is the absence of an indication of the extent to which we are made by our world. Even a person who mustered the strength to stop willing altogether (and thus to stop suffering) would find Schopenhauer's formulation useless in a world populated by other people. Consider the suffering of African-Americans living in the United States before the Civil War. An African-American might suffer because of the gap between what he expected of life and what actually came to him. The expectation of freedom and personal safety is not a frivolous one; there is a strongly social dimension to what a person expects. Schopenhauer overlooks the inevitability of suffering that comes from living in society. He does not want to acknowledge that we cause others to suffer, just by living our lives. Pursuing our ambitions and earning our livings makes us compete with others and, often, to diminish their lives.

Despite the defects of Schopenhauer's account, we must credit him in some part with the theory of *ressentiment*, an idea commonly attributed to Nietzsche. Nietzsche's account of the "slave revolt in morality," the supposed psychological motivation for Jewish and Christian ethics, requires attention to what we are to understand by "slaves." Throughout *On the Genealogy of Morals* Nietzsche describes slaves as poor, impotent, lowly, suffering, deprived, sick, ugly. Nietzsche's thinking about "slave morality" and their perspective owes something to Schopenhauer's reflection on unattractive people who live in dismal apartments. Schopenhauer deserves some credit for anticipating attention to "the slave revolt in morality" and the idea of *ressentiment.*

By focusing narrowly on the disposition of the *schadenfroh* person, Schopenhauer fails to see that we can and do react differently to a variety of bad things that may happen to others. Further, his fear of (or reverence for) suffering prevents him from seeing that *Schadenfreude* delivers a modest interruption from suffering. Anyone who sympathizes with Schopenhauer would make a poor comedian: there is no more reason to assume that only moral monsters feel *Schadenfreude* than to infer that only the lazy experience delight at the approach of weekends. The biggest problem with an account of suffering like Schopenhauer's is that it skews our conceptual grasp of true malignity. We cannot do justice to the profundity of Jewish suffering under National Socialism in Germany if we insist that a slap on the face or life in an unfashionable apartment is on a par with it.

Schopenhauer's well-known ethics of satisfaction shows through his view of pleasure. Simply put, Schopenhauer holds that pleasure isn't worth the effort it takes to obtain it. *Schadenfreude*, however, manifests itself as a function of the invisible hand of justice or of just plain luck. The misfortunes of others which make us happy simply happen; we do not orchestrate them. Schopenhauer's characterization of suffering in *The World as Will and Representation* (that which results from the gap between what we demand or expect of life and what actually comes to us) captures the same element of chance that underlies contemporary discussions of moral luck.

Thomas Nagel describes four types of moral luck: luck in the kind of person one is; luck in the problems and situations one faces; luck in how the will is determined by antecedent circumstances; and luck in the way one's actions and projects turn out.[7] The first and third types are often taken to represent the metaphysical problem of freedom and determinism, while the second and fourth have drawn most interest as representing the problem of moral luck proper. Schopenhauer's account of suffering, in many ways remarkably insightful and useful, anticipates contemporary philosophical discussions of moral luck. These discussions sensitize us to the circumstances of a great deal of human suffering.

Schadenfreude is itself a kind of moral luck. Kant and Schopenhauer both misunderstand *Schadenfreude* as *something persons work to obtain*. In his *Lectures on Ethics* Kant asserts, "Malice is the third kind of viciousness which is of the devil. It consists in taking a direct pleasure in the misfortunes of others. Men prone to this vice will seek, for instance, to make mischief between husband and wife, or between friends, and then enjoy the mishap they have produced" (p. 219). And in *The Metaphysics of Morals* Kant identifies the desire for revenge as the "sweetest form of *Schadenfreude*."[9] Kant claims of *Schadenfreude* that "when it goes so far as to help bring about evil or wickedness it makes hatred of men visible." Immediately after denouncing *Schadenfreude* in *On the Basis of Morality*, Schopenhauer claims that envy and the malicious joy at another's misfortune "are in themselves merely theoretical; in practice they become malice and cruelty" (pp. 135–136). Tying it to the realm of intention, Schopenhauer, like Kant before him, views *Schadenfreude* as preliminary to, and sometimes constitutive of, *acting*, as opposed to a result of being acted upon.

Schopenhauer explains that the pains and sufferings of others are for malice and cruelty an end in themselves, and their attainment is the pleasure of *Schadenfreude*. For this reason, malice and cruelty constitute a greater degree (as opposed to a different kind) of moral depravity than does envy. Schopenhauer concludes that just as *Schadenfreude* is only theoretical cruelty, so cruelty is *Schadenfreude* put into practice; the diseased disposition prone to *Schadenfreude* will become manifest as cruelty as soon as an opportunity presents itself.

Schopenhauer does not ultimately portray suffering with much nuance or subtlety. Childish pranks and inconsequential acts of social rebellion appear the first step on a slippery path to heinous deeds. The sentimental and hyperbolic style of his remarks corresponds to a loaded, univocal, and question-begging description of suffering. That description colors the eventual condemnation of *Schadenfreude*. Because Schopenhauer fails to acknowledge any explicitly unanticipated or unintended sort of pleasure, we may find surprising Alasdair MacIntyre's observation in *A Short History of Ethics* that, "Schopenhauer observed, as perhaps no previous philosopher or psychologist had done, the gratuitous character of malice."[10] MacIntyre seems to mean by "gratuitous" that which is done simply for its own sake, as opposed to the consequence(s) of an act. Schopenhauer *does* miss the gratuitousness of malice, if by "gratuitousness" we mean "not earned or paid for."

The Relevance of Schopenhauer Today

Schopenhauer's position on capital punishment makes it difficult for him to present a coherent condemnation of *Schadenfreude* by virtue of the position he takes regarding punishment. He seems to believe that in committing an offense, the offender forfeits the right not to be made to suffer. To render punishment compatible with justice, though, it is not enough to restrict punishment to those who deserve it. It is necessary to restrict the *kind* of suffering to the sort which a given offense is taken to deserve. Just as justice not only requires a principle of desert and a principle of proportionality between the seriousness of the offense and the punishment deserved, so too does the evaluation of *Schadenfreude* involve both desert and proportionality.

Schopenhauer dismisses proportionality as irrelevant to a discussion of *Schadenfreude* because he insists that any emotional response to suffering is a dispositional, not episodic, matter. Those who enjoy the punishment of a criminal or laugh at even the slightest of misfortunes are guilty. It might be thought that Schopenhauer is an easy target here and that a simple counterexample could be invoked to defeat his position (for an evil deed may be done by someone who is not diabolical, but merely weak or misguided). But Schopenhauer merits study in part because his view endures as an unstated assumption of a good deal of the moral theory written in English. The *Schadenfreude* question for Schopenhauer is not merely one of degree, for he meant to condemn every *kind* of pleasure stemming from another's suffering. No doubt many of us will squirm in the face of such a condemnation. Schopenhauer's is a serious claim not to be lightly rejected.

Endorsement of this claim unites a broad cross-section of believers and non-believers. According to John Atwell, "Schopenhauer provides us, therefore, with a wholly nonreligious account of the misery of life, probably the only one in the history of Western thought."[11] With striking clarity, Schopenhauer presages an explicitly Christian condemnation of *Schadenfreude*. In his essay "Emotions Among the Virtues In the Christian Life" Robert C. Roberts claims in terms reminiscent of Schopenhauer that "cruel hope or joy" is "morally corrupt"[12] and subsequently discusses hope for the death of a rival and joy in another's misfortune as "vicious" and "vices." Like Schopenhauer before him, he never considers such common phenomena as the nasty reactions of children at play or the violent aspects of physical comedy. Schopenhauer's failure can profitably be discussed in the context of two of Roberts's own examples.

The first Roberts passage to reflect Schopenhauer's shortcomings features the word *Schadenfreude*. It is to be found in an article entitled "What is Wrong With Wicked Feelings?"

> What in a morality might support its "belief" that some cases of envy, *Schadenfreude,* pride, hatred, resentment, self-righteousness, contempt, anger, etc., are wicked in themselves, and not only derivatively from actions or other consequences? Only by a fairly concrete analysis of such feelings can one begin to uncover the assumptions behind the judgment that they are wicked.[13]

Calling for "a fairly concrete analysis of such feelings," Roberts ends the essay without having considered whether *Schadenfreude* might be anything other than wicked.

Roberts's example takes shape around the competitiveness between two friends who are academic colleagues. Here it is, in brief: when Mike is promoted to an Ivy League school and offered a contract by Cambridge University Press, Roger is envious. Roberts suggests that Roger's envy may beget "malicious wishes," specifically, the hope that Mike will be accused of plagiarism and subsequently fired. Roberts calls Roger's feelings "unjust" because Mike's success has diminished Roger's self-esteem.

Roberts's discussion misses the same distinction between different kinds of suffering that Schopenhauer's does. As a result, it comes off sounding self-righteous.[14] True, he doesn't explicitly call Roger's feelings wicked, but he does include the example in an article entitled "What is Wrong With Wicked Feelings?" It is worthwhile to note that we can feel

Schadenfreude quite apart from envy and that Roger's admittedly malicious desire does not qualify as *Schadenfreude*, as one can no more feel *Schadenfreude* before a misfortune occurs than one can laugh at a joke before it is made.

Like most emotions, *Schadenfreude* looks backward. For the pleasure which defines *Schadenfreude* to arise, the suffering it celebrates must already have run its course or at least begun. The same is true for pity and sorrow, which *Schadenfreude* in certain respects resembles: if the suffering were not already a fact, these responses would be anachronistic. What is important to understand is that the suffering presupposed by *Schadenfreude* may be something we ourselves actually hoped for (as opposed to caused) in addition to something adventitious. (The suffering we ourselves intentionally cause must be considered an entirely separate case.)

Schadenfreude can in certain instances look forward. It may sometimes follow on the heels of hope, but this hope is not itself constitutive of *Schadenfreude*. For example, the judgment that we are in danger doesn't just happen with the emotion of fear, but contributes to fear. In the same way, my hope that I will be admitted to Yale is not, properly speaking, part of my eventual happiness that I have been offered a place. That happiness depends for its support on some knowledge or at least belief that I have been admitted to Yale, a belief which contrasts with and excludes hoping. The fact of the prior hope may intensify the feeling of happiness, but does not constitute it.

By the same token it does make sense to say that while I am still in the process of applying, I may hope I can enter Yale before I reach old age. In just such a way you could hope that you will someday enjoy hearing of my rejection from Yale. Robert Gordon, from whose discussion of past tense I borrow here, points out the relevance of time to emotion:

> Using tense as our criterion, however, no emotion would be exclusively forward-looking and no emotion would be exclusively backward-looking. We can readily imagine someone hoping or being afraid that a certain train arrived late (past tense), just as we can imagine someone being glad or unhappy that the train will arrive late (future tense).[15]

Though it may make sense to think of looking forward to the day that my rejection from Yale will delight you, it does not make sense to say that that hoping equals *Schadenfreude*. Hoping may lead to (as opposed to produce) *Schadenfreude*, which means that there is a sense, however narrow, in which *Schadenfreude* is a forward-looking emotion. If you are privy to certain confidential information, then, you may be glad to learn that I will receive a rejection letter from Yale next week. That *Schadenfreude* has a forward-looking aspect means that it is difficult to dismiss summarily Schopenhauer's and Roberts's focus on intention.

In sum, just as there are different kinds of suffering, so too are there different kinds of pleasure (finding only green lights on the way to work versus finding a sure cure for breast cancer). The idea that both joy and suffering come in many forms finds corroboration in "Emotions Among the Virtues In the Christian Life." Here Roberts distinguishes between various sorts of joy:

> . . . an emotion's object is constitutive of the emotion; if the object to which the emotion is directed changes, then, while you may have the same type of emotion, you do not have the same emotion. Thus the person who takes joy in another's good fortune has quite a different emotion from the person who takes joy in another's misfortune, even though both emotions belong to the joy-type. (p. 48)

If we press this distinction a bit further, we can similarly distinguish satisfaction over a colleague's arraignment for tax fraud from glee in his or her unflattering student evaluations. The recognition of different sorts of joy does not mean that *Schadenfreude* is a vice *mutatis mutandis*, as Roberts considers it to be. The joy of *Schadenfreude* is not diabolical, because a belief about justice lies beneath and morally justifies that joy.

What Makes Us Different from Others

It seems plausible to maintain that there are different sorts of people as well. However, Schopenhauer is loath to grant this premise. In *On the Basis of Morality*, he prefers instead to have us think of ourselves as though we were other people. Thinking of ourselves as different from others lands us in trouble, he holds:

> The theme of conscience is primarily our actions, indeed, either those in which, because we were guided by egoism or malice, we gave no ear to compassion, which urged us at least not to injure others or even to afford them help and support; or those in which, with the renunciation of egoism and malice, we followed compassion's call. Both cases indicate the extent of the *difference* we make *between ourselves and others*. On such *difference* ultimately rest the degrees of morality or immorality. (p. 196, emphasis added)

The underlying Will of various persons is, according to Schopenhauer, a self-sufficient unity; the illusion of "the principle of individuation" creates the many evils of our lives, specifically through fueling selfishness and malice. Our worst mistake is in insisting that we are unique. Schopenhauer must be wrong here, for it is far from obvious that the more we come to know about strangers, the more we realize our similarity to them. The more we know of some people, the less they seem worthy of compassion. Instead of sympathy, we may feel bafflement, fear, or hatred. Familiarity, we have heard, breeds contempt.

It may well be that Schopenhauer's famous pessimism stems from a stubborn yearning for utopia. Not seeing a perfect world would naturally trouble someone who really wanted to inhabit one. Various writers on utopia have betrayed a willingness to sacrifice human idiosyncrasies in order to achieve human solidarity. Utopias seem boring, even the sexy ones. Several decades before Schopenhauer began to write, the Marquis de Sade set out his vision of the ideal human community. Sade dreamed of a society in which everyone possessed the right to enjoy his or her neighbor sexually. Reduced to their sexual organs, people in Sade's utopia were faceless and interchangeable. Everyone was identical (differences between the sexes a presumable exception). A life of nothing but sex lacks the kind of variety that Schopenhauer's ideal world does. Thoroughgoing differences among people, difficult as they can sometimes be, make life more interesting.

Before Schopenhauer, Adam Smith praised the ability imaginatively to change places with others. In terms that anticipate Schopenhauer's aversion to thinking of ourselves as fundamentally different from others, Smith drew a line in the sand:

> If you have either no fellow-feeling for the misfortunes I have met with, or none that bears any proportion to the grief which distracts me; or if you have either no indignation at the injuries I have suffered, or none that bears any proportion to the resentment which transports me, we can no longer converse. . . . You are confounded at my violence and passion, and I am enraged at your cold insensibility and want of feeling.[16]

Smith was confident that "if you labour under any signal calamity, if by some extraordinary misfortune you are fallen into poverty, into diseases, into disgrace and disappointment...yet you may generally depend upon the sincerest sympathy of all your friends" (p. 43). The reason is that, "When I condole with you...I consider what I should suffer if I was really you, and I not only change circumstances with you, but I change persons and characters" (p. 317). The suffering of others brings on a profound shudder for Smith: there but for the grace of God go I.

Various thinkers have reflected on empathy and have found a problem in such logic. If, sensing my distress, Adam Smith emotionally identifies himself with me in the literal way he says, then he is necessarily unaware of his individual identity as distinct from mine. It is only to an observer that Smith has fellow-feeling with me, for Smith is unaware of the vicariousness of what he is feeling. If Smith immerses himself in my personality, then it becomes confusing to talk of him worrying about me. In order for Smith to care about me, he has to recognize his existence as a person separate from myself. Concern for another person and emotional identification with him, some philosophers have insisted, are mutually exclusive. The more perfectly I identify myself with another, the less sense there is in supposing that I can be disposed to help him.

A century after Adam Smith, Schopenhauer embraces this view and argues for it in terms of the separateness of persons:

> To a certain extent I have identified myself with the other man, and in consequence the barrier between the ego and non-ego is for the

moment abolished; only then do the other man's affairs, his need, distress, and suffering, directly become my own. I no longer look at him as if he were something given to me by empirical intuitive perception, as something strange and foreign, as a matter of indifference, as something entirely different from me. On the contrary, I share the suffering *in him,* in spite of the fact that his skin does not enclose my nerves. Only in this way can *his* woe, *his* distress, become a motive *for me*; otherwise it could be absolutely only my own. I repeat that this *occurrence is mysterious,* for it is something our faculty of reason can give no direct account of, and its grounds cannot be discovered on the path of experience. And yet it happens every day; everyone has often experienced it within himself; even to the most hardhearted and selfish it is not unknown. Every day it comes before our eyes, in single acts on a small scale." (OBM, p. 166)

It is worth pointing out that the difference we make between ourselves and others may prove to be a rich source of fellow feeling. Loyalty to one particular group or ideology may lead to opposition to another; such opposition may strengthen group solidarity and lessen or obscure personal differences among members of a group. Contrary to Smith and Schopenhauer, it seems doubtful that we can empathize with a vast number of persons with quite different interests. Consequently, it is unlikely that we can impartially evaluate persons and positions foreign to us. The goal of taking into oneself the world's wants and sufferings and, at an ideal level at least, feeling all of its pains is a basic motivation of utilitarianism, a doctrine Schopenhauer considers the very face of compassion.

Schopenhauer rebels against the Kantian tradition of moral philosophy that emphasizes the separateness and autonomy of persons and culminates by linking personhood and dignity. He would abhor what contemporary philosophical discussion terms "the separateness of persons." This phenomenon can help to explain that there are some people whose misfortunes or suffering could never supply us with *Schadenfreude*: they are too unlike ourselves. Aristotle, for example, tells us, "And since men strive for honor with those who are competitors, or rivals in love, in short with those who aim at the same things, they are bound to feel most envious of these" (*Rhetoric* 2.10). Schopenhauer's aversion to the social distinctions on which Aristotle's thinking rests is palpable: it is because of such distinctions that envy arises. In fact, however, the reason why I may envy one person stands as the same reason why I may not feel any *Schadenfreude* about another. The separateness of persons works in both a positive and negative way.

Another problem with Schopenhauer's "principle of individuation" is that it fails to allow for competition, a central aspect of life in communities. It must be possible to win promotions, athletic contests, and political elections while maintaining an abiding respect for the persons who lose to us.

What does it mean to speak of the separateness of persons? Some define separateness as physical difference. This kind of separateness is shared by plants, flowers, and paramecia; these, however, lack a point of view. A living thing can possess a subjective point of view if and only if it has (its own) experiences. Various animals share this capacity with us and would seem to deserve the same moral claims we do (Schopenhauer makes a good deal of this observation at the end of *On the Basis of Morality*). Humans differ from animals by having a sense of self; humans have an awareness both of their selves and of their biological and psychological continuity over the course of a life.

Bernard Williams has rejected utilitarianism on grounds that it fails to accommodate personal interests. The problem, Williams contends, is that "Persons lose their separateness as beneficiaries of utilitarian provisions, since in the form which maximizes average utility, there is an agglomeration of satisfactions which is basically indifferent to the separateness of those who have the satisfactions."[17] In *Situation Ethics* Joseph Fletcher equates the Christian notion of agape with utilitarianism because of the central role often assigned to equal regard: "Let's say plainly that agape is utility; love is wellbeing; the Christian who does not individualize or sentimentalize love *is* a utilitarian."[18] Various charges against utilitarianism, that it cannot accommodate moral rights, distributive justice, and the personal point of view, derive from the claim that utilitarianism fails to recognize and appreciate the separateness of persons.

An objection to utilitarianism can be construed as raising the metaphysical question of how separate persons *are*, as opposed to raising the moral question of how separate persons *should be considered*. It is this second line of inquiry that I wish to follow here. In *Ethics and the Limits of Philosophy* Williams insists that persons should be considered separate on the basis of their manifold preferences: "the truth is that this aggregate of preferences is simply unintelligible unless they are understood to be the preferences of *different people*."[19] Williams, unlike Schopenhauer, deliberately avoids claims about the essential nature and identity of persons.

In the same general discussion of separateness in *Ethics and the Limits of Philosophy* Williams criticizes R.M. Hare's attempt in *Moral Thinking*[20] to accomplish what can safely be associated with Schopenhauer's aim to prevent us from thinking of ourselves as importantly dissimilar to those around us. Williams points out that imaginative identification with the feelings of others works to enlighten not only sympathetic persons but also sadistic or cruel persons. He explains that this knowledge helps us to distinguish between the cruel and the brutal or indifferent. The cruel person is someone who prefers not to give help, although that person certainly *knows* about the suffering of his or her neighbor.

To conclude the discussion of the separateness of persons: In *Contingency, Irony, and Solidarity* Richard Rorty takes the separateness of persons as a given, as is evident in his claim that the goal of ethical reflection is "the ability to think of people wildly different from ourselves as included in the range of 'us' [as opposed to 'them']" (p. 192). Rorty's moral paradigm, the "liberal ironist," thinks that mutual susceptibility to pain and humiliation can unite him or her to the manifestly different persons around; Schopenhauer holds that what can unite persons is a recognition of their common human nature. Whereas Schopenhauer urges us to *recognize* an ontological sort of solidarity with other persons, a solidarity that exists before our recognition of it, Rorty encourages us to *create* a more expansive social sense of solidarity.

We see, then, important objections to Schopenhauer's view of the basic similarity of persons. Behind what Nietzsche labels the "herd mentality" lies opposition to Schopenhauer. Nietzsche objects strenuously to thinking of ourselves as others:

Today, conversely, when only the herd animal receives and dispenses honor in Europe, when "equality of rights" could all too easily be changed into equality in violating rights — I mean, into a common war on all that is rare, strange, privileged, the higher man, the higher soul, the higher duty, the higher responsibility, and the abundance of creative power and masterfulness — the concept of greatness entails being noble, wanting to be by oneself, being able to be different, standing alone and having to live independently. (*BGE*, Section 212)

A person who denies his or her individuality is thereafter incapable of either great achievements or great harm. In either event, the goal of morality has been served: the herd no longer has anything to fear.

Finally, Schopenhauer's reverence for genius in *The World As Will and Representation* undermines his own stance with regard to separateness. Schopenhauer certainly does conceive of the genius as a creature decisively dissimilar to the rest of humanity. It was the Schopenhauerian genius who largely inspired Nietzsche's much more famous account of the *Ubermensch*. Nietzsche's insistence that personhood is a function of the ineradicable will to power represents an improvement over Schopenhauer's finally incoherent position.

I do not mean to ridicule Schopenhauer's view, which rises from a wish to tame the fierceness of suffering. One real way in which we as extraordinarily varied people come to resemble one another closely is through the experience of suffering. Schopenhauer understood this, but confused the insight with the infliction of suffering. A torturer aims to reduce a human being to the lowest common denominator through the infliction of pain; a sadist tries to force a person to lose hold of whatever it is that makes that person unique. The sadist's goal is to minimize or deny individuality, which means that sadism and torture depend on Schopenhauer's being wrong about the separateness of persons.

Sharing Suffering: Sympathy

Our moral tradition exalts sympathetic people. Feeling *Schadenfreude* would appear to violate an ethical obligation to cultivate the virtue of compassion, so central to the ethics of duty. Kant postulates that although it is not in itself a duty to share the sufferings (or joys) of others, it is a duty to sympathize actively with them, and, as such, to cultivate the virtue of compassion (*MM*, p. 205). Kant says "cultivate" because he believes that human beings are naturally compassionate. Because everyone already has certain inherent moral endowments, no one could have a duty to acquire them: they are moral feeling, conscience, love of one's neighbor, and respect for oneself (self-esteem) (*MM*, p. 200). These endowments lie at the basis of morality, as subjective conditions of receptiveness to the concept of duty, not as objective conditions of morality. It is by virtue of already having these natural predispositions of the mind that persons can be put under obligation. Freud would obviously disagree, given his sharply divergent notion of human nature.

It might seem odd here that Kant generally disregards the moral import of the emotions, as I have said, even as he postulates an ethical obligation to have a certain emotion (i.e., sympathy). A Kantian understanding of the motive of duty can be stretched to include the motive of sympathy if the sympathy stems from the motive of duty (this differs from attributing moral value to sympathy itself).[21]

Kant's is an ontological claim, one involving a view of human nature. Although philosophical appeals to human nature have become decidedly passé in recent decades, essentialistic notions of human identity still surface with some frequency in discussions of personal obligation. As Kant knew, the most systematic account of the virtues and vices comes from Aristotle, and in the synthesis of Aristotelian and Christian philosophy found in St. Thomas Aquinas. For Kant, as for St. Thomas Aquinas, an account of the virtues and vices depends on what human nature is like. Accordingly, Kant defines vice in *The Metaphysics of Morals* through a particular notion of human nature:

> If vice is taken in the sense of a basic principle (a vice proper), then any vice, which would make human nature itself detestable, is inhuman when regarded objectively. But considered subjectively, that is, in terms of what experience teaches us about our species, such vices are still *human*. As to whether, in vehement revulsion, one could call some of these vices *devilish*, and so too the virtues opposed to them *angelic*, both of these concepts are only Ideas of a maximum used as a standard for comparing degrees of morality. (p. 208)

It is this standard for comparing degrees of morality that requires clarification in a discussion of the moral status of *Schadenfreude*.

Given that Kant refers to *Schadenfreude* in *The Metaphysics of Morals* as "no stranger to human nature," it would hardly seem that he considers *Schadenfreude* an aberrant or epiphenomenal vice. It seems more likely that he regards *Schadenfreude* as all too common to be diabolical in a literal sense. This must be what he means when he calls *Schadenfreude* "*teuflisch*" or diabolical in the *Lectures on Ethics*. When Kant disapproves of *Schadenfreude* as "*teuflisch*," then, he rejects it as a vice on a par with envy, sloth, and greed.

Kant's relatively mild disapproval of *Schadenfreude* finds its most vehement opponent in Schopenhauer, who defends envy but asserts that *Schadenfreude* represents something much worse than an ordinary vice. Because Schopenhauer does not view *Schadenfreude* as universal, he can, without contradicting himself, call the emotion *teuflisch* in a quite literal sense.[22] Schopenhauer's "vehement revulsion" resonates with a number of contemporary moralists and opposes the claim that *Schadenfreude* is all too human to be diabolical (i.e., inhuman) in Kant's subjective sense. Schopenhauer's most glaring error is that he does not come close to persuading us that *Schadenfreude* affects only a limited segment of the populace. Schopenhauer therefore has no ground on which to claim that a *schadenfroh* person is diabolical, both objectively and subjectively.

Our beliefs, attitudes, feelings, and emotions compose our psychological skeleton. In general, moral theorists have tried to show that this structure motivates us to act morally. Some moral thinkers, such as Hume and Schopenhauer, have argued that we have a natural affinity to morality because of our psychological skeleton, but others, such as Kant, have maintained that reason motivates the moral self.

For Kant, we help others because we have an obligation to do so. Our reason guides us and compels us to treat others well. His insistence that inclination cannot form the basis of a truly moral motive has been found both puzzling and outrageous because among the inclinations which Kant debars from moral worth are sympathy for others, fellow feeling, and benevolence. In this regard Schopenhauer differs from Kant — emotions count for something important, as is clear from Schopenhauer's reflection on *Schadenfreude*.

Schopenhauer holds that three fundamental motivations underlie human actions: egoism, malice, and compassion (*OBM*, p. 145). Of these the strongest and most rudimentary is egoism, the desire for one's own well-being (*OBM*, p. 131). Egoism is boundless, and it grounds the desire to keep life free from pain and suffering. Not so much good or bad, it is a simple fact of life for both humans and beasts. Conversely, compassion is explicitly good and malice explicitly bad. The only genuinely moral motivation, compassion gives rise to virtues such as justice and philanthropy. Accordingly, what issues from compassion holds genuine moral worth, but what proceeds from egoism or malice holds none.

Schopenhauer dislikes the idea that an emotionally generous person might receive more compassion from neighbors than an emotionally stingy one. Schopenhauer embraces the force of the thought that if *I* had been subjected to a particular misfortune, I would need or at least appreciate the compassion of others. By counteracting selfish and malicious motives, compassion prevents me from causing another to suffer. Compassion also works positively by inciting me to help another (*OBM*, p. 148).

A simplification of Schopenhauer's position is that sympathy is the only moral motive. Moral value is identified with the motive of sympathy: to act sympathetically is to act morally and to act without sympathy is to act neutrally or immorally (*OBM*, pp. 120–198). Schopenhauer's underlying supposition that sympathy is instinctive has troubled many philosophers. Hobbes for one held that any apparently unselfish sympathy can be more accurately described as disguised self-interest. Nietzsche later agreed with him.

Freud shares with Hobbes a deeply negative view of human nature. With his extreme version of original sin (according to which the abject corruption of humanity is incurable), Augustine can be said to prefigure Freud (it is curious that mainstream Judaism, with which Freud identified culturally, has little to say about original sin). In different ways, Augustine, Hobbes, Nietzsche, and Freud raised the question of whether we are psychologically capable of being moral. Much contemporary discussion in economics,[23] psychology, and ethics reflects uncertainty over this question.

Economics has affected how philosophers and psychologists think about emotions. The economic mindset offers a middle way between cheery and dismal views of human nature. According to this way of thinking, those who labor are entitled to pay, and those who can pay are entitled to the labor of others. Applied to emotional resources, the logic of reciprocity justifies both giving to others who have previously given to us and expecting others to return our gifts. Candace Clark has combined and refined various articulations of this mindset in an engaging work, *Misery and Company: Sympathy in Everyday Life*.[24] A person who follows the etiquette of sympathy — by limiting demands for sympathy, repaying social debts, and so on — can expect sympathy from others. A person who has overdrawn, or failed to replenish sympathy margins (cashed in too many sympathy credits) may find others refusing to sympathize, especially if the grounds are not compelling. A person careful not to overdraw his account may find that others sympathize with him, even when he is to blame for his plight. Of course, Schopenhauer would discount the whole idea of a sympathy margin as an instance of egoism.

For Schopenhauer, emotional well-being hinges on social attachment. He fears the implications of social detachment and theorizes sympathy as not only a natural but an inevitable human response to suffering. He contends that a person who finds pleasure in the suffering of another must pay for that pleasure with the pain that accompanies the inevitable "stings" or "pangs" of conscience (*WWR*, I, pp. 341, 354). Not unlike catching a cold from someone else, these pangs lead us to participate in the suffering of others. Schopenhauer thus adds a new twist to the idea that misery loves company, despite the apparent contradiction between this commonplace and his idea that evil persons (who are by definition miserable) are unrepentant in some permanent way.

Sympathy amounts to an infection for Schopenhauer; to him, such an emotional reaction seems analogous to the movements of flocks of sheep or football crowds. The contagiousness of a *virus* or *disease* certainly makes sense, but what does it mean to speak of the contagiousness of an *emotion*? When I begin to suffer with another over his or her problem, it is correct to say that we experience the same feeling. Seeing a movie with other people who are laughing can make us react quite differently from seeing it with others who are sneering, for example. An interesting feature of Schopenhauer's view of sympathy rests in its insight that intoxication by such mass emotions as racial hatred, religious enthusiasm, and raving depends on an innate susceptibility to infection.

Schopenhauer sees suffering as something that should be shared, in part because he assigns moral value to sympathy. Whether this moral value is unconditional, however, is questionable. Max Scheler argues in *The Nature of Sympathy* that "fellow feeling" cannot be a fundamental moral value. He maintains that the ethics of sympathy does not attribute moral value primarily to the *being* and attitude of persons as such, but seeks to derive moral value from the attitude of the spectator and in so doing invariably presupposes what it is trying to deduce because the sharing of another's pleasure can only be moral when the latter *is itself moral*, and warranted by the context which evokes it. Just as some pleasure is not in itself moral, so some sympathy may not qualify as moral. Scheler calls our attention to the appropriateness of sharing others' suffering. Maybe it's sometimes moral not to sympathize with others when bad things befall them.

The Appropriateness of Sympathy

Withholding sympathy differs from celebrating misfortune. Why would we withhold sympathy? Can sympathy ever be inappropriate? Just as it is sometimes fitting to offer sympathy, in some contexts it is appropriate to withhold or restrict it.

Sympathy and pity have mistakenly been equated. Both emotions depend on an unpleasant sharing of the pain or suffering of another person. Pity involves three separate beliefs: first, that the suffering in question is significant (Aristotle offers as examples loss of friends, loss of city, loss of opportunities, sickness, old age, and childlessness); second, that the person does not deserve his or her suffering; and third, the belief that such suffering could happen to oneself. Some thinkers object to the inclusion of this third belief on the menu of pity, and have argued that pity requires a distance between pitier and pitied that is foreign to compassion. They argue that pity arises instead from perceived inequality between persons, from a belief that the suffering of another simply could not befall them because of their character or conduct (or both). This objection carries some weight, for although we usually welcome compassion, we rarely appreciate pity.

That pity is rarely welcomed by those to whom it is directed means that it differs from other emotions closely associated with virtue, such as gratitude or compassion. The prospect of becoming an object of pity is alarming in part because we suspect that being on the receiving end of that emotion could make matters worse. We consequently regard an aversion to being pitied as morally commendable. That the same cannot be said of sympathy means that pity is more likely to be judged inappropriate than is sympathy.

Pity, which Schopenhauer problematically treats as sympathy, emerges as the opposite of *Schadenfreude*, for in such a state we not only lament the suffering we witness in another, we actively participate in it. The fact that Schopenhauer considers pity a virtue indicates further opposition to *Schadenfreude* as well as a point of intersection with a central feature of Christian morality. Though his thought is atheistic, he borrows certain elements from Indian and Christian sources in such a way as to provide grist for the mill of those who would portray Schopenhauer as a noble, quasi-Christian moralist (this is not my aim). He says, for example:

> Therefore, whatever goodness, affection, and magnanimity do for others is always only an alleviation of their sufferings; and consequently what can move them to good deeds and to words of affection is always only knowledge of the suffering of others, directly intelligible from one's own suffering, and put on a level therewith. (*WWR* I, p. 375)

The only way in which we can effectively help another is to alleviate his or her pain (though no remedy can stop suffering). When we set ourselves to assuage extrinsic suffering we are helping ourselves, because the difference between ourselves and others is illusory. For Schopenhauer suffering generates human goodness. People who suffer misfortunes merit our sympathy (by virtue of their contact with the ferocity of pain) and our appreciation (because they move others to good deeds).

What the world needs now is sympathy, Schopenhauer believes. Those who call upon others' compassion too often, too long, or too boldly may find themselves cut off from friends and family. Those who give sympathy too readily may be sentimentalists who find their emotional reserves exhausted just when they need to muster genuine emotional support. Freud insisted there was such a thing as non-genuine altruism, a reaction formation against sadism. This inappropriate altruism manifests itself in excessive pity, "exaggerated kindness," and the sentimentality that some "friends of humanity and protectors of animals" display (SE 14 "Instincts and Their Vicissitudes" 129, 281–282). It is all too easy, in our age of confessions — group therapy sessions, television talk shows, tell-all autobiographies, where many a person is labeled a victim and where emotion comes easily — to lose a sense of proportion. One moment we cry for the death of Princess Diana, the next for children lost to an urban fire, next for a TV celebrity's marital woes, next for our favorite soap opera heroine's sufferings. Sympathy and compassion are sensationalized.

If we allow ourselves to thrill to rampant emotion, we may find that we are no longer able to distinguish the genuinely pitiable. Removing ourselves from rampant emotion accompanies maturity. Writing in her diary the day of her thirty-second birthday, American food writer M.F.K. Fisher revealed the following:

> I have a much larger capacity for everything. I see a lot more and care a lot less about things like people and whether they like me. . . . I am much less eager, in that way young people have of being eager. I find myself unable or unwilling to give anything of myself, that is. When I was younger, I poured some of my own élan vital into all my contacts with the rest of the world, unthinkingly. Now I am perhaps more cordial, suaver, in my relations with people, even with people I like or love, but I realize with a feeling almost of shock that I am cold and selfish about that pouring out of my élan. I hold it back, saving it.[25]

There is something remarkable about emotional generosity that makes this appealing human characteristic all the more valuable when it is carefully given. Experience sharpened Fisher's sense of when it was appropriate to offer her emotional resources to others. If we pour out our sympathy indiscriminately, we may well have less to spare for others who really need it. Of course, there is a real and important difference between rationing our sympathy for others and celebrating the misfortunes of others; both, however, might offend sentimental people equally.

Sentimentality can lead people into quite drastic actions, good examples of which are found in *Sturm und Drang* drama and Schopenhauer's insistence that *Schadenfreude* is diabolical. Philosophical and religious censure of *Schadenfreude* has enacted sentimentality to a large degree. There has been a genuinely internal connection between *Schadenfreude* and sentimentality (though not vice versa) in that criticism of *Schadenfreude* has been largely drastic.

Idealizing sufferers and demonizing parsimonious sympathizers amounts to projecting the painfulness of the human condition onto the wrong objects. Sympathy can be inappropriate, both with respect to degree and kind. We do a disservice to human suffering by construing it as monolithic and sacred. Some instances of suffering are more terrible than others. Sanctifying suffering offends reason, as it is always possible to argue sincerely and morally for the appropriateness of some instances of suffering.

Is it appropriate to sympathize with a criminal who deserves to suffer? Schopenhauer insists that even when persons can be said to deserve their punishment, we as moral beings must never enjoy their suffering. We must sympathize with sufferers and hope sincerely that their future actions will be more virtuous. For Schopenhauer, there is scarcely an inappropriate instance of sympathy with another person. Agreement on this point has been far from complete.

Scheler suggests in *The Nature of Sympathy* that the moral value of sympathy varies according to the appropriateness of the feelings of the person sympathized with and the value of this person him- or herself.

> . . . the total value of an act of fellow-feeling varies according to the worth of the value-situation which is the occasion of the other person's sorrow or joy. In other words, to sympathize with joys and sorrows which are appropriate to their circumstances is preferable to sympathizing with those which are not. By the same token, it is better to have sympathy for a person of superior worth than for someone of lesser value.[26]

As disturbing an idea as this last one might seem, this same thinking lies at the heart of the culture from which Aristotle's ethics of virtue arose (Aristotle's conception of the good is also highly elitist, centering on affluent, male citizens). In the *Rhetoric* Aristotle asserts that pity is pain at the vividly entertained thought of disaster for someone *like oneself in power and susceptibility*. Aristotle, like Nietzsche, holds that awareness of the pain, suffering, or general wretchedness of someone's life does not automatically mean that it makes sense to pity that person (*Rhetoric* 2.8). If we find another person too alien, we may not sympathize with his or her suffering.

Nietzsche concurs. In *The Will to Power* he writes, "A great man . . . wants no 'sympathetic' heart, but servants, tools; in his intercourse with men he is always intent on making something out of them. . . . There is a solitude within him that is inaccessible to praise or blame, his own justice that is beyond appeal."[27] MacIntyre quotes that passage in his *After Virtue* in the context of an argument to the effect that the only way of rejecting Nietzsche is to embrace the Aristotelian tradition of the virtues. But Aristotle, like Nietzsche, urges us not to sympathize with the weak. Against them both we ought to hold that we sympathize above all with people, not with certain personal qualities. What MacIntyre wants to say is that there is something to value in the suffering of the downtrodden, as well as in the distress of the exalted. Similarly, it is just as worthwhile to sympathize with someone whose fears or anxieties are ill-founded as with someone whose fears or anxieties are well-founded.

We can misconstrue others' interests. The difficulty is not so much whether we can appropriately correct others' preferences when thinking about their interest, but to what extent we have the right to act on the basis of those corrections if the people concerned do not recognize them. For Schopenhauer, everyone has an interest in receiving the compassion of others. We must not expect compassion, however. To do so would be to exercise optimism, which Schopenhauer denounces:

> For the rest, I cannot here withhold the statement that optimism, where it is not merely the thoughtless talk of those who harbor nothing but words under their shallow foreheads, seems to me to be not merely an absurd, but also a really wicked, way of thinking, a bitter mockery of the unspeakable sufferings of mankind. Let no one imagine that the Christian teaching is favourable to optimism; on the contrary, in the Gospels world and evil are used almost as synonymous expressions. (*WWR* I, p. 326)

Being optimistic becomes analogous to being *schadenfroh*. So we are to commit ourselves steadfastly to compassion without expecting to find it in others. For Schopenhauer, it is always appropriate to show compassion, but inappropriate to expect it.

A Mosaic of Suffering

The variety of ways in which people suffer defies ready classification. It is a little easier to grasp the range of our emotional responses to the bad things that happen to other people.

We cannot identify with or have respect or compassion for others without feeling a certain way when they are violated. This response is connected to the feelings of guilt we would experience were we the ones who perpetrated the violation and to our own need for sympathy, had the misfortune befallen us. This emotional state calls for compassion, but the questions of whether compassion is appropriate in situations involving trivial suffering and what the limits of a person's sympathy might be find no satisfactory answer in Schopenhauer's reflections.

Of course, the broad category of suffering certainly includes misery. We should not, however, limit ourselves to dark and heavy examples in the course of evaluating responses to suffering. Many light and transient ones are no less worthy of attention for their levity. Further, not all suffering is to be deplored completely: some people deserve to suffer. The defects of *Schadenfreude* as a moral category present a fundamental problem in Schopenhauer's and Roberts's conception of *Schadenfreude* as a moral experience. The best way to see the weakness of this theoretical conception is by looking at the everyday distinctions their accounts fail to accommodate.

In a world without suffering, there would be no *Schadenfreude*. This is the world for which Schopenhauer longs. Schopenhauer recommends extrication from the phenomenal world to which suffering is ineluctably attached. He advises us to quicken "the will's self-elimination" because "at every step the will of the individual is crossed and thwarted by the chance of inanimate nature, by contrary aims and intentions, even by the malice inspired by others" (*WWR* I, p. 188). But if the price of steering clear of *Schadenfreude* is living less, then the prize seems hardly worth the fight.

Five

Celebrating Suffering

INDEED, THIS IS PRECISELY WHAT NIETZSCHE, THE RELENTLESS YES-SAYER, maintains: Schopenhauer's prize comes at too high a cost. Without the personal separateness which *Schadenfreude* presupposes, there would be precious little personality at risk of being bruised by laughter — not so much because we are immune to pain, but because there is no particularly distinctive personality left to harm. Nietzsche holds that *Schadenfreude* is not something that should alarm us, even as he acknowledges that being the object of *Schadenfreude* can be unpleasant. Being laughed at, either silently or overtly, bothers Nietzsche quite a bit less than it does Schopenhauer.

Nietzsche's critique of Schopenhauer captures the moral problem of *Schadenfreude*: although both take human suffering quite seriously, they thoroughly disagree on how to respond to it. Like Wittgenstein, Nietzsche first approached the discipline of philosophy under the spell of Schopenhauer. Nietzsche read the works of his much-admired teacher avidly, and Schopenhauer's thoughts and words cascaded through his writings throughout the 1870s. The motivation for Nietzsche's subsequent about-face provides one of the most forceful illustrations of problems we encounter in thinking about suffering.

Nietzsche's various works contain countless references to the problem of envy. Happy people must constantly beware of unhappy people, Nietzsche admonishes. The thinker whose Zarathustra at one point exclaims, "How could they endure my happiness, if I did not put around it accidents, and winter-privations, and bearskin caps, and enmantling snowflakes!," believes he has identified the genesis of the moral problem of *Schadenfreude*. In Part II, Section 27, of *Human, All Too Human* (from 1886) we find Nietzsche's account of how *Schadenfreude* comes to be:

Explanation of *Schadenfreude*. — *Schadenfreude* originates in the fact that, in certain respects of which he is well aware, everyone feels unwell, is oppressed by care or envy or sorrow: the harm that befalls another makes him our equal, it appeases our envy. — If, on the other hand, he happens to feel perfectly well, he nonetheless gathers up his neighbor's misfortune in his consciousness as a capital upon which to draw when he himself faces misfortune: thus he too experiences *Schadenfreude*. The disposition bent upon equality thus extends its demands to the domain of happiness and chance as well: *Schadenfreude* is the commonest expression of the victory and restoration of equality within the higher world-order too. It is only since man has learned to see in other men beings like and equal to himself, that is to say only since the establishment of society, that *Schadenfreude* has existed.[1]

Sounding a good deal like Rousseau (specifically, *Second Discourse* 156), Nietzsche ties *Schadenfreude* to inequality and sees both everywhere. The contrast between Nietzsche's and Schopenhauer's moral assessment of *Schadenfreude* could hardly be more pronounced. I will examine the implications of the separateness and inequality of persons for thinking about compassion and human solidarity at the conclusion of this chapter. For now, a crucial inference from this "explanation" demands emphasis: Nietzsche takes *Schadenfreude* to be as *universal* a phenomenon as the civilization with which he associates it. Nietzsche believes that no society can be effective or even attain a tolerable social climate if it does not employ a belief that will bring the underprivileged man to see, if not himself, then the effect of blind chance as a cause of his condition. Otherwise, the unfortunate person may blame a neighbor for his misfortune, with potentially disastrous social effects.

Nietzsche believes that we have been socially conditioned to view the setbacks of other persons in terms of our own well-being. Ever worried that people around us may be flourishing more than we are, we view their suffering as a chance to even the score, as it were. In Nietzsche's genealogy of *Schadenfreude*, our pleasure comes not just from the actual suffering of others but also from the fact that they suffer. How curious that Nietzsche, a consummate philologist, uses the word *Schadenfreude* this loosely:

literally, *Schadenfreude* should refer to pleasure in the suffering of others, not in the justice to which that suffering attests. I have followed Nietzsche's broader usage of the word "*Schadenfreude.*"

For Nietzsche, *Schadenfreude* is a thoroughly social emotion, one that, like guilt, shame, love, and jealousy, connects people. The social interaction on which it depends can be real or imagined. Without the social glue of *Schadenfreude*, we would be more distant from each other and would likely feel more alienated from a society that causes us to suffer almost daily. *Schadenfreude* disrupts the sense that the rest of the world forms some unified force: the experience of *Schadenfreude* makes the identities of separate persons more distinct, more concrete. This grounding effect makes it easier for us to relate to others as unique personalities in a social constellation, instead of as faceless members of enemy forces. In Nietzsche's social understanding of *Schadenfreude*, enjoying the misfortunes of others puts us in their debt, for they have given us pleasure. We repay that debt by offering up our own misfortunes to them.

Nietzsche's use of the phrase "the disposition bent upon equality" pierces to the heart of his understanding of *Schadenfreude*. For Nietzsche, *Schadenfreude* says more about people who feel it than about those who suffer. Equality rests on the conviction that we deserve as much as our neighbors, which means that Nietzsche understands *Schadenfreude* to include an important consideration of what we take our neighbors to deserve. Nietzsche's cynicism about our ability to make such a determination selflessly ran quite deep. This cynicism colored Nietzsche's view of modern ideas about corporal punishment and social justice.

Another pregnant reference to *Schadenfreude* surfaces in Nietzsche's laconic "definition" of laughter found in *The Gay Science*: "Laughter: being *schadenfroh* with a good conscience."[2] Nietzsche's vitality, astute eye, and remarkable intuitions converge in this aphorism and deserve to be taken seriously. In this remark and throughout the second essay in *On the Genealogy of Morals* Nietzsche indicates that taking pleasure in the sight of the suffering of others is a *universal* characteristic of human beings. It should not seem farfetched to infer from Nietzsche's *aperçu* that even he possesses firsthand knowledge of *Schadenfreude*, in contrast to his probably disingenuous claim in *Ecce Homo* ("Why I Am So Wise," Section 5) never to have experienced resentment, which is closely related to *Schaden-*

freude. My analysis of *Schadenfreude* owes much to Nietzsche's penetrating insights into laughter.

Walter Kaufmann details in a lengthy footnote to Section 294 of *Beyond Good and Evil* the extent to which Nietzsche's estimation of laughter, especially at the defects of others, borrows and diverges from Hobbes's. For Nietzsche, laughter is a symbol of a joyous affirmation of life and of the refusal to bow before the spirit of gravity. Yet Nietzsche also refers to laughter as a vice. How can it be that he interprets a weakness, albeit an "Olympian" one, as a sign of strength? The answer must lie in his distinction between being *schadenfroh* with a good conscience and being *schadenfroh* with a bad conscience. This distinction rests on the working of *Mitleid*, which in turn depends on a certain understanding of the separateness of persons.

The aim of examining these fine points is, first, to infer from this "definition" of laughter and relevant passages in other works Nietzsche's assessment of the moral status of *Schadenfreude* and, second, to question the pivotal distinction between enjoying *that* someone suffers and enjoying his or her suffering. I want to put forth Nietzsche's understanding of *Schadenfreude* as for the most part exemplary: with Nietzsche, I conclude that we should think of *Schadenfreude* as pleasure both *that* someone suffers and *in* his or her suffering. I share much of Nietzsche's cynicism about justice, though not all of it. And so I take a softer view of *Schadenfreude* than he ultimately does: though he looks with scorn on the idea of selfless beliefs about justice, I do not.

Schadenfreude and Conscience

Nietzsche locates the origin of bad conscience and guilt in primitive concepts of obligations to the gods, obligations which bequeath a burden of outstanding debt. He attributes to the rise of Christianity responsibility for the dissemination of the sense of indebtedness, that is, guilt. Freud took up this point in *The Ego and the Id* and, following Nietzsche's lead, depicted guilt as a (frequently unconscious) means to inflicting suffering on oneself. Bad conscience and guilt accomplish the aims Nietzsche imputed to ascetic priests. Given his close association of bad conscience with Christianity, Nietzsche would seem to be saying that Christians are generally capable only of *Schadenfreude*, not of laughter.³ The self-directed aggression at work in bad conscience, which Nietzsche certainly and Freud perhaps takes to be an enduring state, trumps the other-regarding aggression underlying laughter.

Nietzsche views Christianity as a cancer eating away at modern morality, which he calls "a veritable cult of suffering" in which "what is baptized as pity in the circles of such enthusiasts" has come to be regarded as the epitome of moral sensitivity (*BGE,* Section 293). The very notion of a moral conscience, which plays so central a role in both Christianity and Schopenhauer's thought, is for Nietzsche not a set of problems but a problem in itself. For Nietzsche, the morality Schopenhauer espouses amounts to a morality of pity; significantly, he regards this morality as largely compatible with Christianity. As for Christian mores, Nietzsche's disgust is fathomless:

> Who has not pondered sadly over what the German spirit could be! But this nation has deliberately made itself stupid, for practically a thousand years: nowhere else are the two great European narcotics, alcohol and Christianity, so viciously abused.⁴

Throughout the *Anti-Christ* Nietzsche denounces both the ideals of institutionalized Christianity and the failure of this religion to live up to its own perverse standards. Nietzsche's target in *The Anti-Christ* is not simply institutional Christianity: he also repudiates even the purest exemplification of Christian values (namely Christ), though he acknowledges Christ's "perverse achievement" of *perfect* decadence. Christians, says Nietzsche, fall short of Christ's ideal; they preach decadence but practice *ressentiment*. Because of *ressentiment*, a "transvaluation of values," the laughter of Christians involves bad, not good, conscience.

Nietzsche's thinking is, of course, notoriously unsympathetic to Christians. It would be unwise, however, simply to discount his conclusions as *ad hominem* or ill-founded. Sympathy with Christian views or the idea that we should love our neighbors as ourselves should not commit one to embrace Schopenhauer's full-blown censure of *Schadenfreude* too quickly. For it does not follow that Schopenhauer's moral philosophy is false if Nietzsche's is true and *vice versa*. In a much stronger sense Schopenhauer's moral philosophy is pitted squarely against Nietzsche's by virtue of the position each takes on pity or fellow feeling.

For Nietzsche, the will to power of noble individuals affirms their difference from others. They do not want others to be like them any more than they want to be like others. For the rest of the world, however, the differences between individuals must become as small as possible, if the "slave morality" is to dominate.⁵ For Nietzsche, *Mitgefühl* (fellow feeling) has a conditional value: it is desirable when one sympathizes with a noble or worthy individual, but undesirable when one feels it toward an unworthy individual (*BGE*, Section 284 and *Will to Power*, Sections 864 and 1020). Schopenhauer's moral assessment of *Schadenfreude* collapses personal differences; Nietzsche's account accentuates them.

Pity is fundamentally linked to suffering, as the German terms *Mitleid* and *Leid* indicate. In German, suffering implies community, as the word *Mitleid* connotes that one suffers *with* others. But because *Mitleid* focuses on the negative states of others, Nietzsche regards it as life-denying and without positive value. Nietzsche's use of *Mitleid* suggests that he distinguishes between compassion and pity only ambiguously. To the extent that *Mitleid* (presumably "compassion" in these instances) involves a genuine concern for the good of others, it is fundamentally life-affirming and positive. This means that though *Mitleid* is *principally* negative for Nietzsche, it is not wholly so. In any event there can be no doubt that Nietzsche is attacking, rather than praising, when he refers to Christianity as *the* religion of *Mitleid* ("die Religion des Mitleidens," *GS*, Section 377; *BGE*, Section 206; *GM*, III, Section 25; *A*, Section 7).

Nietzsche maintains that a proclivity to pity or fellow feeling leads to a perverse privileging of sadness. He says, "Quite in general, pity crosses the law of development, which is the law of *selection*" because it "conserves all that is miserable" even while lamenting its misery and consequently condemning life thereby (*A*, Section 7). Sounding quite Nietzschean, Lawrence Blum points out that it is possible for a compassionate person to be insensitive to the pleasures of others.⁶ A focus on misery and suffering in the absence of regard for others' joys and pleasures constitutes a limitation in the moral consciousness of the merely compassionate person.

I pointed out in the previous chapter that Schopenhauer advocates a passionate participation in the sufferings of others, which leads him to demonize an aversion to pity. Schopenhauer judges Kant's declaration in the *Critique of Practical Reason* that a right-thinking person desires to be free from "the feelings of sympathy (*Gefühl des Mitleids*) and soft-hearted fellow feeling (*weichherzigen Teilnehmung*)"[7] thoroughly repugnant. For in such a world as Kant's, only a "slavish fear of the gods"or "frankly self-interested concerns" could move a hard heart to help a sufferer (*OBM*, p. 66). What is particularly striking here is an unusual example of agreement between Nietzsche and Kant. Though in *The Metaphysics of Morals* Kant takes sympathetic feeling to be a duty, he qualifies the obligation:

> . . . when another suffers and I let myself (through my imagination) also become infected [*anstecken lasse*] by his pain, which I still cannot remedy, then two people suffer, although the evil (in nature) affects only the one. But it cannot possibly be a duty to increase the evils of the world, or therefore to do good from pity [*Mitleid*] . . . (p. 205)

David Cartwright has noted Nietzsche's obvious debt to Kant's critique of pity.[8] Nietzsche objects to pity because it erodes the self by immersing us in the plight of a sufferer. Throwing ourselves into the problems of others does no good to anyone. Misery may love company, but this abject company escalates suffering. Nietzsche, like Kant, considers acting from pity an indulgence of one's inclinations to the extent that it is oneself that really benefits. For both Kant and Nietzsche, pity transmits suffering.

Nietzsche concurs with Schopenhauer that suffering is contagious: for him, however, this happens because of, rather than despite, pity. He says: "Suffering itself becomes contagious through pity . . . Schopenhauer was within his rights in this: life is denied, made *more worthy of denial* by pity — pity is *practical* nihilism" (*A*, Section 7). Pity is the most agreeable feeling among those who have little pride and no prospects of great conquests; for them easy prey — and that is what all who suffer are — is enchanting.

In *Human, All Too Human* we are told that we should *manifest* pity, but take care not to feel it, for "the unfortunate" are so stupid that the manifestation of pity constitutes the greatest good in the world (p. 38). Children weep and wail in order to make themselves pitied; they, like invalids and the mentally afflicted, display their misfortunes in order to hurt others. The pity they manage to evoke is a consolation for the weak and suffering, inasmuch as it shows them that, all their weakness notwithstanding, they possess at any rate one power: the power to hurt, to drag others down with them. In this feeling of superiority, derived from inducing others to pity, the "unfortunate man" gains a sort of pleasure: he is still of sufficient importance to cause affliction in the world. The thirst for pity is thus a thirst for self-enjoyment, and that at the expense of one's fellow men. Pity becomes not the antidote to the *Schadenfreude* of others but, curiously, a means toward achieving *Schadenfreude* for ourselves.

For this reason it appears that Nietzsche and Schopenhauer *agree* that *Schadenfreude* is objectionable, though for sharply opposed reasons. Schopenhauer holds that it violates the principles of compassion and Nietzsche regards it as a correlate of *ressentiment*. Because Nietzsche seems to have in mind a certain contrast between "*Schadenfreude* with a good conscience" and "*Schadenfreude* with a bad conscience," it seems safer to conclude that Schopenhauer and Nietzsche agree only that some *Schadenfreude* is objectionable.

Pity that produces *Schadenfreude* stands as a good example of what Nietzsche describes as "being *schadenfroh* with a bad conscience," because its only affirmation is of the power to hurt. This kind of hurting is indirect, like the pouting or groaning that aims to interrupt the tranquility of others. This "power" perversely imitates what Nietzsche takes to be bona fide power, which he associates with nobles. Another example of this sort is the joy that comes from *observing* the hurt of others. Nietzsche's sharpest objection to this perverse imitation of power surfaces in the acerbic remarks on St. Thomas Aquinas and Tertullian in the first essay of *On the Genealogy of Morals*. Nietzsche reacts with astonishment and revulsion to St. Thomas's assertion (in *Summa Theologiae*, III, Supplementum, Q. 94, Art. 1) that the joy of the saints in heaven will derive in part from a view of the suffering of the damned in hell. (In the third article of this supplement, to which Nietzsche does not refer, the saints take joy in the *justice* of God's order.) The weak, finally made strong in heaven, rejoice over the power to look down on the very nobles whose various strengths tortured them on earth.

How do nobles react to the suffering of others? In *Thus Spake*

Zarathustra Nietzsche does not consider Zarathustra's sensitivity to the misfortune of others appropriate, although he judges Zarathustra's shame at seeing the sufferer suffer preferable to the behavior of the merciful, who feel blessed in their pity.[9] Further, he says, "if I do pity, it is preferably from a distance." Nietzsche attacks only one kind of pity and neighbor-love, the kind that entails commiseration or an indulgence of others' weaknesses. To be sure, if a friend should suffer, one will suffer with him, though "it might be better to hide this feeling under a hard shell" (Z I, Section 14). A friend succeeds morally if he helps the sufferer regain his self-mastery. Pity exemplifies the bad kind of love we might have for ourselves or others; the struggle for self-perfection represents the superior love. The irony of Nietzsche's position is that, sneering aside, it is by far more compassionate than the judgment of Schopenhauer, who works to ensure that persons who do on occasion feel *schadenfroh* suffer inexorable guilt as a result.

Nietzsche's reflections on humor, particularly the humor of the noble or the laughter of children, suggest that only the strong can experience "being *schadenfroh* with a good conscience." We may take as an example of this phenomenon Julian Young's suggestion that the early Nietzsche's Dionysian worldview is an expression of *Schadenfreude*.[10] That view figures prominently in Nietzsche's work *The Birth of Tragedy* (1872), which has religion as its fundamental concern. Art is to fill the void left by the demise of the Christian God and the role of the tragic theater in Greek life is to provide a model for the regeneration of modern culture.

Nietzsche avers that the Greek theater provides metaphysical consolation for the horrors of human life no less than a Christian church does. The Apollonian spectator rejoices in the annihilation of the tragic hero. Just as barbarians celebrated their ecstatic absorption into the primal oneness in acts of real violence performed on real individuals, the Greek audience performed the same act symbolically. The performance of a tragedy offers a symbolic sacrifice to Dionysus. The manifestly therapeutic *Schadenfreude* of the Greek spectators exuberantly endorses supraindividual identity, an affirmation aptly thought of in terms of burning money in celebration of sudden accession to great wealth. Nietzsche does recognize a salubrious strain of *Schadenfreude*, then, one which can be indulged with a good conscience.

I too affirm a healthy kind of *Schadenfreude*, despite my disagreement with a number of Nietzsche's views on human interaction. His anti-Judaism and anti-Christianity, contempt for democracy, justification of slavery, misogyny, and enthusiasm for eugenics are all reasons to exercise caution in accepting Nietzsche's aphorisms. One need not accept all of Nietzsche's reflections on human interaction to endorse his view of *Schadenfreude*, though. Although Nietzschean morality undermines to some important extent the most vital sources of human love, it clarifies the ramifications and potential of human strength. In a world in which we must compete with one another for any number of scarce goods, even compassion, our very will to survive jeopardizes the chances that someone else will find happiness. Beyond this, our holding moral beliefs and principles will in some real sense exacerbate the inevitable suffering of others who do not agree with us.

Briefly put, *Schadenfreude* and malicious glee are episodic concerns, where *ressentiment* is a dispositional one. Malicious glee indicates something about a person's character, where *Schadenfreude* indicates something about how a person views justice and moral triviality. I have questioned the moral appropriateness of condemning some instances of malicious glee (specifically, those of self-esteem and of comedy). This same sort of defense can be expanded, with minimal modification, to cover resentment. This is not the case with *ressentiment*, however, which bespeaks a genuine moral shortcoming.

Resentment versus *Ressentiment*

Ressentiment, in the *Oxford English Dictionary* interchangeable with the word "resentment," remains a somewhat vexing aspect of Nietzsche's legacy because it has eluded consistent translation; because no criteria help us to discern when hostility and *ressentiment* are really the same thing; and because the application of *ressentiment* beyond religious morality is in some respects dubious. I argue that *ressentiment* and resentment are not in fact linguistic equivalents, and that *ressentiment* has more to do with envy than with hostility.

The two principal expositors of the phenomenon, Nietzsche and

Scheler, relied on the French word *ressentiment* because they believed that it could not be reduced to the psychological notion of indignation. Agreeing with them, I adopt the convention of using the French *ressentiment*. *Ressentiment* has become widely accepted within the German language, although there is no full equivalent for this term in English.[11] Derived from the French word *sentire* (to feel), the English word resentment indicating indignation or bitter feelings against some person or situation carries less weight than the French notion of *ressentiment*.

Scheler has offered a sound reason for retaining the French word, but in so doing, he has slanted the meaning Nietzsche intended:

> We do not use the word *ressentiment* because of a special predilection for the French language, but because we did not succeed in translating it into German. Moreover, Nietzsche has made it a terminus technicus. In the natural meaning of the French word I detect two elements. First of all *ressentiment* is the repeated experiencing and reliving of a particular emotional response reaction against someone else. The continual reliving of the emotion sinks it more deeply into the center of the personality, but concomitantly removes it from the person's zone of action and expression. It is not a mere intellectual recollection of the emotion and of the events to which it "responded" — it is a re-experiencing of the emotion itself, a renewal of the original feeling. Secondly, the word implies that the quality of this emotion is negative, i.e., that it contains a movement of hostility.[12]

While the English noun "resentment" possesses marked similarities to the French word "*ressentiment*," Scheler's characterization of the phenomenon rules out the employment of the two words synonymously. (Scheler does not comment on the problems of English translation; "sour grapes" must be the closest linguistic and conceptual equivalent.) The English verb "to resent" derives from the same Latin prefix and verb as "*ressentir*." However, the English verb pertains to cases in which someone merely feels or shows displeasure at (a person, act, remark, etc.) from a sense of injury or insult. Although I believe Scheler exaggerated the link of *ressentiment* to physical violence, I think he was correct to insist that by expressing our occasional "resentment," we could avoid developing within ourselves the disposition called "*ressentiment.*"

As will become clear in examining Nietzsche's speculations in the following section, *ressentiment* is essentially about the ongoing lack of and desire for some value or good, whereas resentment arises much more generally, in the context of feeling mistreated in a particular way. Sir Peter Strawson's well-known essay "Freedom and Resentment" classifies resentment as a morally reactive attitude, a response that follows the perception that other people aren't treating us, or others who deserve respect and goodwill, well enough. Although resentment is not necessarily a constructive sentiment, it may help change attitudes or behavior we find objectionable. Resentment is considerably less worrisome than *ressentiment*, both psychologically and morally. What we speak of in English as resentment often accompanies what Nietzsche means by *ressentiment*. I will now explain the difference this makes.

Nietzsche's Theory of *Ressentiment*

Fredric Jameson has called Nietzsche "the primary theorist, if not, indeed, the metaphysician of *ressentiment.*"[13] Walter Kaufmann similarly termed *ressentiment* "one of the key conceptions of Nietzsche's psychology and the clue to many of his philosophic contentions."[14] According to Kaufmann it is this state of mind or state of being that perhaps best illuminates the separation of Christian ethics from Nietzsche's own (though whether Nietzsche endorsed the philosophical enterprise of arguing for ethical actions or emotions is not entirely clear). *Ressentiment* involves the feelings and emotions in a fundamental way. When explicating Nietzsche, Scheler had argued that no "perversions of value feelings" correspond to the perversions of desire, only illusions and delusions of value feeling. Scheler found this understandable, for "feeling" or "preferring" a value is an act of cognition. Therefore a man who slanders the unattainable values which oppress him may still be aware of their positive character.

I have said that Schopenhauer must have contributed to Nietzsche's reflections on *ressentiment*. Schopenhauer speaks in *The World as Will and Representation* of the "bitterest of all human sufferings, dissatisfac-

tion with our own individuality" (I, p. 307). Nietzsche's insight that the
weak suffer from themselves bears the influence of Schopenhauer:

> Where does one not encounter that veiled glance which burdens
> one with a profound sadness, that inward-turned glance of the
> born failure which betrays how such people speak to themselves —
> that glance which is a sigh! "If only I were someone else," sighs
> that glance: "but there is no hope of that. I am who I am: how
> could I ever get free of myself? And yet — I am sick of myself!"
> (*GM* III, Section 14)

In his last book and philosophical autobiography *Ecce Homo*, Nietzsche
repeats nearly verbatim Schopenhauer's insight into the deep pain caused
by thoroughgoing dissatisfaction with the self ("Why I Am So Wise," Section 6). In this essay Nietzsche articulates the link between *Schadenfreude*
and *ressentiment*.

Nietzsche's understanding of *ressentiment* reflects an apprehension,
absent in Schopenhauer, of the *dispositional* (or habitual, as opposed to
episodic) nature of this reactive attitude. People who yearn to be someone
else, those who fundamentally dislike themselves, exhibit a properly dispositional trait. They are fertile soil for *ressentiment*. Someone simply
having a bad day, on the other hand, doesn't necessarily dislike him- or
herself. A sporadic or temporary crisis of self-esteem differs in scope, du-
ration, and consequences from the state of mind that leads to *ressentiment*. This second class of persons may, when rationally assessing the
misfortune of another, include in their thought process an element of feeling inferior. (Of course, this feeling of inferiority or disempowerment is
continuously subject to revision.) Nobles may feel resentment, but they do
not suffer from *ressentiment*.

Difficulties of all sorts befall us. Difficulties, regardless of their extent,
bother some of us more than others. Nietzsche's view of human life, a
view he shares with Schopenhauer, is not cheery:

> Here we must beware of superficiality and get to the bottom of the
> matter, resisting all sentimental weakness: life itself is *essentially*
> appropriation, injury, overpowering of what is alien and weaker;

suppression, hardness, imposition of one's own forms, incorpora-
tion and at least, at its mildest, exploitation — but why should one
always use those words in which a slanderous intent has been im-
printed for ages? (*BGE,* Section 259)

For Nietzsche, this omnipresent suffering is a consequence of the will to
power. The most repellent aspect of human misery for Nietzsche is its irra-
tionality. Nietzsche cares about suffering, but he warns us not to allow
preoccupation with it to interfere in the task of living our lives.

Nietzsche views *ressentiment* as a lasting mental attitude caused by the
systematic repression of certain emotions and affects. Later, Scheler identified these emotions: *Rache* (revenge), *Hass* (hatred), *Bosheit* (malice),
Neid (envy), *Scheelsuch* (impulse to detract), *Hämischkeit* (spite) *Groll*
(rancor), *Zorn* (wrath), *Rachsucht* (vindictiveness, vengefulness), and
Schadenfreude. In *On the Genealogy of Morals* I, Section 8, Nietzsche associates the *modus operandi* of this repression with Judaism. Though he
initially blames Judaism for *ressentiment,* Nietzsche takes pains to make
clear that Christianity is just as guilty, because Christianity eagerly ab-
sorbed the perversion of values underlying *ressentiment.*

Invoking God to justify the suffering of others lies at the heart of "the
slave revolt in morality." As I have said, Nietzsche accuses the Jews of ini-
tiating that revolt. Their misery over failing to attain the values of "the
noble, the powerful, the masters, the rulers" led Jews to substitute a new
system of values such that

the wretched alone are the good; the poor, impotent, lowly alone
are the good; the suffering, deprived, sick, ugly alone are pious,
alone are blessed by God, blessedness is for them alone — and you,
the powerful and noble, are on the contrary the evil, the cruel, the
lustful, the insatiable, the godless to all eternity; and you shall be in
all eternity the unblessed, accursed, and damned! (*GM* I, Section 7)

Christians subsequently embraced this revolt wholeheartedly. Nietzsche
calls the ideal of Christian love, agape, the "triumphant crown" of "Jewish hatred." First the Jew and then the Christian learned to transfer to

God the vengeance he himself could not wreak on the great. *Ressentiment* thus began as a distinctly religious phenomenon.

It is a mistake to think of *ressentiment* as *necessarily* a function of religion. It would be more accurate to think of envy as the culprit. The success of *ressentiment* does not hang on religious belief. *Ressentiment* poisons the consciences of life's winners, who start to doubt whether they deserve to prosper. Even the strong have their weary hours, Nietzsche tells us. Once life's winners start doubting their right to happiness, *ressentiment* has worked its black magic. Even an atheist, though, might worry about the misery he sees around him: he doesn't need a religious voice to compel him to look at the suffering of others. Religion may fuel *ressentiment,* but religion is not a necessary cause.

Further, it is a mistake to dismiss cynically all of the Jewish/Christian morality. Against Nietzsche, Scheler defended the concept of Christian love as an expression of strength rather than weakness, as a sign of vitality rather than decadence. He suggested that Nietzsche had confused authentic love with Schopenhauer's version of Christian culture. Scheler regarded the culture of bourgeois society as the most profound manifestation of negative *ressentiment*. In particular, he condemned the bourgeois endorsement of utilitarian philosophy as a perversion of true values and a subversion of genuine feeling and Christian love. These reservations notwithstanding, Scheler was one of the first serious thinkers to understand the extraordinary importance of Nietzsche's moral insight.

The following passage from *On the Genealogy of Morals* most clearly explains how the "transvaluation" underlying *ressentiment* works:

> The slave revolt in morality begins when *ressentiment* itself becomes creative and gives birth to values: the *ressentiment* of natures that are denied the true reaction, that of deeds, and compensate themselves with an imaginary revenge. While every noble morality develops from a triumphant affirmation of itself, slave morality from the outset says No to what is "outside," what is "different," what is "not itself"; and this No is its creative deed. This inversion of the value-positing eye — this *need* to direct one's view outward instead of back to oneself — is of the essence of

> *ressentiment*: in order to exist, slave morality always first needs a
> hostile external world; it needs, physiologically speaking, external
> stimuli in order to act at all — its action is fundamentally reaction.
> (I, Section 10)

Like *Schadenfreude, ressentiment* is a function of reaction, not action. *Ressentiment* involves a distortion of reality, a distortion of facts. Recent philosophical attention to sentimentality has focused on how this emotional indulgence distorts the world.[15] Sentimentality causes people to falsify the object of their emotions. They may actively cultivate false beliefs about some object in order to make an object appear appropriate to their feelings. A film or novel, for example, might sentimentally portray a child molester by emphasizing his own sad childhood (the loss of a mother, the cruelty of a father, the death of a pet) instead of focusing on his pattern of damaging the lives of children. As John Kekes has put it, sentimental people change the world (in fantasy) to accommodate their feelings, as opposed to changing their feelings to accommodate the world.

Why is *ressentiment* any worse than sentimentality? First of all, remember that sentimentality enjoyed a great deal of popularity until this century. What Nietzsche calls *ressentiment* never has. European literature in the mid-eighteenth century was dominated by a cult of feeling, itself a reaction to a tendency in philosophy to scorn emotions.[16] At base, sentimentality represents a misguided attempt to do something good: to make someone or something objectionable appear more favorable. On some level, however, sentimentality also represents an attempt to deceive and thereby to protect the self. Here sentimentality emerges as closer to moral acceptability than *ressentiment*, for where *ressentiment* also represents an attempt to deceive and thereby protect the self, *ressentiment* requires a downward, as opposed to upward, valuation. *Ressentiment* represents a misguided attempt to do something bad. Instead of awarding more credit than is due (as in sentimentality), *ressentiment* gives less. Sentimentality touches on emotional generosity, but *ressentiment* resembles a hardened cynicism.

Nietzsche explains that by transvaluing, the weak enjoy "the ultimate, subtlest, sublimest triumph of revenge." How does *ressentiment* lead to revenge? And what sort of revenge is in question here? Nietzsche's answer: the weak reach inside the strong and compel the strong to desire weakness. The weak achieve their revenge when the strong turn against themselves. The mental revenge turns on malice, a hope that things will not go well for the noble or strong. This perversion explains why *ressentiment* is much more morally objectionable than sentimentality: maliciousness is more serious than making believe that something is not so bad as it really is. It also indicates that Nietzsche views *ressentiment* as a mental, not a physical, operation.

According to Nietzsche, the essence of *ressentiment* consists in consciously, perversely denying or denigrating everything one is not. Thus if one is not strong, powerful, or wealthy, one designates such attributes bad, wrong, evil. In the weak this mental revolt takes the place of the revenge they are helpless to exact. For the strong, the story is quite different: they certainly can avenge themselves, though they characteristically refrain from doing so. To have claws and not use them, to be above any *ressentiment* or desire for vengeance: that is for Nietzsche the true sign of power (and love) (*A*, Section 40).

Though the weak may experience their impotence or inferiority in any number of circumstances, the justification for it becomes, according to Nietzsche, in large part (though certainly not exclusively) a *religious* phenomenon. He alleges that the priests, the "truly great haters in world history," have perfected the means for achieving the consolation *ressentiment* delivers. This consolation does not imply physical violence, for Nietzsche does not view Christianity as a threat to the bodily safety of others (the Crusades and Inquisition notwithstanding).

True, impotence can trigger aggression and rage. An extremely powerful and biological response to the subjective experience of endangerment and cruelty, aggression contributes to the shaping and the vitalization of the self. The rage is a response to a perceived sense of threat and danger, a response that, over time, can become the central, organizing force behind personality. The inclination to rage in a persecuted minority such as the ancient Jews and early Christians incurs Nietzsche's scorn, though one might expect a more compassionate response. Nietzsche's outrage that Christians were winning the battle for cultural supremacy in the West nearly two thousand years later made compassion unthinkable.

The notion of impotence underlying Nietzschean *ressentiment* figures even more prominently in Scheler's analysis:

The *ressentiment* of cripples or of people of subnormal intelligence is a well-known phenomenon. Jewish *ressentiment,* which Nietzsche rightly designates as enormous, finds double nourishment: first in the discrepancy between the colossal national pride of "the chosen people" and a contempt and discrimination which weighed on them for centuries like a destiny, and in modern times through the added discrepancy between formal constitutional equality and factual discrimination. Certainly the extremely powerful acquisitive instinct of this people is due — over and beyond natural propensities and other causes — to a deep-rooted disturbance of Jewish self-confidence. (*Ressentiment*, pp. 33–34)

Scheler, who was born Jewish but later converted to Roman Catholicism, attributes to Jews a "powerful acquisitive instinct" and general impotence to satisfy that instinct. Here "chosen people" is understood not as "chosen to serve" but "chosen for special privileges." European Jews were, of course, manifestly disempowered, hence an obvious reason for their impotence to acquire material goods. It seems odd to overlook this social fact in alleging their susceptibility as a group to *ressentiment*. Be that as it may, we are to understand impotence as a necessary, though not sufficient, cause of *ressentiment*. Today, psychoanalysts call "narcissistic injuries" grave wounds to one's self-esteem which are coupled with feelings of impotence. *Ressentiment* in the sense I borrow from Nietzsche would be the emotional culmination of various, particular narcissistic injuries.

The Value of *Schadenfreude*

Nietzsche distinguishes between good and bad *Schadenfreude*, but even *Schadenfreude* of the debasing sort escapes Nietzsche's censure. Despite some ambivalence about *Schadenfreude*, Nietzsche recognizes certain benefits in our own setbacks. He maintains that the noble stand to profit a great deal from precisely what the Judeo-Christian injunction to love others as ourselves aims to prevent:

Examine the lives of the best and most fruitful people and peoples and ask yourselves whether a tree that is supposed to grow to a proud height can dispense with bad weather and storms; whether misfortune and external resistance, some kinds of hatred, jealousy, stubbornness, mistrust, hardness, avarice, and violence do not belong among the favorable conditions without which any great growth even of virtue is scarcely possible. The poison of which weaker natures perish strengthens the strong — nor do they call it poison. (*GS*, Section 19)

Nietzsche remarks in several different places that whatever adversity does not kill us will make us stronger (*Twilight of the Idols* I, Section 8 and *Ecce Homo* I, Section 2). These passages recall Nietzsche's acknowledgment of the ultimate value of bad conscience (*GM* II, Section 18), and his vigorous affirmation of the value of the apparently negative. Zarathustra says that "pain too is a joy" and maintains that to say "yes" to a single joy is also to say "yes" "to all woe," because "all things are entangled, ensnared, enamored" (*Z* IV, Section 19). An analysis of Nietzsche would be incomplete without mentioning the life-giving dialectic between negative and positive forces in his thought.

Because Nietzsche deemed self-mastery the highest degree of power, he prized suffering and struggle as contributing "style" to character. Ultimate power consists not only in overcoming the negative in existence but also in controlling and channeling one's impulses — not in condemning and fighting them, as Christians are enjoined to do. Though he may condescend to Christians in particular or the weak in general, Nietzsche neither fears nor abhors "being *schadenfroh* with a bad conscience," nor does he demonize those who succumb to *Schadenfreude*. Just as Nietzsche compassionately allows that many people can't survive without Christianity, so too does he believe that the lives of many people would be sadder still without *Schadenfreude*.

Strong people do not need the consolation *Schadenfreude* offers. What does a strong person, one of life's winners, look like? Nietzsche tells us:

A well-turned out person . . . has a taste only for what is good for him; his pleasure, his delight cease where the measure of what is good for him is transgressed. . . . He exploits bad accidents to his advantage; what does not kill him makes him stronger. . . . He is always in his own company, whether he associates with books, human beings, or landscapes. . . . He believes neither in "misfortune" nor in "guilt": he comes to terms with himself, with others; he knows how to *forget* — he is strong enough; hence everything must turn out for his best. (*Ecce Homo* I, Section 2; VI, Sections 266 and 267)

Winners do not fixate on misfortunes — their own or anyone else's. Winners do not hold grudges. Winners do not have to banish feelings of bitterness and resentment toward others, because winners never really have these feelings. Where Schopenhauer insists that all suffering is deadly serious, Nietzsche's winner denies that any suffering is.

For Nietzsche, strong people cannot be harmed. This sounds a lot like Socrates's claim that a good person cannot be harmed (Plato, *Apology* 41D, 30, D–C). The bad things that can happen to us, Nietzsche and Socrates concur, are of no real importance. The strong do not need the compassion or pity of others, for the strong have themselves. That is enough. Being good or strong, we instinctively focus on and care for ourselves in order to deprive the external world of power over us.

Finally, it cannot be said of Nietzsche that his genius lay more in knowing how to dismiss Schopenhauer's objections to *Schadenfreude* than in his practical insights on how to undermine or circumvent the *Schadenfreude* of others. Nietzsche recognizes that it can be unpleasant to discover that others are celebrating our misfortunes. Sounding Machiavellian, he warns that "he who exercises a great inner influence upon another must allow free rein to that other from time to time, and on occasion even induce resistance in him: otherwise he will inevitably make for himself an enemy" (*HH* I, p. 576). Nietzsche also advises us to display our unhappiness, "and from time to time be heard to sigh; for if we let others see how happy and secure we are in spite of suffering and deprivation, how malicious and envious we would make them" (*HH* II, p. 334)!

How well Nietzsche would have understood the media's concentration on the sufferings of movie stars, supermodels, rock stars, princesses, themselves often all too ready to speak of unhappy childhoods, bad marriages, aging problems, difficult offspring. We, like the media, simultaneously revere and fear the distance we perceive between divas and ourselves. The suffering of a superstar bridges the gap between him and us; savvy superstars know how to benefit from their own struggles. Our pain and suffering can deflect the envy of others. One of the best ways to circumvent the envy of others is to persuade them that we are struggling in some importantly difficult way. Our public suffering amounts to our private advantage because of the proclivity of others to take pleasure in our misfortunes.

Ressentiment holds no positive value for Nietzsche, unlike *Schadenfreude*. I have argued in this and previous chapters for the moral acceptability of our own *Schadenfreude*. Should we extend this moral acceptability to the *Schadenfreude* of others? Should we call their celebration of our setbacks moral? Yes.

We moderns like to think that we can control our aggression better than our forebears. We do not turn to spears and beatings nearly so often to express our dissatisfaction with others. At the dawn of a new millennium, however, the objections of others take a different shape. Moral beliefs do battle with one another in the minds of people who do not think alike. Sometimes these battles show up in our public speech; more often, though, we keep them to ourselves. Civilization evolves, and we now find ourselves in the West in a political culture significantly different from that of the last century.

When we object to the political or moral views of others, we more often than not find ourselves changing the subject of conversation. We have learned to be, or at least appear, tolerant. Curiously, we find ourselves in the same position of the high priests who, according to Nietzsche, thought up *ressentiment* as a way of mentally avenging ourselves on people we cannot stop.

Nietzsche offers us a way out of this impasse. Far from simply (and falsely) denying that we take pleasure in the setbacks of other people (particularly people who disagree with us), we ought to recognize *Schadenfreude* as a largely inevitable consequence of living in community with others. We ought to strive to make ourselves the sort of people who do not revel in the misfortunes of others. And we ought to recognize how useful the laughter of others can be. As others prey upon our misfortunes as evidence of our supposed mistakes, we ought to examine our lives carefully. Either we will agree with others and recognize the folly of our ways, or we will disagree with them and strengthen our resolve to live as we see fit. The objections of others can strengthen us. Such strengthening, however, will reinforce and deepen the moral divisions between us and them. *Schadenfreude* will live on and on.

Our civilization has in fact advanced, at least with regard to the frequency of physical attacks on others. The spears of yesterday have become the *Schadenfreude* of today. Luckily for us, *Schadenfreude* does not kill. The greatest value of *Schadenfreude* attaches to the legal institution of punishment, I will argue in the next chapter. Punishment restores and preserves social equality, the disruption of which Nietzsche locates at the heart of *Schadenfreude*. The failure to punish wrongdoers will not only erode political authority, but will also erase a social opportunity to celebrate the suffering of a wrongdoer. Like Emile Durkheim, Nietzsche views popular passions as the driving force of legal punishments.

Six

Punishment and Its Pleasure

A CENTRAL ASSUMPTION IN MY ANALYSIS OF *SCHADENFREUDE* IS THAT social and criminal justice inform and shape one another. Our emotional responses to the suffering to which criminals are sentenced can tell us something about our emotional responses to the suffering that befalls our neighbors.

Wrongdoers anger us. We feel a need to punish wrongdoers because we love justice and abhor injustice. We resolve not to tolerate further injustice from wrongdoers. Our anger is not immoral, contrary to what utilitarians may tell us. We should not be ashamed of our convictions, nor of our emotional pleasure in learning that a wrongdoer has been punished. We do well, however, to remember that we, like wrongdoers, are liable to make errors of judgment. We should make sure that our judges and lawgivers exercise great caution in punishing, and we should make sure that we examine our consciences carefully before celebrating the punishment of others.

The Point of Punishment

The unpleasantness of punishment (for example, incarceration) is intrinsic to it, not an accidental accompaniment. Utilitarians such as Bentham and non-utilitarians such as Kant agree. Plato (*Protagoras* 324–325, *Laws* IX, *Gorgias* 479–480) and Aristotle (*NE* II.1104b 15–19) hold that punishment cures the soul by virtue of its being painful. In *Discipline and Punish*, where we find the most complete expression of his account of punishment, Foucault says there is no such thing as a non-corporal punishment, for depriving the body of its rights is the same as inflicting pain.[1] Because this is not obviously the case, I filled in the contours of a general philosophical distinction between pain and suffering. I disagree that even if we treat our prisoners well (which is hardly the case in the United States), we necessarily cause them pain.

When we do inflict pain through punishment, do we hope to benefit someone else or ourselves? This question is very difficult to answer. Because punishment is a cultural vehicle for the expression of resentment of injury received, it raises the possibility of a juridical kind of *Schadenfreude* — the pleasure of just people in the legally imposed injury of a punished person. If it is true that our modern penal policy is a disguise for primitive torture devices, then we would expect the emotional responses to modern-day punishments more or less to mimic the emotional responses of our ancestors to public displays of remonstrance. If our high-minded theories of justice conceal a basic desire for revenge, then punishment benefits us more than it does the wrongdoer who endures it. I do not claim that an examination of *Schadenfreude* provides an analytical advantage to thinking about punishment. I mean only to suggest that how we think about punishment bears importantly on the ways we understand the suffering of other people.

W.D. Ross argues that the state has, prima facie, the right and the duty to punish the guilty, because of its implied promise to do so.[2] Curiously, Ross does not explain the origin of this right. The moral problem posed by a legal institution of punishment involves the deliberate and intentional infliction of suffering. Mercy, remorse of the wrongdoer, or recognition and acceptance of the uncharacteristic nature of the wrong perpetrated might lead us not to inflict harm proportional to the offense of the wrongdoer. On occasion, however, persons who have been wronged seek legal redress. Under what circumstances is the infliction of suffering through punishment justified and why?

Throughout the Hebrew Bible we find instances of God punishing the Israelites for their various transgressions. After someone suffered, the slate was wiped clean, and the Israelites made themselves worthy again of divine favors. The medieval system of penance served a similar end. Our system of criminal justice, though secular, does not differ dramatically in aim. Or so we are to believe.

The philosophical justification of punishment turns on three standard normative theories: the reformatory, the retributivist, and the utilitarian-deterrent.[3] The reformatory theory seeks to reform or improve offenders, help them or "socialize" them, and thereby reduce offenses. Reform theories tend to portray criminality as a disorder or disability. The deterrence theory requires that punishment be directed primarily at something other than granting satisfaction to the victim(s) of a crime; it depends upon consequences of punishment other than the *Schadenfreude* of victims of offenses. It need not ignore these satisfactions, but it rightly finds them of relatively small importance. Of supreme importance is the stipulation that punishment *prevents* offenses. The retributivist theory calls for inflicting on a wrongdoer the same amount of suffering he or she has caused others.

Theories of reform and deterrence involve well-known difficulties. The central problem is that both theories could justify the punishment of an innocent person — the deterrent theory if someone were mistakenly believed to have been guilty or likely to commit the crime in the future, and the reformatory theory if he or she were a bad person though not a criminal. The deterrent theory has an additional weakness: it is the threat of punishment and not punishment itself that deters. Deterrence seems to depend on actual punishment but, in fact, depends on a belief that guilty parties receive punishment. So reform can come about if people merely believe that punishment has occurred. In a truly just society, it might be thought, we would deceive the populace into thinking that any given criminal had been punished. Horror for torturing people would justify deception. As Bentham saw, apparent justice is everything for a utilitarian; real justice is irrelevant.

Utilitarians believe that each person's happiness or welfare carries the same weight as that of any another person, and that the most effective way to enhance general welfare is to make happy the greatest number of people possible. In deliberating a course of action, one must therefore take into account its effects on everyone, and consider the interests of all impartially. The suffering of the wrongdoer, taken on its own, makes no less a claim on us than the similar suffering of the virtuous. Why, then, should punishment be confined to wrongdoers? Critics have argued that utilitarians are committed to punishing innocent people if such punishment maximizes happiness.

Another problem involves the pivotal distinction between the fact of my suffering and my actual suffering. This distinction might suggest that simply making people believe that a wrongdoer suffers would suffice for purposes of criminal deterrence. However, it may turn out that actually punishing people may be the best way to produce such a belief, and so deterrence. It is hard to think of a society that only pretends to punish wrongdoers in order to deter others from crime. That societies really have to punish wrongdoers reinforces the distinction between enjoying *that* another suffers and enjoying his or her suffering.

The utilitarian theory applies to all cases of punishment. It lays down both necessary and sufficient conditions for the justification of punishment. From the utilitarian point of view, moral desert cannot be a necessary condition for justifying punishment because if the best consequences are produced by punishing the innocent, or others who do not deserve punishment, then punishment is still justified: utilitarian considerations are sufficient. Moral desert also cannot be a sufficient reason because it would not justify punishment unless punishment also produces the best consequences: utilitarian considerations are necessary. For the utilitarian, the only good reasons for punishment have to do with the consequences of such punishment. Insofar as moral desert embodies reasons for punishment which are independent of the desirable consequences, moral desert by itself cannot justify punishment.

Retributivists depart from the utilitarian attitude toward the suffering of wrongdoers. Retributivists hold that the offender's wrongdoing requires punishment and that punishment should be proportionate to the extent of the wrongdoing. It is the offender's desert, and not the beneficial consequences of punishment, that justifies punishment. Some retributivists seek to explain how punishment is supposed to give the moral wrongdoer what he or she deserves, while others believe such punishment derives from a fundamental axiom of justice, that wrongdoers deserve to suffer. Still other retributivists try to connect punishment with broader issues of distributive justice, or justice in the distribution of the benefits and burdens of social life: the offender is viewed as someone who has taken an unfair advantage of others in society, and punishment restores fairness by what it takes away from the offender.

Some people believe that we inflict pain through punishment in order to *help* a wrongdoer, by reforming him or her. They reason that we base our moral and legal decision to inflict pain on beliefs about social justice.

Nietzsche holds contempt for the ideas of social justice which underlie and justify corporal punishment. In *Zarathustra* he exhorts us:

> Mistrust all in whom the impulse to punish is powerful. . . . Mistrust all who talk much of their justice! Verily, their souls lack more than honey. And when they call themselves the good and the just, do not forget that they would be pharisees, if only they had — [worldly] power. (Part 2, Section 7)

Nietzsche believes that punishment has evolved in such a way that we pretend what we do to criminals in courts has nothing to do with what we used to do to criminals on torture racks. He blames human pettiness for the legal institution of punishment:

> Throughout the greater part of human history punishment was not imposed because one held the wrongdoer responsible for his deed, thus not on the presupposition that only the guilty one should be punished: rather, as parents still punish their children, from anger at some harm or injury, vented on the one who caused it — but this anger is held in check and modified by the idea that every injury has its equivalent and can actually be paid back, even if only though the pain of the culprit. And whence did this primeval, deeply rooted, perhaps by now ineradicable idea draw its power — this idea of an equivalence between injury and pain? . . . in the contractual relationship between creditor and debtor, which is as old as the idea of "legal subjects" and in turn points back to the fundamental forms of buying, selling, barter, trade and traffic. [*GM*, II, Section 4]

We have become weak, Nietzsche would have us believe, and we abuse the institution of punishment. The intentions of those who administer punishment have changed, and not for the better. In Section Six of the same essay Nietzsche refers to punishment as "a warrant for and title to cruelty." In *The Gay Science* Nietzsche urges us to move beyond the practice of punishment:

> Let us stop thinking so much about punishment, reproaching, and improving others. . . . Let us not contend in a direct fight — and that is what all reproaching, punishing, and attempts to improve others amount to. Let us rather raise ourselves that much higher. . . . No, let us not become darker ourselves on their account, like all those who punish others and feel dissatisfied. Let us sooner step aside. Let us look away. (Section 321)

A century after Nietzsche we have not looked away from punishment. Nor does it seem we will anytime soon, as punishment still lies at the heart of various systems of justice in Western nations.

Retaliation for wrong by inflicting pain without any object for the future is revenge (*die Rache*), Schopenhauer holds, and has no other purpose than seeking consolation for the suffering one has endured through witnessing the suffering one has caused in another. Calling revenge "wickedness and cruelty" (*Bosheit und Grausamkeit*), he deplores it, while upholding punishment as worthwhile (*WWR* I, p. 348). The difference between revenge and punishment turns on the *emotions* of those who have been wronged — and those who enjoy seeing punishment administered generally.

When we hear of a villain being sentenced in court, we may derive pleasure from the belief that justice has been served, that the villain will suffer, or both. According to Nietzsche, we are predisposed to enjoy the actual suffering of a criminal, even if we know very little about his or her crime. Crowds thronging athletic events and crying for the defeat of a particular team resemble crowds thronging executions. They can take pleasure in the loss of a particular sports team even if they know little about either team. Of course, competition takes other forms, most commonly economic. Economic competition must stand as one of the primary sources of cruelty and suffering in society.

The sports analogy threatens Schopenhauer's separation of justice from revenge. Schopenhauer specifies that our pleasure in courtrooms may center exclusively on justice, on the smooth functioning of the state. He declares that justice permits enjoying *that* another has been made to suffer. He justifies state punishment only if it is based on a single-minded and genuine effort to reform a wrongdoer, not on a response to public outcry against the criminal. Presumably, Schopenhauer would take a similar view of athletic competitions: the joy of winners should derive exclusively from the fact of victory and not from the thought that rivals suffer because of defeat.

About the law Schopenhauer says: "Thus the law and its fulfillment, namely punishment, are directed essentially to the *future*, not to the *past*" (*WWR* I, p. 348). Schopenhauer is quick to condemn Kant, believing that Kant's account of punishment regards only the past, not the future, and so is a disguised form of revenge. He says: "Therefore, Kant's theory of punishment as mere requital for requital's sake is a thoroughly groundless and perverse view" (*WWR* I, p. 348). Kant, for his part, had cautioned against the desire for revenge: "[T]o insist on one's own right beyond what is necessary for its defence is to become revengeful . . . such desire for vengeance is vicious" (*MM*, p. 214). If it is true that Kant is a retributivist, it must also be true that he favors the putative justice of punishment and does not revel in any pleasure that might come from seeing a wrongdoer suffer. Schopenhauer does not give Kant enough credit on this score; perhaps Schopenhauer focused too closely on a few passages from the section on punishment in Kant's *The Metaphysical Elements of Justice*, in which Kant does espouse the typically retributivist view that wrongdoing stands as a necessary and sufficient condition for the just imposition of punishment. Kant cares about punished people more than Schopenhauer seems to allow. Further, Schopenhauer's insistence that those who take pleasure in the suffering of another should be "forever shunned" raises the question of his own retributivistic leanings. Schopenhauer endorses punishment for its deterrent value, yet the goal of deterrence is to receive a wrongdoer back into society after repentance and forgiveness.

Schopenhauer's revulsion toward *Schadenfreude* leads to a virtual recommendation of revenge. It is the retributivistic way of thinking about punishment, with its problematic dependence on the notion of desert, that underlays primitive revenge rituals. Nonetheless, Schopenhauer relies on the distinctness of modern punishment from its predecessor. In Schopenhauer's defense, modern penal codes do represent an advance over primitive thinking about revenge. Our system of criminal justice does not unreflectively punish offenders simply because they have violated laws: mitigating circumstances such as accident, duress, and reasonable mistake are all considered. The penalty we impose upon someone guilty of a misdemeanor does not correspond to the punishment we inflict upon someone guilty of a felony: the two misdeeds differ in kind, just as the two judicial responses to them do. Note too that it's one thing to say that vengeful passions help fuel the legal institution of punishment, another to say that retribution is conceptually wound up with them. But numerous moralists have nonetheless insisted that our institution of retributive justice amounts to revenge, both historically and conceptually. One frequently quoted thinker, Joel Feinberg, has said: "I think it is fair to say of our community, however, that punishment generally expresses more than judgments of disapproval; it is also a symbolic way of getting back at the criminal, of expressing a kind of vindictive resentment."[4] This claim returns us to the *lex talionis* of "an eye for an eye" that reverberates throughout Greek tragedy and the Hebrew Bible. In his *Jewish Social Ethics* David Novak maintains that vengeance can only be sublimated; to do more than that actually destroys criminal justice.[5]

The principle embodied in the *lex talionis* is one of appropriateness, of making the criminal suffer as much as the person whom he or she has harmed. The notion of an equivalence between a crime and its punishment must be a moral one if proportionality is to justify the punishment. The *lex talionis* gives no consideration to the mental state of the offender, or to the mitigating or aggravating circumstances of the crime. Yet someone who kills another out of negligence or recklessness, we feel, does not deserve the same punishment as a criminal who kills out of hatred, in a calculated fashion. The *lex talionis* seems ill-suited for punishing satisfactorily the person who deliberately aims a gun at another in order to kill, but who misses his or her target and fails. Additionally, the formula required for applying the *lex talionis* seems too crude and sometimes yields (as in the case of sadistic murderers) morally unacceptable punishments. For this reason we have a system of jurisprudence which purports to administer punishments with an eye to future good, not to revenge.

While I disagree with Schopenhauer on many scores, I nonetheless concede the possibility that some people seek justice without desiring revenge. Such people seek no personal benefit from the suffering of a wrongdoer; their only pleasure derives from a belief that the world has been made safer by the wrongdoer's punishment. This conceptual possibility strains the word "*Schadenfreude*" because the operative joy or satisfaction for such people is not in suffering, but rather in justice. If there were such a word as "*Gerechtigkeitfreude*" (the joy of justice), Schopenhauer would probably have used it in opposition to *Schadenfreude*. Ambivalence characterizes my defense of *Schadenfreude*: it is only because so many people agree with Schopenhauer's view of justice that my defense of *Schadenfreude* makes any sense, yet I do not myself agree with Schopenhauer.

Some moralists believe there is no point whatsoever to punishment, because punishment involves doing to others something we generally consider wrong. Philosophers still debate whether punishing people according to what they deserve can be defended by the principles of justice. Mercy and clemency, various writers have argued, accomplish more than punishment does. Mercy toward offenders follows the principle that it is better to prevent wrongdoing than to punish it. It may well be preferable to accept human vulnerability in a spirit of forgiveness and understanding than to punish offenders out of rage. Our emotional reactions to insult and injury might then be directed not to revenge, but to reform. This premise fortifies much of Jewish and Christian moral thinking.

Forgiveness does not come cheaply in Judaism and Christianity, however. God forgives repentant sinners, but genuine repentance must precede forgiveness, and punishment exists to ease genuine repentance. Some Jews and Christians justifiably worry that mercy and forgiveness collude with evil; mercy and forgiveness tolerate sin, it may seem. It would be naive to accuse Jews or Christians of hypocrisy when they read God into the suffering of others. Jews, Christians, or members of any religion naturally defend rules and beliefs and, correspondingly, resent infringements of them. We cannot blame religious believers for adhering to rules, although we may reasonably object to the rules to which they adhere.

Most of us believe that compassion toward others can solve many of the world's problems. We care about the world's problems precisely because we care about the world's people. We want others, like ourselves, to live well. We do not want the wicked to prosper, because we want the wicked to see the error of their ways. Should we show compassion to the wicked? The stronger our moral beliefs, the more difficult it will be to show compassion to others whose lives we consider fundamentally immoral, particularly if their immorality threatens us or our community in some way (think of rapists and child molesters here). Forgiveness may not come easily to us, for our moral beliefs may seem too important to compromise. We may come to think of mercy in certain instances as indifference, or as a betrayal of our convictions.

Those whom we consider wicked (or at least deeply misguided) may consider us wicked (or deeply misguided) too. This is quite often the case. In part for this reason, and in part because of ongoing disputes over the moral justification of punishment, it remains a challenge to argue that punishment does not represent revenge. Nietzsche, for one, insists that such arguments can only fail.

The Pleasure of Seeing Another Punished

If we have learned the misery of suffering from personal experience, why would we make others suffer? How we respond to wrongdoing tells us something about our common morality (to the extent that we have one) and our cultural aspirations. It also no doubt reflects broad patterns of how individuals in a particular culture treat and respond to one another. It further indicates the extent to which we feel justified in meting out suffering and imbuing it with meaning. More to the point, our response to wrongdoing says something about how we are properly to respond to punishment emotionally.

Punishment aims to cause suffering, and perhaps even pain. According to Nietzsche, the legal institution of punishment represents a socially acceptable way of coming to grips with our own aggression. The legal institution of punishment amounts to a muted festival of cruelty, he holds, in which citizens are free to exercise their base emotions and their indirect enjoyment of power. Is Nietzsche right? If so, then part of the point of punishment is to provide enjoyment to onlookers, and there is a clear parallel between *Schadenfreude* and our emotional responses to the punishment of others.

Consider Edmund Burke's challenge in *A Philosophical Enquiry*, issued a century before Nietzsche took up the question:

> Chuse a day on which to represent the most sublime and affecting
> tragedy . . . and when you have collected your audience, just at the

moment when their minds are erect with expectation, let it be reported that a state criminal of high rank is on the point of being executed in the adjoining square; in a moment the emptiness of the theatre would demonstrate the comparative weakness of the imitative arts, and proclaim the triumph of the real sympathy.[6]

Burke's "real sympathy" is the delight ("and that no small one") we take "in the real misfortunes and pains of others" (p. 45). Burke does not believe that crowds at public executions had assembled to rejoice in the spectacle of justice; rather the crowd thrills to the sight of brutality. For Burke, we cannot make the problem of *Schadenfreude* disappear by claiming that love of justice extinguishes love of suffering.

Against Burke and Foucault, various moralists have credited moral progress for the disappearance of public spectacles of torture: whereas premodern societies reveled in savage spectacles, we moderns have no taste for such violent displays of revenge. We prefer courtroom justice. It may well be that we moderns have no time to march off to the public square to watch a hanging: we are too busy watching violent films and videos. Torture now takes place all around us — in televised court cases particularly.

Pieter Spierenburg has written a highly engaging but idiosyncratic book that details how much crowds appreciated public spectacles of torture in previous centuries.[7] What is quite surprising about *The Spectacle of Suffering* is that it does not mention Nietzsche. Instead, it focuses largely on Dutch society and theorists. Nonetheless, Spierenburg's conclusion fits neatly with Nietzsche's disdain for "the herd." Spierenburg argues that the popular toleration of violence began to change in the Netherlands and elsewhere by about the middle of the eighteenth century; after 1800 the shift accelerated and led to what is recognizably our own sensibility toward violence, suffering, and the fate of others. According to Spierenburg, this shift was imposed on the masses by social elites, who had become disgusted by the crudeness of public displays of brutality, and by the evident enjoyment on the faces of those who watched the torturing. Only gradually did a studied and cultivated sensibility begin to take root among the masses.

Little by little, public executions were banned in Europe. Concurrently, enjoyment of the punishment of others was driven underground.

Schopenhauer is one of the first philosophers to discern that this enjoyment continued. His attention to the mental state of punishers predates Durkheim's slightly more developed account of the same phenomenon. David Garland's formidable work *Punishment and Society*, which contains an exemplary account of the emotional aspect of administering punishment, presents Durkheim's findings as a key for unlocking a larger cultural text such as the nature of social solidarity or the disciplinary character of Western reason.[8] In *The Division of Labor* (1895) Durkheim argues that the punitive passions emerge from collective sentiments and convey the moral energy of the citizenry against its criminal enemies. Durkheim explains:

> In the first place, punishment constitutes an emotional reaction. This characteristic is all the more apparent the less cultured societies are. Indeed primitive people punish for the sake of punishing, causing the guilty person to suffer solely for the sake of suffering and without expecting any advantage for themselves from the suffering they inflict upon him The proof of this is that they do not aim to punish fairly or usefully, but only for the sake of punishing. Thus they punish animals that have committed the act that is stigmatised, or even inanimate things which have been its passive instrument. When the punishment is applied solely to people, it often extends well beyond the guilty person and strikes even the innocent — his wife, children or neighbours, etc. This is because the passionate feeling that lies at the heart of punishment dies down only when it is spent.[9]

Durkheim rejects the argument that modern societies now punish as a deterrent to future wrongdoing. For Durkheim, we do not punish out of a conviction that the consequences of punishment are good; instead, we punish out of a sense that such punishment is intrinsically good and fitting. He insists on a sense of proportionality between crimes and punishments in such a way as to make Burke's challenge seem unreflective:

> . . . reaction to punishment is not in every case uniform, since the emotions that determine it are not always the same. In fact they

vary in intensity according to the strength of the feeling that has suffered injury, as well as according to the gravity of the offence it has sustained. . . . Since the gravity of the criminal act varies according to the same factors, the proportionality everywhere observed between crime and punishment is therefore established with a kind of mechanical spontaneity, without any necessity to make elaborate computations in order to calculate it. What brings about a gradation in crimes is also what brings about a gradation in punishments; consequently the two measures cannot fail to correspond, and such correspondence, since it is necessary, is at the same time constantly useful. (p. 57)

Durkheim characterizes punishment as a social institution that reflects and enhances social solidarity. Punishments issue forth from strong bonds of moral solidarity and, when inflicted, reaffirm and strengthen these same social bonds.

As Garland has pointed out, Durkheim's work can be taken as a reaction against turn-of-the-century criminologists who aimed to remove all traces of moral censure from penal law in order to give it a purely technical character. Durkheim insisted that the essence of punishment is not rationality or instrumental control but rather irrational, unthinking emotion stirred up by a perceived violation of the sacred. For Durkheim, punishment is not so much a means to an end as a release of psychic energy. The end or objective of punishment is not reform of the offender, but the common expression of social outrage, an expression that unites people and creates solidarity.

Garland's analysis proceeds from Durkheim to Nietzsche, for whom there is more than dutiful moral sentiment in the fact of punishment — there is positive pleasure. As usual in Nietzsche's vision, the least noble sentiments are to be found among the common people, the lower classes, the herd. It would be pointless to search for evidence to support the truth of Nietzsche's snide view. But in the case of punishment, there is a specific explanation for this social distribution of cruel delight — for the act of punishing brings with it power. In punishing the debtor, the creditor shares a seignorial right. The creditor feels that finally he or she can bask in the glorious feeling of treating another human being as inferior — or if the actual punitive power has passed on to a legal "authority," of seeing another person despised and mistreated.

According to Nietzsche, the pleasures of punishment are vicarious rather than direct, since in modern society it is the state which punishes, using the punitive machinery for its own purposes. Of course, the penal institutions of modern society deny their association with cruelty, but Nietzsche insists that beneath this hypocrisy these passions continue to exist. Particularly in the Second Essay of *On the Geneaology of Morals,* Nietzsche advances the claim that "pleasure in cruelty is not really extinct today; only given our greater delicacy, that pleasure has had to undergo a certain sublimation." Pleasure gets so well disguised that it can untimately pass muster before "even the tenderest hypocritical conscience."

An examination of the sentiments typically expressed by reformers, by penal agents, and by different sectors of the public makes clear that the punishment of offenders can evoke a whole range of feelings from sympathy and compassion to anger and indignation. It makes little sense to reduce this diversity to a single sentiment. Nor does it seem useful to debate whether the predominant sentiment is high or low in some moral hierarchy, since a key aspect of emotional life is ambivalence, that is, the coexistence of contradictory impulses and emotions toward the same object. Psychological attitudes often meld high moral sentiment and selfish ulterior motives, so we should not expect that punitive emotions will prove simple or single-minded. David Garland has the last word here.

I want to emphasize that I do not deny the possibility that anyone might, in fact, take pleasure simply in knowing that a transgressor of some sort suffers. My skepticism about the likelihood that pleasure can be restrained in such a way derives from the psychological difficulty of controlling ourselves perfectly. Along with this skepticism goes admiration for the creativity with which people explain their drives and actions to themselves and others. Schopenhauer's point lends itself to easy comparison with the much maligned principle of double effect in Roman Catholic theology. This famous principle justifies what amounts to an abortion procedure on a Catholic woman whose pregnancy is ectopic or whose uterus has been invaded by cancer according to the following logic: the death of the fetus at the hands of a physician is a foreseen but unintended consequence of the medical procedure through which the uterus is removed. The distinction between what is foreseen and what is intended accounts for the "double effect." The physician removes the fetus without intending to kill it. The physician resists thinking about the inevitable death of the fetus just as we might resist thinking about our pleasure in knowing that a criminal has been sentenced to spend the rest of his or her life in prison. Roman Catholic physicians can claim that they are not performing an abortion just as persons who delight in the triumph of justice can claim that they do not feel *Schadenfreude*. Nietzsche would scoff at either defense.

Soft on Sin?

Numerous writers have shared Nietzsche's conviction that our penal code thinly veils old-fashioned revenge. While sympathizing with this conviction, I have acknowledged the conceptual possibility that we punish wrongdoers not to get back at them, but to deter them from future wrongdoing. Taking pleasure in the suffering of others is no more and no less morally acceptable than endorsing various systems of justice in the West. For at the heart of *Schadenfreude* lies the same question that lies at the heart of our endorsement of penal codes in the West: do we enjoy the suffering of another (as in revenge) or do we enjoy the confidence that this suffering will serve as a deterrent to future wrongdoing?

I have explored some of the disagreement over this question. If it were true that our system of justice amounted to sanitized revenge, then it seems that *Schadenfreude* would too. Then there would be no moral justification for *Schadenfreude*, for there would be none for our system of justice. Just as some voters accuse politicians of being "soft on crime," so some moralists might accuse those who tolerate *Schadenfreude* as being "soft on sin (or vice)." It might be thought that talk of self-esteem, social injustice, and even comedy can only *sanitize Schadenfreude*, as opposed to *justifying* it morally. Some moralists will insist that it is impossible ever to excuse feeling good when bad things happen to other people; at most, we can only make ourselves feel better about our pleasure.

I have enlisted Nietzsche's help in establishing a case for the moral acceptability of *Schadenfreude*. This move is complicated, for I have portrayed non-trivial *Schadenfreude* as a function of justice, and Nietzsche views justice as sanitized revenge. Following Nietzsche, it would be possible only to sanitize *Schadenfreude* and revenge, not to justify them. I have moved beyond sanitization.

Seven

Cheering with the Angels

Does disaster befall a city unless the Lord has done it?
—*Amos 3:6*

STRANGE AS IT MIGHT FIRST SEEM, DEFENDING *SCHADENFREUDE* BENEFITS religious believers. Defending *Schadenfreude* as morally acceptable gives permission to believers to adhere to their moral convictions wholeheartedly. Believers need not deny to themselves or to others that they see the hand of God in human suffering. We may not like the idea that religious believers insist we deserve our suffering, but they may not like our convictions either. Getting along with others in the world requires a certain ability to avoid dwelling on the moral beliefs of the people around us.

Orthodox Jews share with various evangelical Protestant sects (called "postmillennialist") the belief that the Messiah will only come to earth once we have put our world in order. These Jews believe that the Messiah will come only when all *Jews* (as opposed to all *people* for most of the postmillennialist Protestants) observe the commandments. These Jews suffer when they encounter other Jews who do not keep the commandments and may naturally yearn to find a way to induce errant Jews to abide by God's laws. Similarly, some evangelical Protestants seek to help those whom they deem destined for hell in order to speed the return of Jesus. Interpreting suffering as a sign of divine dissatisfaction suggests itself as a ready way to persuade skeptical neighbors.

Defending *Schadenfreude*, as we have seen, raises a problem. Thinkers such as Seneca, Marcus Aurelius, and Nietzsche have exhorted us to resist thinking of suffering in terms of cause and effect: much of our suffering, they insist, simply happens. If they are right, as I believe they are, then a believer's impulse to explain suffering in terms of God's will amounts to a bad idea, although not an immoral one.

Since the Enlightenment, many non-believers have sharply criticized believers as hypocrites. A prominent moralist, Judith Shklar, has gone so far as to call Christianity in particular a "vast engine of cultural dishonesty and humiliation" (*Ordinary Vices*, p. 39). Regardless of the ethical objections we might raise against Judaism or its offshoot Christianity, we should not simply dismiss religious belief as incoherent. The same leap of faith believers make to reach God underlies their conviction that they can see God's hand in human suffering.

Religious beliefs of various sorts could survive without the idea that we can see God behind suffering. But believers will no doubt continue to think of suffering in terms of (human) cause and (divine) effect. These terms hold a moral appropriateness of their own.

To think of God as an agent who promptly punishes those who have sinned is to think of at least some suffering as a function of divine justice. This is only one way of looking at God, albeit an entirely understandable one. The moral difficulty with the belief that God causes (sinful) people to suffer is that self-deception about the desert of others remains a permanent possibility and consequently an obstacle to distinguishing *Schadenfreude* from hatred and envy.

A subset of the problem of theodicy, or why a just God allows evil in the world, is the problem of suffering, or why the good God allows the physical pain or mental afflictions of persons. The temptation to view the sufferings of others as a sign of divine disfavor continues to hold many Jews, Christians, and Muslims in its grip. All three Western forms of monotheism include an apocalyptic element that bestows value on current events. Western believers are conditioned to view present conflicts as images or prototypes of the final decisive battle between the forces of good and evil. This means that virtually any instance of extrinsic suffering may accommodate the aims of religious writers or believers, who may interpret strife in such a way as to safeguard and validate a particular belief system. Judaism, Christianity, and Islam are not the only religions to link suffering and pain to sin — the same tendency has surfaced in Native American and African religions as well. The social difficulty with the belief that God causes (sinful) people to suffer is that we are less likely to concern ourselves with the regulation of suffering here on earth.

On Seeing God in Suffering

The Hebrew Bible, especially in the Psalms, frequently refers to God's infliction of suffering and its dramatic effect. The appropriateness of such suffering is not questioned: we understand that Israel deserves its suffering for having sinned, just as Israel's enemies do. Suffering caused by God must surely be appropriate, for God is just. This certainty provides little guidance, however, as long as uncertainty about God's involvement in any given instance of suffering lingers.

Theodicy concerns innocent suffering, not guilty. Because theodicy must by definition include reference to God, it seeks to reconcile a belief in a good God with the fact of innocent suffering. Note that Buddhism, with no requirement of belief in a god, neither invites nor requires theodicies. Buddhism does not allow for the possibility of innocent suffering, but instead posits that a suffering person is repaying wrongdoing from a previous lifetime.

The presence of evil and innocent suffering in the world stands as the most widely raised objection to belief in God in Western and Eastern philosophy. Such an objection to the reasonableness of belief in God usually assumes one of two forms: according to the *deductive* or *logical* version, the presence of *any* evil in the world makes God's existence unlikely; according to the *probabilistic* version, the *extent* of evil in the world makes God's existence unlikely. Religious believers have responded to these objections by rationalizing suffering in various ways: as a trial designed to strengthen the faith of a believer (according to the Talmud suffering can be a process of purification — "afflictions of love" or *yissurin shel ahnvah*); as a redemptive opportunity to move closer to God (according to the Talmud all human suffering represents a means for intensifying our attachment to God); and as punishment for sin.

One could well argue that both the Jewish and Christian traditions have *discouraged* the temptation to view suffering as punishment for sin. In the Book of Job God ultimately refutes Job's friends, who blindly uphold the belief in divine retribution. In the New Testament Christ explicitly instructs his disciples not to think of those who perished under the tower of Siloam as especially wicked (Luke 13:4). Moreover, Jews and Christians alike have long emphasized the redemptive value of suffering, even innocent suffering.

The simplistic equation of suffering with sin excludes the possibility of *innocent suffering*, which is a real problem. Abraham and Job both reproached God for unjust suffering, and God conceded to Job the unsettling possibility of innocent suffering. The Book of Job's unique effect is to have silenced God himself. Notably, it was over the question of appropriate suffering that God withdrew from direct conversation with human beings for the rest of the Hebrew Bible. As Jack Miles has noted:

> God's last words are those he speaks to Job, the human being who dares to challenge not his physical power but his moral authority. Within the Book of Job itself, God's climactic and overwhelming reply seems to silence Job. But reading from the end of the Book of Job onward, we see that it is Job who has somehow silenced God. God never speaks again, and he is decreasingly spoken of. In the book of Esther — a book in which, as in the Book of Exodus, his chosen people faces a genocidal enemy — he is never so much as mentioned. In effect, the Jews surmount the threat without his help.[1]

An extraordinarily vast body of critical literature focuses on the Book of Job; it is a work to which Jewish (though not only Jewish) thinkers return again and again.

The reason why some Jews and Christians view suffering as divinely caused likely derives from a false analogy between the hereafter and the here and now. I will turn to that analogy shortly. For now, I want only to establish the point that the association of suffering with sin survives in popular belief. In American writer David Leavitt's novella "The Term Paper Artist" a college student, who is a committed Mormon, confesses to the narrator in a private garden at UCLA:

> Well, in the church we have this very clear-cut conception of sin. And so I always assumed that if I ever committed a really big sin,

like we're doing now . . . I don't know, that there'd be a clap of thunder and God would strike me dead or something. Instead of which we're sitting here in this courtyard and the sun's shining. The grass is green.[2]

In a similar vein, Rabbi Harold Kushner explains that the impetus for his enormously popular work *When Bad Things Happen to Good People* came in part from "all those people whose love for God and devotion to Him led them to blame themselves for their suffering and persuade themselves that they deserved it."[3] Here Kushner puts into play the idea that persons can and do persuade themselves to adopt certain beliefs about desert and, consequently, suffering. This capacity to persuade ourselves, whether about our own desert or someone else's, stands as the central issue underlying questions of the appropriateness of suffering. Thinking of suffering as divine punishment inclines us to feel guilty about our own suffering and righteous about the suffering of others.

A certain rudimentary problem with the idea of seeing God in suffering should be noted here before moving on. If God's love is in fact the highest good of life and itself a supreme consolation, believers must explain how it is that non-believers are seemingly denied this consolation and therefore made to suffer quite a bit more than they otherwise would. The great philosopher Wittgenstein, regularly tormented by his competing Jewish and Catholic identities, remarked to his friend M. O'C. Drury in 1929, "I think one of the things you and I have to learn is that we have to live without the consolation of belonging to a church."[4] Forty years after having seen an otherwise unextraordinary play in Vienna, Wittgenstein told his friend Norman Malcolm he suddenly felt himself spoken to in the words, "Nothing can happen to you! No matter what occurred in the world, no harm could come to *him*!"[5] It was then that Wittgenstein first perceived the possibility of religious belief. According to Norman Malcolm, Wittgenstein remembered throughout his life a play he had seen at the age of 21 and longed for faith, a faith which looks remarkably like Socrates's assurance in the *Apology* that no harm can come to a good person.

A more jarring example of this deprivation is the suffering of Mary Tyrone, the mother in Eugene O'Neill's play *Long Day's Journey Into Night*. Mary attributes her mental anguish, immediately caused by the drug addiction, which she has once again failed to conquer, to divine punishment.[6] The malaise pervading the play, and the lives of the Tyrone family, seems to stem from Mary, who is looking desperately for something (here I quote selectively):

> Something I miss terribly. It can't be altogether lost.
>
> Something I need terribly. I remember when I had it I was never lonely nor afraid. I can't have lost it forever. I would die if I thought that. Because then there would be no hope.
>
> [Longingly]
>
> If only I could find the faith I lost, so I could pray again!
>
> pause
>
> "Hail, Mary! Full of grace! Blessed art thou among women . . ."
>
> [Sneeringly]
>
> You expect the Blessed Virgin to be fooled by a dope fiend reciting words! You can't hide from her!

Mary suffers because she cannot believe as believers do. Her suffering cannot be considered redemptive, for it does not bring her closer to God, who she feels has turned his back on her. Her consciousness of thought should be viewed over and against unconscious believing and wanting. She has lost her faith in God, yet she is no atheist. She interprets her lack of belief as punishment for wrongdoing rather than as evidence of the belief's falsity.

A useful Catholic answer to the question of why it is that not everyone possesses faith points up the randomness of suffering. Arthur Danto has remarked that faith is often viewed as a gift from God, in a sense just good luck:

> There is a theory, a version of which is exemplified in the Third Meditation of Descartes, that having a belief in the existence of God is a mark of grace, there being no way save through the mediation of grace that believing in God can be accounted for: it is a gift.[7]

As Danto points out, this explanation is largely sound, since it links the *causes* of having a belief with the conditions which make the belief true. By believing in God, the believer is committed to hold that his believing is explained with reference to whatever makes the belief true. Assent to the observation, "Some rise by sin, and some by virtue fall" (*Measure for Measure*, ii.I.38) attests to the role of luck in evading suffering and undermines the belief that suffering signifies sin. Like the gift of faith, the affliction of suffering should be understood as random and inexplicable.

God's ways are not our ways, we learn with Job. The moral of the Book of Job might be that God does not work as an accountant, perfunctorily meting out earthly reward or punishment on the basis of discrete actions or desires. Were he to do so, Satan's question would be a damning one: Job, like other mortals, might well adore God purely or principally in the hope of obtaining divine favors. In any event, we are at God's mercy. For everything good and evil comes from God (Amos 3:6; Isaiah 45:7; Job 2:10). The Hebrew Bible diverges from the Greek tradition here; a relationship with God might be easier if we could believe with Plato: "For good things are far fewer with us than evil and for the good we must assume no other cause than God, but the cause of evil we must look for in other things and not in God" (*Republic* II.379). Accepting Plato's counsel, though, requires us to think of God as less than all-powerful. So there does not seem to be any entirely satisfactory way of thinking about God's role in our suffering.

Suffering in the Hereafer

Heaven and hell are all about suffering. The reflex to think of suffering as both secular woe and spiritual punishment would seem entirely reasonable, given that Jewish and Christian understanding of the hereafter includes not only a clear distinction between the virtuous and the wicked, but also divine justification for their divergent lots.

What role does thinking about the hereafter play for believers? According to Nietzsche, the concept of heaven serves an important psychological function. Ceaselessly afflicted by a world of contradiction, plurality, flux, and falsity, Christian philosophers sought a world beyond suffering in compensation for pain and death. Nietzsche held that thoughts of heaven express our hatred for a world that makes us suffer. Hell complements and completes the expression of human hatred of suffering, even as it perpetuates and infinitely magnifies that suffering. Nietzsche's aim to deflate the realm of heaven stemmed from a drive to liberate our energies so that we could turn to the elimination of the causes of suffering rather than merely "narcoticizing" their effects. In *Nietzsche: Life as Literature,* Alexander Nehamas has suggested that Nietzsche sometimes succumbed to the appeal of such comfort, though: Nietzsche's anguished demand for consolation over the death of God in *The Gay Science* (Section 125) can be taken to indicate the depth of his own yearning for heaven, or at any rate consolation from the ravages of suffering.

Thinking about the hereafter not only provides relief from suffering; it can also explain away the obvious injustice of a world in which "some rise by sin and others by virtue fall." Bad people who succeed on earth will get their due after death; good people who do not prosper on earth will get their reward in heaven. Heaven entails the absence, and hell the intensification, of all suffering. Although Christianity is more prone than Judaism to rely on the imagery of hell to reinforce the consequences of sin, the New Testament did not invent the notion of hell. Quite the contrary: it incorporated into the new tradition a notion it borrowed from later Judaism. Hebrew Scripture includes the idea of an afterlife in Sheol, a place for departed souls. One of the thirteen principles of Maimonides derived from the Bible is that God will resurrect the dead. Although the word *hell* in not used in the Hebrew Bible, its counterpart *Gehenna* represented the final destination of the dead bodies of those who had rebelled against Yahweh (Isaiah 66:24). Extrabiblical Jewish writings frequently refer to the place as a fiery abyss. Nowhere does suffering bear a clearer meaning than in hell. In hell God punishes the damned for their sins. No suffering is random or accidental there.

We find mention of Gehenna seven times in the gospel of Matthew, three times in Mark, and once in Luke.[8] The Book of Revelations describes the place as the final destination of the wicked; earlier in the New Testament it appears as a place of weeping and gnashing of teeth (Matthew 8:12; 13:42, 50; 22:13; 24:51; 25:30), a place where the worm does not die (Mark 9:48), yet also a place shrouded in darkness (Matthew 8:12; 22:13; 25:30). The devil is to be found in hell: the Fourth Lateran

Council of 1215 speaks of "perpetual punishment with the devil" for those in hell. Curiously, hell is not mentioned in the documents of the Second Vatican Council, nor in Pope Paul VI's *Credo of the People of God* of 1968. Roman Catholic belief in hell has by no means faded into the background, however, for reference to "eternal punishment for the sinner" can be found in the Congregation for the Doctrine of the Faith's "Letter on Certain Questions Concerning Eschatology" of 1979. Certainly, belief in hell as the climax and paradigm of suffering endures in many of the Protestant churches as well.

Hell is a function of justice, then. Judaism teaches that the ultimate goal of compassion, both our own and God's, is justice. The Hebrew Bible is replete with instances of God punishing, sometimes quite viciously, his chosen people (and others) for their transgressions of the law. God's love for Israel entails the enforcement of justice; the punishment suffered returns Israel to a proper love for God. The punitive aspect of God's compassion manifests itself in the New Testament as well. In the gospel of Matthew we find a clear parallel with the emphasis on justice that runs throughout the Hebrew Bible:

When the Son of Man comes in his glory and all his angels with him, he will sit on his glorious throne. Before him will be gathered all the nations, and he will separate them one from another, as a shepherd separates the sheep from the goats, and he will place the sheep at his right hand, but the goats at the left. . . . Then he will say to those at his left hand, "Depart from me, you cursed, into the eternal fire prepared for the devil and his angels; for I was hungry and you gave me no food, I was thirsty and you gave me no drink, I was a stranger and you did not welcome me, naked and you did not clothe me; sick and in prison and you did not visit me." (Matthew 25:31–33, 41–45)

Judaism and Christianity share a retributive view of justice. These words of Jesus evince Jewish influence. Even though Jesus himself does not seem particularly concerned with hell in the New Testament, this excerpt stands in the way of anyone who views the very idea of hell as antithetical to Jesus's gospel of love.

In this passage Jesus contrasts heaven with hell and reveals that the just will reap glorious reward on the day of judgment. To illustrate the import of this event, he admonishes that the unjust will *not* be rewarded, but will instead suffer terribly. His message is bracing. Though he says nothing about celebrating the fate or the imminent torments of the damned, nothing in his message indicates that God will eternally regret their awful punishment. The damned will be left to suffer the horrific fate they *deserve.*[9]

The agreement between Jewish and Christian sources is not complete, however. A cursory glance at leading figures in either tradition will bring out some discord relevant to a discussion of emotional responses to punishment. The tenth-century Jewish philosopher Saadya ben Joseph, known better as Saadya Gaon, sought to demonstrate that the assertions of the (Hebrew) Bible do not insult or oppose valid philosophical argument. Saadya, like Maimonides after him, remained convinced that reason could explain even the most difficult passages in the Bible. Consider what Saadya has to say in his magnum opus *The Book of Beliefs and Opinions* about the interaction of the just and the unjust in the hereafter:

> In regard to the tenth question, namely, whether those to be requited in the hereafter will meet each other, let me say, on the basis of my studies and findings, that, so far as the righteous and the wicked are concerned, they will only look at one another with their eyes. Thus Scripture says concerning the righteous: *And they shall go forth, and look upon the carcasses of the men that have rebelled against me* (Isa. 66:24). Whenever, then, they regard their sufferings, they will say: "Praised be He who saved us from this torment!" and they will rejoice and be glad over their own condition.

> Likewise Scripture remarks concerning the wicked: *The sinners in Zion are afraid; trembling hath seized the ungodly: Who among us shall dwell with the devouring fire? Who among us shall dwell with everlasting burnings?* (Isa. 33:14). In amazement they will watch the righteous abide in the burning fire without being in the least hurt by it, and they will sigh regretfully over the reward which they forfeited.

Further [bearing out this view] is the analogy given elsewhere in Scripture of people who are invited to a banquet whilst others are brought there merely in order to be tormented, with the result that the latter, when they see the former eat, give vent to sighing. That is the import of the statement: *Behold, My servants shall eat, but ye shall be hungry; behold, My servants shall drink, but ye shall be thirsty; behold, My servants shall rejoice, but ye shall be ashamed; behold, My servants shall sing for joy of heart, but ye shall cry for sorrow of heart, and shall wail for vexation of spirit* (Isa. 65:13, 14).[10]

Note the distinct lack of pleasure in the sufferings of the unjust in Saadya's account. In the first section quoted above, Saadya's commentary on Scriptures contains no suggestion of rejoicing over the suffering of those who rebelled against God. The just experience relief, which is a self-regarding emotion, as opposed to *Schadenfreude*, which is an other-regarding emotion. What is further striking about Saadya's depiction are the regretful sighs — as opposed to violent shrieks — of the unjust in the "devouring fire." Saadya does not conceive of the separation of the just from the unjust in the way we find in Dante's widely familiar isolation of paradise from both purgatory and hell. Rather, the just and the unjust rub elbows, as it were. That Saadya speaks of the *sighing* (as opposed to, say, shrieking) of the unjust in the fire suggests a certain reluctance on his part to portray the punishment of the unjust as monstrously painful. Rather, the distress in question is likened to hunger or wistfulness.

Now consider how Aquinas rearranges the stage in order to introduce pleasure, to which he assigns an expansive, if crucially ambiguous, role. Here are St. Thomas's answers to the questions 1) whether the saints in heaven will see the suffering of the damned in hell and 2) whether the saints will delight in the torments of the damned (Supplement to the *Summa Theologiae*, Question XCIV):

I answer that, Nothing should be denied the blessed that belongs to the perfection of their happiness. Now everything is known the more for being compared with its contrary, because when contraries are placed beside one another they become more conspicuous. Therefore in order that the happiness of the saints may be more delightful to them and that they may render more copious thanks to God for it, they are allowed to see perfectly the sufferings of the damned (Article 1).

I answer that, A thing may be a matter of rejoicing in two ways. First, in itself, when one rejoices in a thing as such, and thus the saints will not rejoice in the punishment of the wicked. Secondly, accidentally, by reason namely of something joined to it; and in this way the saints will rejoice in the punishment of the wicked, by considering therein the order of Divine justice and their own deliverance, which will fill them with joy. And thus the Divine justice and their own deliverance will be the direct cause of the joy of the blessed, while the punishment of the damned will cause it indirectly (Article 3).

Given that the *Supplement* to the *Summa* was assembled by Aquinas's pupils from his earlier writings after his death, some caution is in order here. Thomas writes at length on the beatific vision in the *Summa Theologiae* (Ia.12; IIa 1–5) and it should not seem farfetched to take these passages from the *Supplement* as generally representative of his mindset. In fairness to St. Thomas, recall that the author of the Book of Revelations invites (Christian) readers to identify with God and to take pleasure in the great suffering awaiting the damned.

Whereas Saadya and Aquinas concur that the saved and the damned will be able to see one another in the hereafter, Aquinas adds that this sight is something of a privilege. According to Aquinas all the saints will see God, but those in whom charity is stronger will see him more perfectly. Although the beatific vision is not subject to degrees, some saints are better able to enjoy that vision than others. Enjoyment, an act of the will, follows an act of the intellect. The essence of beatitude follows from the intellect, whereas joy stems from the will. The enjoyment of Aquinas's saints tells us something important about their character.

These passages from the *Summa Theologiae* are presumably those that astounded Nietzsche (in the first essay of *The Genealogy of Morals*) because of their profound cruelty. For my purposes it is unfortunate (although perhaps not accidental) that Nietzsche does not refer to Saadya in this essay. While Nietzsche regarded Judaism and Christianity as essentially different sides of the same coin, it must in fairness be noted that Saadya strives to lessen the horror of the scene to which Aquinas introduces pleasure.

In the same spirit of fairness, it must also be noted that Aquinas makes a pivotal distinction in the second passage — a distinction between the direct and indirect cause of the saints' joy. It is not the operative suffering *in itself* that will please the saints, but rather contemplation of the order to which that suffering testifies. The fulfillment of God's justice is not a result of the suffering of the damned, at least not in any causal sense; their suffering is an expression of that justice. The damned do not merit anything by their suffering, nor does their suffering bring them closer to God. They suffer because of their sinfulness. What is of value is the overall state of affairs, within which suffering plays an integral part. This distinction fails to mitigate Nietzsche's revulsion in *The Genealogy of Morals*. No one can deny the force of Nietzsche's charge of rationalizing malicious glee; this does not mean, though, that this charge cannot be answered. We might ask, first, whether Aquinas's distinction is tenable, and, secondly, what Nietzsche risks in ignoring this all-important sleight of mind.

Aquinas is not alone in making a teleological distinction in order to assess the moral status of joy that comes from the misery of others. In the twenty-seventh canto of Dante's *Paradiso*, St. Peter bemoans the demise of the papacy into a sewer of blood and stench.[11] Dante's Satan delights not so much in the present troubles of the papacy as in the hope that such troubles raise. In this canto Satan does not derive much pleasure, if any, from the actual suffering of an actual pope, but rather from pleasant reflection on the spectacle of the imminent ruin of an institution that had fallen into terrible corruption. Dante's characterization of Satan lends credence to the distinction Aquinas lays out in the *Supplement*, though it is important that Dante depicts Satan as *more evil* for focusing on the sweet contemplation of the defeat of God's system of justice than on the suffering of a pope. We are left to conclude that Nietzsche either fails to grasp the point of Aquinas's distinction (which seems most unlikely, given his consummate interpretive powers), or that he suspects Aquinas of a rationalization of hatred. The latter possibility, in any event, resonates with Nietzsche's general stance toward suffering. Nietzsche sees no interesting difference here between taking pleasure in the suffering of another person (Aquinas's direct cause) and taking pleasure *because* another person suffers (Aquinas's indirect cause).

I will be discussing the same sort of mental dodge in Bernard Häring's disavowal of *Schadenfreude*. For now, there is one more detail to add to this brief sketch of Jewish and Christian meditations on suffering in the hereafter: theological uncertainty about the concept of hell. Because its organizational structure makes Catholicism somewhat easier to generalize about than various Protestant churches, I will limit myself to a telling uncertainty in the Roman Catholic tradition.

In his sweeping catechetical work *Catholicism*, Richard McBrien has cautioned that biblical passages regarding hell are to be interpreted according to the same principles which govern the interpretation of apocalyptic literature.[12] The New Testament passages regarding hell are not to be taken literally, nor as a balanced theological statement of the hereafter (note, for instance, that St. Matthew describes hell as both a pit of fire and a place of darkness). Jesus never stated that persons actually go to hell or are there now. Like Jesus, the Catholic Church restricts itself to the *possibility* that persons may suffer eternally in hell. Not insignificantly, hell lends itself to other interpretations: it can be viewed as God's yielding to our own freedom to choose evil instead of good, to turn our backs to God resolutely. Catholics are to understand Jesus's own descent into hell after his death as a sojourn to the underworld, where those who had died before him remained, and not to the place of fire.

For most Western believers, hell stands as the *locus classicus* of suffering. The less believers understand hell, the less they understand suffering. Ecclesiastical reservations or disagreements about hell (how awful it is, whether people will actually be sent there for eternity) might reasonably discourage believers of relevant faiths from thinking they understand God's rationale for punishing. A Jew or a Catholic, in any event, might prudently insist that we cannot make sense of human suffering without attacking or opposing religious tradition.

Earthly Suffering and Divine Retribution

For believers, the idea of attributing the reason for human suffering to God's anger is not so much preposterous as presumptuous, in so far as such attribution claims a familiarity with God that enacts the sin of pride.

What is the basis for reading God's will into the physical or emotional state of a person? Pentateuchal and prophetic doctrine proclaimed exclusively earthly rewards or punishments for those who fulfilled or transgressed the obligations of God's covenant (Jer. 11:1–12). Those rewards mentioned in Proverbs were all related to this world as well, for example wealth and honor, land and possessions, and numerous, healthy children. The folly of wickedness, on the other hand, brought sudden and early death (Prv. 8:17–21; 10:27; 22:22–23). Jack Miles takes the following passage in Isaiah to be a crucial turning point after which God punishes discriminately the sinful:

> Therefore the Lord says,
>> the Lord of hosts,
>> The Mighty one of Israel:
> "Ah, I will vent my wrath on my enemies,
>> and avenge myself on my foes.
> I will turn my hand against you
>> and will smelt away your dross as with lye
>> and remove all your alloy.
> And I will restore your judges as at the first,
>> and your counselors as at the beginning.
> Afterward you shall be called the city of righteousness,
>> the faithful city." (I:24–26)

According to Miles, God had thought of punishment differently prior to this point (*God,* p. 206). When punishing the generation of Noah, for example, he thought mankind as a whole incorrigible. This remained God's view throughout much of the Hebrew Bible. With the exception of II Samuel 7, when God said that he would be a strict father to David's house but no more than that, punishment had not been understood as discipline before the example in Isaiah. What Miles does not state explicitly is that such discipline took place in the here and now and that only in the latest books of the Hebrew Bible did the hereafter figure into the notion of punishment and reward.

The only passage in the New Testament that holds out a specific promise of earthly rewards is found in Mark 10:30: those who have left all to follow Christ will "receive now in the present time a hundredfold as much, houses, and brothers, and sisters, and mothers, and children, and lands — along with persecutions . . ." There is less explicit evidence in the New Testament than in the Hebrew Bible to support a nexus between sin and suffering here on earth.

Numerous philosophers and theologians in both the Jewish and Christian traditions have woven into their reflections on divine justice a similar concession regarding a correlation between sin and suffering. Saadya carefully reserves for the "realm of compensation" the bulk of God's judgment upon humans, yet allows that God rewards and punishes us in this life as well:

> . . . God does not leave His servants entirely without reward in this world for virtuous conduct and without punishment for iniquities. For such requitals serve as a sign and an example of the total compensation which is reserved for the time when a summary account is made of the deeds of God's servants. That is why we note that He says of such *blessings* as those listed by Him in the section of the Torah [beginning with the words] *If in My statutes* (Lev. 26:3): *Work in my behalf a sign for good* (Ps. 86:17), and again of the *curses* listed in the section [beginning with the statement] *But it shall come to pass, if thou wilt not hearken* (Deut. 28:15): *And they shall be upon thee for a sign and for a wonder, and upon thy seed for ever* (Deut. 28:46). (*Book of Beliefs*, pp. 208–209)

Saadya instructs that the rewards and punishments we observe in the lives of our neighbors are a "specimen and a sample" of what each respective person may reasonably expect in the next life. While qualifying the belief that God punishes discriminately the sinful, Saadya simultaneously endorses it. Saadya believes that evil in the world is fairly distributed, even when we cannot understand precisely how this takes place. In Saadya's thought, God works and thinks much as mortals do, rewarding and punishing on the basis of desert.

Despite his insistence on the incommensurability of God and man, the twelfth-century philosopher Moses Maimonides (1135–1204) echoes Saadya's conclusions about the meaning of suffering. In *The Guide of the Perplexed*, an exegetical rather than speculative work, one of the great theological rationalists of the Middle Ages explains:

> It is likewise one of the fundamental principles of the Law of *Moses our Master* that it is in no way possible that He, may He be exalted, should be unjust, and that all the calamities that befall men and the good things that come to men, be it a single individual or a group, are all of them determined according to the deserts of the men concerned through equitable judgment in which there is no injustice whatever. Thus if some individual were wounded in the hand by a thorn, which he would take out immediately, this would be a punishment for him, and if he received the slightest pleasure, this would be a reward for him — all this being according to his deserts.[13]

According to Maimonides, all events, whether they are of nature, acts of will, or outcomes of pure chance, are causal and can be ascribed to God (*Guide* II, Section 48). Maimonides's agreement with Saadya ends over the question of determining the appropriateness of suffering, for Maimonides goes on to aver that, "we are ignorant of the various modes of desert." Maimonides emphasizes, where Saadya minimizes, the distance between the works of God and the minds of men. Maimonides cautions us against confidence in assessing what others deserve in the way God can and does determine. A minor point to be taken from Maimonides's position with respect to the question of whether God punishes discriminately the sinful in this life is the idea that *Schadenfreude* might be cognized as a gift from God.

Calvin, to offer a later example of theological association of temporal suffering with sin, stridently declared that the experience of the reprobate was a foretaste of hell. Calvin enjoyed enormous popularity in England.

Fifteen editions of *The Institution of Christian Religion* appeared between 1574 and 1587; toward the end of the sixteenth century, this work became required reading for all students at Cambridge and Oxford.[14] Calvin's well-known doctrine of predestination included a lens through which to interpret suffering. "By dogmatizing about God's treatment of the reprobate on this side of the grave Calvin encouraged the idea that predestination worked itself out in the everyday detail of life."[15] Crucial to Calvin's exposition was a vision of how the suffering of the just differs from the suffering of the unjust in this world. The experiences conveyed distinctly divine attitudes: "For the order of playne teachyng, let us cal the one kinde of judgement, the judgement of Revenge, the other of Chastisement" (*Inst.* 3.4.31). The sufferings of the unjust were "a certayne entrie of hell, from whense they doe alredy see a far of their eternall damnation"; this suffering served to prepare them for "the most cruell hell that at length abideth for them" (*Inst.* 3.4.32). Worldly events lent themselves to interpretation of God's plan for an individual, but Calvin did not hold that this plan was immediately comprehensible. Calvin's theology and its wild popularity cultivated in yet another sphere the popular belief that God punishes discriminately the sinful in this world. In contemporary Protestantism, the divine mystery of love has been emphasized more than the significance of punishment.

These, then, are several instances of how explicitly religious thinkers have linked, however tenuously, earthly suffering and divine dissatisfaction. They have allowed that punishment for sin may take place in this world *in addition to* the hereafter. Not surprisingly, persons who themselves suffer may believe that God is punishing them for some sin, as O'Neill's Mary Tyrone did. In his moving *Devotions Upon Emergent Occasions*, John Donne pondered whether his own grave illness represented God's punishment. Today, reflection on the AIDS epidemic frequently includes similar speculation. In describing a family coming to grips with an HIV-infected member, the physician Sherwin Nuland has stated:

> I prefer to believe that God has nothing to do with it. We are witnessing in our time one of those cataclysms of nature that have no meaning, no precedent, and, in spite of many claims to the contrary, no useful metaphor. Many churchmen, too, agree that God

plays no role in such things. In their *Euthanasie en Pastoraat . . .* the bishops of the Dutch Reformed Church have not hesitated to deal quite specifically with the age-old question of divine involvement in unexplained human suffering: "The natural order of things is not necessarily to be equated with the will of God." Their position is shared by a vast number of Christian and Jewish clergy of various denominations; any less forbearing a stance is callous and a further indecency heaped upon people already too sorely tried.[16]

Rabbi David Novak has echoed this conclusion:

> . . . AIDS seems to raise what was thought by most moderns to be an ancient superstition long behind us, namely the whole issue of God's punishment of sin through physical maladies. Yet, as anyone with either therapeutic or pastoral experience knows, the first question most often raised even today, even by many "nonreligious" people, who have discovered serious disease in themselves is: "What did I do for God to do this to me?"[17]

Although Novak ties the contraction of the HIV virus to behavior he views as sinful (that is, male homosexual activity and intravenous drug use), he affirms a categorical duty to care for the sick, irrespective of ways in which people become ill. According to Novak, infected gay men and IV drug users cannot be called passive victims; nor, for that matter, can chain smokers who die from lung cancer. Novak maintains that we bring certain illnesses upon ourselves. About other diseases Novak urges caution. Curiously, he dismisses as "an ancient superstition" the "whole issue of God's punishment of sin through physical maladies." That "superstition" plays a pivotal, if not mystical, role in other thinking about God.

Bernard Häring, likely the most influential Roman Catholic moral theologian of this century, offers another reason for thinking of human suffering as a sign of divine dissatisfaction: the sins of others. The reason that innocent people suffer is that they are paying for the sins of the guilty.

Apropos of nothing explicitly sexual, Häring asserts in *Free and Faithful in Christ*, "the sick person must ask himself whether he has properly resolved the erotic or moral crises of his life."[18] Coming as they did just several years before public awareness of the AIDS crisis, Häring's words might appear an uncanny omen. However, Häring's cautious interpretation of human suffering obviates the supposition that he would unreflectively view the AIDS of gay men as divine punishment.

Häring's view of suffering surfaces in several works, including his magnum opus *The Law of Christ*. Although illness is only one example of suffering, it is a particularly good one in so far as it resonates with virtually everyone. Häring ties our physical problems to guilt:

> Illness points to guilt, though indeed not always to personal or individual guilt. In our sickness we bear the guilt of our first parents and our ancestors. Many unfortunately in their illness suffer the consequences of sins which their parents committed in the time of their conception and upbringing. . . . Not rarely is a disease the consequence and manifestation of personal sins.[19]

This reasoning extends the link of suffering to sin across generations. It is of a piece with some passages relating to retribution in the Hebrew Bible. By his adultery and murder, for example, King David doomed his son to death and his royal line to perpetual warfare and violence (2 Samuel 12:7–14). The classical statement about punishment meted out by Yahweh on the presumably innocent children of evil men appears in Exodus 34:7. The same passage assures us that God's mercy and forgiveness will endure "for a thousand generations."

Häring deepens the difficulty of separating suffering from sin by raising the possibility that even a living saint may suffer because of the sins of a forebear. As if the range of causal antecedents to suffering were not already sufficiently vast, Häring expands the list of possible reasons for divine retribution to include punishment for the sins of others:

> Even though personal defect may not lie at the root of the illness, it still may be (and should be) borne patiently in the spirit of penance for the actual sins from which none of us is altogether free. Above all it should also be borne in atonement for the sins of others, for at the root of all illness there lies in some way the guilt of the race

with which we are united in the solidarity of the original fall. (*LC*, III, pp. 224–225)

Some suffering, then, is not the result of personal wrongdoing, but rather *human* wrongdoing. The dialectic of self and other in his thinking leaves permanently open the possibility that other people are a part of the bad things that happen to us. Häring exhorts the innocent sufferer to endure pain for the sake of humanity (that is, for other people). Häring espouses a certain ancient Hebrew logic according to which repayment for the crime or virtuous act of an individual affected the group to which the person belonged. Hebrew tribal background produced this idea, as did the belief that God had chosen the Israelites as a people, not as individuals. It was only logical to conceive of God as punishing the nation for one person's sin and as rewarding it for the good action of another. The most obvious example of group punishment for the sins of individuals is the expulsion from the Garden of Eden (Genesis, Chapter 3). Later in Israel's history the *lex talionis* (Exodus 21:24) served to control the indiscriminate vengeance that could decimate entire tribes and families. The compensation of "an eye for an eye, a tooth for a tooth" curbed excessive revenge and focused attention on the crime and its perpetrator, rather than on the group to which the perpetrator belonged. Separating the guilty individual from his innocent group prefigured the Israelite idea of the justice of God in avenging sin.

We are all guilty in Häring's view. My suffering should matter to you, then, for the reason that I am paying for our collective debt. In Häring's thought we all become fellow-sufferers. Because its cause may be far removed in both space and time, suffering should not be expected to bear a readily apparent meaning of much specificity. Häring greatly weakens our capacity to see sin in suffering, even as he affirms it.

Häring says that ours is not to know why some people seem to suffer more than others; what we can conclude is that such persons enjoy a special opportunity to reduce the total sum of human transgression. The idea of vicarious suffering was fully developed by Isaiah in his "Servant of the Lord Oracles" (Isaiah 42:1–4; 49:1–7; 50:4–11; 52:13–53:12). This idea runs throughout the New Testament as well, where the suffering of Christ is presented as wholly vicarious. The Christian, as a redeemed member of

Christ's mystical body, must share in Christ's suffering if he wishes to participate in Christ's glory. St. Paul rejoiced in his own suffering, because it consoled others (2 Corinthians 1:4–7) and contributed to their salvation (2 Timothy 2:10).

Häring comes up with a new way of saying that hell is other people. Other people put us through hell on earth because we have to pay for their sins. This is as strong a sense of human community as we will find anywhere. Because other people can and do atone for our sins, we are a part of the bad things that happen to other people.

Interpreting God's will is not easy. Neither wholly inscrutable nor transparent, the will of God seems best understood as somewhat noncompliant with human ambitions for it. What is clear are certain risks: that mortals make God an accomplice in their various injustices, and that, while supposedly glorifying God, persons in fact idolize good fortune and demonize suffering. If it is true that God's ways are not our ways, then we should think twice about seeking a message from God in any given instance of human suffering. Even a believer, who must concede that all events unfold according to God's will, can conclude that some suffering simply happens or that some suffering simply defies theological explanation. Aquinas wisely steers us to a reasonable *via media*: he stresses that the notion of Divine Providence does not exclude the operation of chance or luck (*Summa Contra Gentiles*, III, lxxiv).

Even the Nicest Priests Feel It

What makes Häring so interesting for my purposes is that even someone so open-minded can remain deeply loyal to a set of beliefs. If asked to name a priest who strove heroically to make the world a kinder, gentler place, many liberal Catholics throughout the world would think of Häring. Father Häring, who died in 1998 at the age of 85, led the way to many of the reforms wrought by the Second Vatican Council. Häring worked to break down walls between Catholics and non-Catholics and to make the Church of Rome more explicitly respectful of other religious faiths.

Having carefully conceded that suffering can properly be considered a function of sin, Häring appeals to God in order to condone joy which springs from even, or perhaps especially, the terrible suffering of others:

> Nor is it the sin of rejoicing over the misfortune of another [*Schadenfreude*] if one is glad that the proud enemies of God are crushed and humiliated, or that the suffering of a fellow man has led him back to God. (*LC*, I, p. 376)

In this terse and finally enigmatic passage Häring disavows *Schadenfreude*. This disavowal, which is also an avowal, would not merit attention if it weren't for the idea, in evidence here, that there must be instances in which it is appropriate to take pleasure in the suffering of another person (for example, the child murderer who fails to win an early release from prison or the self-righteous minister who gets caught in a sex scandal). Although he does not entirely oppose the impulse to see sin as the reason for suffering, Häring shifts our thinking about *Schadenfreude* away from the appropriateness of suffering to the inappropriateness of sympathy. Just as sympathy for the criminal who is sentenced to life in jail is in some sense inappropriate, Häring considers inappropriate that sympathy for reprobate persons whose suffering may teach them a valuable lesson. Otherwise stated, sympathy for the "proud enemies of God" who suffer is inappropriate because that very suffering may lead them to a proper understanding of God. The suffering of St. Paul as Saul might be a good case in point. What is perhaps most disturbing about Häring's supposed disavowal of *Schadenfreude* is that he allows for the possibility that we might rejoice over terrible (as opposed to relatively trivial) suffering.

It might be objected that this interpretation takes a few words from Häring out of context. At issue here, however, is not just a brief passage but the whole way of thinking behind *The Law of Christ*. It is not my aim here to portray Häring as draconian or afflicted with *odium theologicum*. Quite the contrary: he is valuable precisely because he supported ecumenical reform in the Second Vatican Council. The conviction upon which all of Häring's extensive theology rests must be insistence on an internal connection between religion and morality. Häring has insisted that ethics for the Christian is a *religious* ethics; his moral theology is thoroughly Christocentric.

In the passage quoted above, note that Häring does not defend *Schadenfreude*; in fact, he considers it a sin. As with Shakespeare's case of "cruel to be kind," Häring regards suffering as a *means*, not an end. There is some reason to conclude that Aquinas would approve of Häring's disavowal of *Schadenfreude*, for both thinkers aim to ensure a proper understanding of God's will and both insist on a distinction between direct and indirect causes of joy. Disallowing *Schadenfreude* per se and allowing pleasure in the humiliation of "the proud enemy of God" entails the same mental adroitness required by Augustine's exhortation to hate the sin and love the sinner. It may be logically possible to rejoice in the justice of a punishment, yet to regret or even to feel sorrow over the suffering of the one being punished. Psychologically, however, this must be quite a challenge.

Another difficulty with Häring's disavowal lies in the temptation to decide which instances of happiness in others' suffering we find acceptable and then to justify our joy through the hope that this suffering will prove instructive, much as Saul's suffering did immediately before his conversion. But even this insight is more suggestive than conclusive, for it begs the question of whether the pleasure Häring condones is *Schadenfreude* or a thinly disguised rationalization for hatred. It is well known that religious beliefs may cloak or incorporate intolerance. The means for rationalizing suffering as appropriate are as varied as human creativity will allow and one could argue here that Häring is rationalizing hatred as justice.

Careful analysis can usually differentiate between conscientious application of religious ethics and the use of religious precepts as a cover for personal animosity. In what remains of this chapter I will caution against convicting Häring of malice and hatred. The case of Bernard Häring furthers our understanding of suffering by focusing attention, as neither Saadya, nor Maimonides, nor Aquinas did fully, on the appropriateness of sympathy for sufferers in the here and now.

Häring's *Christian Renewal in a Changing World*, first published in 1961, can illuminate what Häring makes of the attitude of the faithful to others. Referring to sentiments and dispositions as "thoughts of the heart," Häring declares, "Even involuntary sentiments and inclinations of the heart, which are morally indifferent as such, are important indications of the true state of our hearts."[20] Häring clearly does not take *Schadenfreude* to be morally indifferent, perhaps because he distinguishes carefully in *The Law of Christ* between rejoicing over the misfortunes of others and the simple taking of pleasure. According to Häring,

> Men's free will is called into action whenever good or evil impulses make themselves felt in his heart. If not confirmed by the will they remain mere tendencies or inclinations. Through the assent of the will they become true sentiments and dispositions of the heart. (*Christian Renewal*, p. 144)

Taking pleasure in the suffering of the "proud enemies of God" would, for Häring, amount to a disposition — a morally acceptable one at that. Häring calls dispositions "infallible guides to man's true state of heart" and asserts that, "unpremeditated and purposive sentiments, if they are deep and lasting, will most effectively contribute to 'the treasury of the heart' from where they predetermine the true possibilities for future motives and actions" (*Christian Renewal*, p. 150).

Conduct issues from character, Häring instructs. Putting our emotional lives in order prepares us to act morally toward others. This is precisely what I take him to mean in *The Christian Existentialist*, when he says, "It is an essential constituent of the Christian religion to tear down all walls of separation between peoples and cultures."[21] This work is particularly useful as a record of Häring's interpretation of Vatican II. Häring tells us that the power of the Catholic Church "arises from the fact that [it] in our time of pluralism is freed from temporal commitments; that she considers with loving eyes and in the spirit of adoration everything that God works, even in those parts of Christianity separated from Rome" (*Christian Existentialist*, p. 43). In *Free and Faithful in Christ* he calls for an ecumenical ministry to persons in mixed marriages and advises that spouses decide without anguish about the baptism and education of children in one or the other church according to the greater probability of ensuring a permanent commitment to some faith (II, pp. 276–333). This sympathy for the religiously different and their spiritual beliefs confounds the idea that Häring is a crusader or a spiritual imperialist.

In several works Häring displays a careful and sincere regard for the faithful of other religions, particularly Jews. At times it seems that the mere fact of participating earnestly in an organized religion is all that

Häring hopes for others, though at other times his profound reverence for and allegiance to the Church of Rome almost suggest another goal (see the section "Zeal for Our Neighbor's Salvation" (*Christian Renewal,* pp. 233–257). In any event, embracing the love of God means hating evil, as Häring tells us: "Zeal for God's kingdom may manifest itself in a variety of ways in keeping with the individual's endowments. The predominant sentiments may be grief over the sins and evils of the world or hatred for the intrigues of the devil" (*Christian Renewal,* pp. 148–149). Unlike St. Paul, who in the Second Epistle to the Corinthians refers to fellow believers who disagree with his version of the Christian message as agents of Satan, Häring never ties any religious creed to Satan (although he does call "total" pride "satanic" in *The Law of Christ* [III, pp. 67–68]). It is, rather, the pride of those who deny God's sovereignty that earns his disapproval:

> In the event that man should fail to surrender himself to the loving designs of a personal God in a proud attempt to deny God's sovereignty, his self-glorification reaches a frightening and an alarming degree. Such an egotistic attitude excludes an interior readiness and openness for the light of moral truths, especially if these run counter to man's pride and sloth. (*Christian Renewal,* p. 106)

The careful phrase "proud attempt" recalls the substance of the passage in which Häring approved of the suffering of the "proud enemies of God." I take Häring to mean that celebrating extrinsic suffering is acceptable only (but not always) when the operative pleasure serves as a tribute to God and when the operative misfortune involves pride (the worst of the seven deadly sins).[22] The question not satisfactorily answered is how to identify a proud enemy of God.

A defense of Häring relies on the idea that I should be cheered by Häring's telling me that he is not celebrating my suffering, but rather the justice to which my suffering attests. Any disagreement I have with Häring's vision of justice will only exacerbate the difficulty of accepting this defense. By accepting this defense, moreover, I implicitly prepare a moral justification for my emotional response to his suffering. In order to justify this way of thinking about suffering, we must show not only that the suffering does some good, but also that no available alternative would achieve as much or more good at a lower cost. Making an example of the guilty exalts justice over persons. By subsuming suffering under beliefs about justice, we exacerbate suffering.

For the Good of the World

The ordinary notion of good can convey at least two distinct concepts: that of well-being or welfare and the seemingly more esoteric notion of an intrinsically good state of affairs or things. Given this distinction, it is important for a form of ethics to make clear whether the notion of good to which it ties its ethical ideals is that of a good state of affairs (St. Thomas Aquinas, Häring), or that of being well-off by having things good (Nietzsche). For Nietzsche, who remained horrified at the ostensible purposelessness and inexorableness of human suffering, the intrinsically good state of affairs responsible for his rejection of Aquinas is a world as free of suffering as possible. For Häring, good consists in part of a world in which "proud enemies of God" are brought to a proper understanding and appreciation of God. Häring's is a consequentialist view of suffering: the rightness or wrongness of suffering depends solely on its overall consequences.

The idea that one must be cruel to be kind implicit in Häring's conception of good invites mention of historical instances or events in which persons taken to represent "the proud enemies of God" have actually been "crushed and humiliated" (for example, the Crusades, the Inquisition). In 1987 John Mahoney contended that "until very recently indeed in the making of moral theology, the attitudes and the enterprises of others were of little, if any, concern to Roman Catholic moralists, far less to the leaders in their community, unless to condemn them."[23] It is not difficult to see where this line of reasoning leads. Although Häring is careful not to defend *Schadenfreude*, his drawing of the line between *Schadenfreude* proper and the cognate rejoicing over the spectacle of divine justice leaves him open to a charge of legitimating religious intolerance and cruelty. I do not accuse Häring of either religious intolerance or cruelty; my aim has been to bring to light his nuanced notion of the appropriateness of suffering. We all suffer for the good of the world in Häring's eyes: the suffering of the faithful lessens the sum total of humanity's collective guilt, and the suffering of the "proud enemies of God" reforms infidels.

Häring argues convincingly for the role of character and the emotions in the moral life. Good people practice good works, he wants to say. This sounds perfectly fine until examples of good works appear. In *Christian Renewal in a Changing World* Häring instructs us to correct our neighbors and to do so sympathetically:

> On the whole, we should always try to take a positive attitude toward our neighbor's difficulties. It reveals a deep understanding to penetrate to the real and hidden concern of our neighbor and to use this insight whenever we have to correct his erroneous ideas. (p. 241)

The most obvious problem with such thinking is that the person who finds him- or herself helped by Häring may not consider him- or herself in need or want of help. The presence of good motives alone cannot ensure that the actions or emotions of a person will be moral.

The task of articulating a religious notion of appropriate suffering returns us to a contest of wills. Catholicism differs little from many Protestant sects in its desire to assert its correctness. In a discussion of medieval social tension, Bernard Lewis argues that Christianity has shared this characteristic with Islam:

> When Christians and Muslims called each other infidels, each understood what the other meant, and both meant more or less the same thing. In so doing, they revealed their essential similarity.[24]

Despite the terrible postwar examples of strife between Catholics and Protestants in Northern Ireland, between Jews and Muslims in Israel, between Christians and Muslims in the former Yugoslavia, and a host of other examples, it can nonetheless be argued that most believers choose not to interfere in the lives of others. This does not mean, however, that they are indifferent to the "errors" of others. Tolerance does not eliminate the occurrence of *Schadenfreude*: it is certainly possible that tolerance will increase the frequency of *Schadenfreude*.

God and *Schadenfreude*

In the ninth century Popes Leo IV and John VII promised eternal life to all those who lost their lives in battles against the Arabs or the Vikings. Two centuries later, crusaders heard a similar promise. Montaigne worried that religious institutions pose a threat to society by holding out hopes of divine reward for attitudes and actions which undermine social solidarity. His worry reverberates throughout Enlightenment thought. The historic controversy over Salmon Rushdie's novel *The Satanic Verses* notwithstanding, the idea of a modern-day crusade seems scarcely plausible. Nonetheless, some religious believers continue to evince great confidence in the determination of the desert of others and, as such, are likely to rationalize or justify their *Schadenfreude* through reference to God. This phrasing is perhaps unacceptable to believers, who may insist that they do not feel *Schadenfreude*, but rather joy at the spectacle of divine justice.

Various forms of religious devotion, like various narratives of history, underscore the fluidity of notions of appropriate suffering. We call a religious zealot or a screaming soldier a fanatic; he provokes scorn, fear, and even revulsion in us. In those of his religion or national origin, however, he stirs admiration. We call heroic or virtuous acts undertaken for our advantage and fanatical those undertaken for someone else's. While we may want to insist that our moral notions of appropriateness descend from the heavens above or spring from objective reason, we recognize that a conversion from one religion or political ideology to another can transform our views. Embarrassing reminders of what we used to believe, like unsettling stories of what others still believe, complicate the process of assuring ourselves that we are right this time about what someone else deserves.

At the dawn of the twenty-first century, many Western believers, whatever their denomination, are not religious in any traditionalist sense. Their far looser, secularized notions of suffering and what other people deserve nonetheless come into focus against the background of many of the earlier conflicts of our culture, as between reason and faith, philosophy and theology, secular and sacred learning. For them or for traditionalists, assessment of the appropriateness of suffering will often turn on intuitions about what God wants.

The curious strategy by which Bernard Häring disavows *Schaden-freude* — one that bears the influence of Aquinas — indicates how formidable is the perennial difficulty against which believers struggle to make sense of suffering. Although Häring succeeds in moving us beyond the temptation to link suffering to sin in a simplistic or overly confident way, his carefully qualified justification for rejoicing over another's suffering returns us to the very problem of moral appropriateness with which we began.

Eight

Outlaw Emotions

Revenge, envy, the impulse to detract, spite,
Schadenfreude, and malice lead to *ressentiment* only
if there occurs neither a moral self-conquest (such as
genuine forgiveness in the case of revenge) nor an act
or some other adequate expression of emotion, and
if this restraint is caused by a pronounced awareness
of impotence. . . . *Ressentiment* can only arise if
these emotions are particularly powerful and yet
must be suppressed.

—Max Scheler, *Ressentiment*

IF MORALLY ACCEPTABLE PLEASURE IN THE MISFORTUNES OF OTHERS IS AS
common as I have made it out to be, why is it that we do not have a name
for it? Why do we deny the experience, and how? Misogyny has a lot to
do with answers to these questions. Striving to portray justice as blind, re-
mote, and impersonal may mask a longing to make justice masculine. Various thinkers have sought to excise the emotional element deep within
justice; such cutting away seems a necessary step to insisting that justice is
not, in fact, disguised or sanitized revenge. Purifying justice of anything
traditionally considered feminine comes at the cost of outright denial of
Schadenfreude or identifying *Schadenfreude* with femininity.

In addition to a sustaining interest in the problem of human suffering,
Schopenhauer and Nietzsche share credit for drawing philosophical attention to psychological disavowal. Both Schopenhauer and Nietzsche appreciate, for different reasons, the social importance of disavowing

Schadenfreude. The revulsion with which various commentators have condemned the emotion makes it easy to understand why people who feel it might disavow it. *Schadenfreude* belongs to the category Alison Jaggar calls "outlaw emotions": those responses which are distinguished by their incompatibility with dominant perceptions and values in a community. Jaggar, like Annette Baier, Cheshire Calhoun, and others working within the field of feminist ethics, alerts us to the privileges our moral theories may extend to certain kinds of people (for example, male, Christian, white heterosexuals). In the late twentieth century, predominantly female thinkers have refined moral philosophy, or rather those who think about it. These philosophers have prompted us to attend out of habit to the motives of people who come up with theories about morality. Consequently, the way in which I have framed *Schadenfreude* requires some mention of Schopenhauer's and Nietzsche's mutual contempt for women.

Frailty, Thy Name Is Woman

Contempt for women grows out of the Western philosophical tradition. Kant, like others before him, equated emotions with passivity and women with both. Emotions, we learn from (male) philosophers, are feminine, actions are masculine. Even orthodox emotions (such as love and compassion) raise suspicions, because emotions allegedly threaten to undermine reason. Kant saw little or no moral significance in the emotions: for him, morality centered on actions — what he took to be the realm of men.

It is not surprising that so-called feminist philosophers have to a large extent fastened upon the emotions, for the association of emotions has been not just symbolic, but also normative. This means that disdain for emotions amounts to disdain for women. Work in feminist ethics has tried to expose a moral double-bind: men have confined women to a certain realm of experience or behavior and then blamed women for their imputed behavior. Emotions rule women, our moral tradition told us, and so women are unsuitable for public life. Women belong at home because we have been conditioned to see women as suited for domesticity.

This synopsis simplifies what feminist philosophers have shown us, but nonetheless captures a bona fide fear of emotions that has pervaded Western philosophy. The misguided idea that emotions signify personal weakness and, further, subvert reason gave men an additional reason to hide their *Schadenfreude.*

We learn to disguise our *Schadenfreude* for the same reason that our forebears came to ban public executions. Anger toward criminals had to disappear from ready view in order to sustain a belief in a non-vengeful justice. We have learned a dubious lesson, namely that emotions and justice have little if anything to do with one another. This lesson harbors uneasiness over the idea that the legal institution of punishment might rest to some important extent on emotional responses to transgressions. Mentally separating the emotions from justice recalls a tradition of segregating women from reason.

What Remains Unsaid

What does it mean to stifle emotions? It means we don't allow ourselves to reflect on a thought that presents itself. Sometimes we have good reason to do this, namely to make our lives easier in society. Emotional conformity often confers identity in a particular group. Cheering over the electrocution of a hardened criminal, for example, may well land us outside of a group to which we want to belong. Silence may earn us the admiration of desired peers.

Emotions, like actions, follow social cues. In Thomas Hardy's *Return of the Native,* an ambitious mother happens upon her worldly and well-educated son working in the fields as a common laborer. Mrs Yeobright observes her child Clym "wearing the regulation dress of the craft, and apparently thinking the regulation thoughts, to judge by his motions."[1] To succeed as a field laborer, Clym has programed himself to think and feel as a field laborer. By watching him closely, his mother can sadly tell that her son has adapted to a socially inferior position.

Can our communities really dictate our mental responses to the world around us? Listen to what Simone de Beauvoir tells us in her autobiography *Memoirs of a Dutiful Daughter* about the thrill of suddenly understanding her fondness for a girl: "All at once conventions, routines, and the careful categorizing of emotions were swept away and I was overwhelmed by a flood of feeling that had no place in any code. I allowed myself to be uplifted by that wave of joy which went on mounting inside me, as violent and fresh as a waterfalling cataract, as naked, beautiful and bare as a granite cliff."[2] This first-person account describes the experience of an outlaw emotion. (It is just one description, however, as the experience may not always be pleasant.) As a young girl, the renowned French philosopher already knew something about non-conformist emotions. The violation of an unspoken code thrilled her.

In my earlier discussion of emotion management, I praised Arlie Russell Hochschild, who has argued that we instinctively mold our emotions to conform to reigning standards of appropriateness. Alison Jaggar's account of outlaw emotions advances Hochschild's contribution to moral thinking. Jaggar illustrates what it means to disavow or repress emotion, and what she writes can illuminate *Schadenfreude*. She offers both a useful description of disavowal and a compassionate justification of it. Against Scheler, who warns that the disavowal of *Schadenfreude* leads to the generation of *ressentiment*, Jaggar points to the redundancy of avowing outlaw emotions in a culture that expects them of you.

Strategies for disavowing *Schadenfreude* disguise a rationalization of self-interest while they reveal cultural ideas. These strategies attest to the force of emotions generally, as well as to the susceptibility of the socially privileged to turn away from the suffering of others.

According to Jaggar, the apparently individual and involuntary character of our emotional experience is often used as evidence that emotions are "gut reactions." Such an inference is, however, quite mistaken. One of the most obvious illustrations of the processes by which emotions are *socially constructed* is the education of children, who are carefully taught appropriate responses to any number of situations: to fear strangers, to relish spicy food, or to enjoy swimming in cold water, for example.[3] Children also learn what their culture defines as appropriate ways to express the emotions that it recognizes. Although any individual's guilt or anger, joy or triumph, presupposes the existence of a social group capable of feeling guilt, anger, joy, or triumph, this does not mean that group emotions precede or are logically prior to the emotions of individuals. Rather, it indicates that individual experience is simultaneously social experience.

Values both derive from social experience and presuppose emotions to the extent that emotions provide the experiential basis for values. If we had no emotional responses to the world, it is inconceivable that we should ever come to value one particular state of affairs over another. Further, it would be in many instances virtually impossible to claim knowledge without some significant familiarity with the emotions. If, for example, someone feels no fear when confronted with apparent danger, his or her lack of fear requires further explanation. Similarly, if he or she is afraid when no danger can be identified, his or her fear is denounced as irrational or pathological. Without characteristically human perceptions of and relations to the world, Jaggar points out, there would be no characteristically human emotions.

Jaggar maintains that feminists can learn from outlaw emotions how to reeducate, refine, and eventually reconstruct their emotional constitution. Moreover, social alienation enables outsiders to see and understand patterns which elude insiders. Ironically, outsiders understand systems of domination better than those who construct or enforce them. Insiders need outsiders to explain how a community can be improved:

> Oppressed people have a kind of epistemological privilege insofar as they have easier access to this standpoint ["a perspective that offers a less partial and distorted and therefore more reliable view"] and therefore a better chance of ascertaining the possible beginnings of a society in which all could thrive. (p. 162)

The very idea of defending or valuing outlaw emotions raises difficult questions about social stratification and what we are to understand by the facts of inclusion and exclusion. Those difficulties aside, I want to highlight Jaggar's contention that those who are excluded from a morality might enjoy a privilege unknown or unknowable to those who are included by it. It is a thesis that sounds remarkably like Nietzschean *ressentiment*. For Nietzsche, the kind of knowledge that the weak possess is frankly not worth having: more important is the knowledge or wherewithal one needs to become strong. Jaggar would insist here that people struggling under a system of domination are not weak, but rather oppressed. There is an important difference.

We might view the elite as the oppressed, particularly given Nietzsche's account of the "herd mentality."[4] I do not want to criticize Jaggar for not filling out the notion of oppression in part because Nietzsche leaves the same question unanswered and in part because any normative answers introduce an illusion of neatness into what is a very ambiguous concept. Descriptive answers to the question of what oppression is — and they are enormously varied — suggest an infinite number of possible outlaw emotions.

Jaggar forces us to rethink what we mean by male dominance. She focuses our attention on control, evaluation, and exclusion. Male-dominated cultures control women's conduct; they label women the intellectual, moral, or spiritual inferiors of men; and they exclude women from the religious and political centers of a society. Jaggar recognizes that people (not just men) are highly motivated to seize meanings and resources out of a sociocultural environment that has been arranged to provide them with the meanings and resources that suit them.

The point of identifying *Schadenfreude* as an "outlaw emotion" is to expose a moral system of domination. I want to look more closely at the social position of women, among whom *Schadenfreude* is reputed to flourish and to lurk. The first of two strategies for repressing *Schadenfreude* illustrates the effect of names on concepts, and the second reveals an assumption of the moral inferiority of women. The assumptions underlying these strategies limit in advance the applicability of the moral theory they produce. They also show that strategies for repressing *Schadenfreude* mask both the expression and production of *ressentiment*.

First Denial Strategy: The Disavowal of *Schadenfreude*

A central part of the experience of *Schadenfreude* involves the denial that one takes pleasure in the actual suffering of another. As with the sentencing of "enemies of the people" and those guilty of "crimes against humanity," morally acceptable pleasure in the injury of other people must spring from love of justice. The underside of justice is the emotional satisfaction of revenge (for those who were directly harmed by the criminals) or *Schadenfreude* (for those whose belief in justice sustains the conviction that criminals deserve to suffer) or of malice (for those who simply take sadistic pleasure in the suffering of others, whether or not they are guilty of serious acts). It is not farfetched to assert that a conviction won in a war crimes court entails not only joy that a particular side has won the case but also (for the allies of the winning side) active pleasure that the other side has suffered defeat.

Denying *Schadenfreude* is one of the simplest ways to claim that one takes pleasure only in justice prevailing. Refusing to name *Schadenfreude* is one of the simplest ways to deny it, much in the way that a heterocentric society might have refused to name homosexual impulses, desires, or domestic arrangements. Let's circle back to the identification of *Schadenfreude* as a discrete emotion in order to see how naming *Schadenfreude* (or refusing to do so) amounts to an act of symbolic formulation.

In the American play *Suddenly Last Summer* (1958) by Tennessee Williams, Violet Venable, a reclusive grande dame played by Katharine Hepburn, is puzzled when a young doctor asks her if she is not a widow. "Yes, of course," she confirms, but points out that much more important to her, she is a woman who has lost her only son. "Why is it," she wonders aloud, "that they have a word for a woman who has lost her husband, but not for a woman who has lost her son?"

Like Violet Venable, someone might wonder why there is no English word for "pleasure in the misfortune or suffering of another." Few English speakers avail themselves of the term, most likely because of their unfamiliarity with it. If at first *Schadenfreude* seems like a term English speakers can do without, we should recognize a strong case for arguing to the contrary, given the ubiquitousness of what it signifies. For the brand of happiness it names is so much a part of our daily lives, and so central to our narratives of them, that it seems futile to protest that the would-be label sounds too foreign or simply pretentious. We are conditioned to think of *Schadenfreude* as a pleasure that dare not speak its name.

Schadenfreude in America

Why haven't Americans adopted the German term? The reason may be simple: we manage just fine without it. Though such a reason may explain why we have no word for "a woman who has lost her only son," it seems an implausible answer to the *Schadenfreude* question. For it can just as easily be argued that Americans would immediately be able to use the word discriminately upon acquiring it as it can be argued that they do not need a word for *Schadenfreude* because they manage just fine without it. Claiming that a society can do without a particular word or device neglects the possibility that that word or device might quickly assume a useful function in a society. As Yale historian John Boswell notes:

> English appears to have no real equivalent for the French term "fiancé," but this is certainly no indication that the idea of heterosexual engagement was unknown in the British Isles prior to its adoption. Why foreign words for social relations ("protége," "gigolo," "madame," etc.) catch on and supplant indigenous terms is a complex issue; the notion that the phenomena they describe were unknown before importation of the word belongs among the least likely explanations.[5]

What is especially puzzling about *Schadenfreude* — unlike the hypothetical word for "a woman who has lost her only son" — is that the term has *not* caught on in America. For what it signifies is not something peculiar to a few sinister or morally weak persons, but something that occurs, no doubt with variable frequencies, to virtually all non-infantile, non-comatose human beings — not just to Germans.

That *Schadenfreude* is often disguised, qualified, or denied explains in part why it rarely shows itself. Gossip and laughter may indicate *Schadenfreude*, but *Schadenfreude* does not always end in gossip or laughter — for people may repress their laughter out of fear that others will perceive their enjoyment as evil. In this respect *Schadenfreude* resembles envy, jealousy, malice, and hatred. Of course, such repression is not always rational; more often than not, as Nietzsche's theory of *ressentiment* explains, this is a matter of instinct. For this reason we should not expect characters in novels to experience *Schadenfreude* in ways which are readily identifiable, even to themselves. Dorrit Cohn has remarked, "Modern novelists who know their Freud, therefore, would be the last to resort to direct quotation in order to express their characters' unconscious processes."[6] We should not expect literary sources in either English or German to report on the prevalence of *Schadenfreude*.

The reading and interpretation of a confession or a letter such as

Kafka's can develop readers' sensitivity to problems of self-esteem and justice, so they can understand *Schadenfreude*. In reading Kafka's *Brief an den Vater*, some readers may infer from the expression of *Schadenfreude* a need for subterfuge. We can, then, accept Jaggar's main point: outlaw emotions may be culturally relegated to silence and new ways of describing them may be socially discouraged.

This point should not seem controversial. Remember, the *Oxford English Dictionary* reports that *Schadenfreude* first appeared in the English language in 1852. The term arrived embedded in a warning:

> What a fearful thing is it that any language should have a word expressive of the pleasure which men feel at the calamities of others; for the existence of the word bears testimony to the existence of the thing.

And so, the logic might go, if we can successfully keep *Schadenfreude* out of the English language, we can successfully deny the existence of the emotion it names. What is puzzling is why Trench even discussed the very word he hoped to debar from the English language. Curiously, Trench seemed to assume that people need to be taught any but the most obscure vices. It would be extreme and, in fact, erroneous to infer from Trench that the silent celebration of the accidental misfortunes of others was unknown in Europe or America before or after his study.

The *Oxford English Dictionary*, in identifying *Schadenfreude* with malice, perpetuates Trench's anxiety. Taboos can be prolonged *ad infinitum* if they are never questioned, but they certainly profit from periodic reinforcement, a good example of which is found in the writing of Nicholas Rescher:

> From the standpoint of ethical legitimation, the positive vicarious affects have an altogether different ethical footing than the negative. For the negative (that is, antipathetic) vicarious affects in fact represent unworthy, morally negative attitudes: hostility, malice, envy, jealousy, *Schadenfreude,* and the like. From an ethical point of view they merit nonrecognition and dismissal as reprehensible.[7]

Over a century after R.C. Trench's unambiguous advice to close the linguistic gates in the face of *Schadenfreude*, the idea that "outlaw emotions" ought to be banished from ethical thought endures. That something is prohibited, however, is hardly indication that it did or does not take place.

The disavowal of *Schadenfreude* appears ironic because if outlaw emotions achieved expression, they would be quantifiable and therefore less problematic. Free and frank discussion would be perhaps the most effective means of countering *Schadenfreude*. Openly displayed emotions are less dangerous than concealed ones because their release can be observed by all; they are thus subject to public control.

The agenda I impute to Trench and Rescher *inter alia* has enjoyed some success. Unlike other German words such as "kindergarten," "sauerkraut," or "kitsch," *Schadenfreude* is no more familiar to us now than it was a hundred years ago. Were it even slightly common in our vocabulary, it seems unlikely that the 1989 Vintage edition of *The Gay Science* would include the following footnote to Nietzsche's use of the word *schadenfroh* (a cognate of *Schadenfreude*): "The word is famous for being untranslatable: it signifies taking a mischievous delight in the discomfort of another person."[8] We are left wondering just *where* this word is famous and *why* it has not been adopted if it is in fact untranslatable.

That it does not enjoy wide circulation in America should surprise us more than the knowledge that it is not used in, say, Italy, Japan, Russia, or Spain. An estimated eighty percent of the English vocabulary is derived from other languages, such as Danish, Latin, Greek, Swedish, Hebrew, Arabic, Bengali, and Native American tongues. The *Oxford English Dictionary* lists some 500,000 entries. By contrast, German has only 185,000 words; French a meager 100,000. It is probably English's greedy appetite for "loan words" that makes it such a rich and yeasty language.[9] The absence of a one-word equivalent of *Schadenfreude* from, say, Italian or Spanish vocabularies thus has little bearing on the claims I make here.[10]

Much caution needs to be exercised in assessing a linguistic deficiency, even one just within the context of American parlance. About etiology and verbal deficiency Alasdair MacIntyre has pointed out,

Notice that there is no word correctly translatable by our modern word "morality" in any ancient or medieval language. And this lack of word is a symptom of the different ways in which different forms and aspects of social life were classified in the societies in which those languages were spoken and written. . . . Ethics, in both Greek practice and Aristotelian thought, was part of politics; the understanding of the moral and intellectual virtues, in both medieval practice and Thomistic thought, was part of theology. To abstract the ethics from its place in either is already to distort.[11]

MacIntyre by no means wants to say that morality is a function of modernity, only that we moderns have a different way of referring to, and therefore understanding, a familiar concept. Further, this concept has evolved in such a way that a simple glance from one society or era to another will frustrate our attempt to compare the role of *Schadenfreude* in other places.

Disavowing the reality of the emotion represents one strategy for disavowing pleasure in the suffering of others. The American disavowal stems from cultural dissatisfaction with the idea that *schadenfroh* persons dwell in their midst or that such a response figures regularly in their own emotional lives. This dissatisfaction produces *ressentiment* in those who feel *Schadenfreude*, because they perceive themselves as powerless or unwilling to resist the emotion and thereby to achieve a moral standard that precludes *Schadenfreude*. A moral culture that inculpates everyone by demonizing *Schadenfreude* defies us to transform common assumptions and sensibility. Transforming sensibility matters, particularly when that same moral culture discourages familiarity with *Schadenfreude*. Now I will turn to a closely related but distinct disavowal strategy: characterizing it as culturally foreign.

Schadenfreude across Cultures

That the German language is uniquely qualified to express a mischievous delight in the suffering of another is not self-evident. But in his 1965 essay "Auf die Frage: 'Was ist deutsch?,'" Theodor Adorno claims that "the German language seems to have a special elective affinity for philosophy and especially for its speculative element [*Moment*]" and that in the domain of one's mother tongue, it is that very language which stands in for one's fellow human beings.[12] To Adorno, it might seem natural to find a word for "the largely unanticipated delight in the suffering of another which is cognized as trivial and/or appropriate" in German, not because anything in the German character might indicate unusual receptiveness to that pleasure, but because something in or about the German language is hospitable to the distinctions upon which the notion plays.

Even if the Kafka and Peter Gay cases were unique, that would not explain why *Schadenfreude* or any other German word would not move easily into another language. Adorno holds that it is precisely the extraordinary capacity for fine distinctions characteristic of German that makes exportation of native *mots justes* impossible:

> Yet the impossibility of non-violently transposing into another language not only highly developed speculative thoughts but even particular and quite precise concepts such as those of spirit [*Geist*], the element [*Moment*], and experience [*Erfahrung*], with all the connotations with which they resonate in German — this impossibility suggests that there is a specific, objective quality to the German language. (p. 130)

Like Heidegger, who insisted to Victor Farias that any number of philosophical or etymological distinctions could not be exported from the German language,[13] Adorno privileges his maternal tongue. If the upshot of Adorno's or Heidegger's position is that *Schadenfreude* cannot be imported, this means only that we don't understand *Schadenfreude* exactly as Germans do, not that we don't understand it at all. In spite of the manifest difficulty of ascertaining whether any two cultures understand exactly the same thing by joy, virtue, or melancholy, I believe that non-German cultures can comprehend the sense of *Schadenfreude* every bit as well as Heidegger or Adorno.

What does it matter, then, that *Schadenfreude* originates in German? The German language does differ fundamentally and significantly from English in the unusual ease with which it accommodates compound words. One noun is added to another and in turn to another until we are left with the comically long words for which German is ridiculed. A word like *Schadenfreude* is unremarkable in German, merely one such conglomeration among many others. But that the Germans do not have a corresponding opposite for *Schadenfreude* only draws more attention to the distinctiveness of this term. For a word like *Freudenfreude* (joy at another's joy) simply never happened or gained currency.

The demonization of *Schadenfreude* outside of Germany is a *cultural* matter for the same reason that the understanding of *Schadenfreude* in any milieu is a cultural task. Anthony Kenny makes this point about emotions in general:

> Wittgenstein has shown that a purely mental event, such as Descartes conceived an emotion to be, is an *Unding* [an inconceivable and so inexpressible thing]. Any word purporting to be the name of something observable only by introspection, and merely causally connected with publicly observable phenomena, would have to acquire its meaning by a purely private and uncheckable performance. But no word could acquire a meaning by such a performance; for a word only has meaning as part of a language; and a language is something essentially public and shareable.[14]

What *Schadenfreude* names must be generally recognizable, for if the experience of *Schadenfreude* acquires meaning for each of us by a ceremony from which everyone else is excluded, then none of us can have any idea what anyone else means by the word. Nor can anyone know what they themselves mean by the word, for to know the meaning of a word is to know how to use it correctly.

Not having any sociological research at hand, I can only assert that Kafka and Peter Gay are representative of Germans in their use of the word *Schadenfreude*.[15] Psychologists of emotion have pointed out that, as with most other aspects of culturally shared knowledge, there seems to be considerable agreement on the adequacy of particular emotional reactions to specific antecedent situations, without explicit criteria for such judgments.[16] It is fairly easy to elicit agreement on how angry a person might properly become when he or she misses a train or loses money on the stock market. On the other hand, it would be difficult if not impossible to elicit an abstract definition of the necessary and sufficient antecedent conditions for anger in general.

Other psychologists have concluded that the validity of conclusions on the cross-cultural variations of emotions may very often be challenged because the field lacks standards of comparison.[17] It is not my aim here to provide such standards for comparing the *Schadenfreude* of Germans to the *Schadenfreude* of non-Germans.

Second Denial Strategy: The Feminization of *Schadenfreude*

Max Scheler views women and Jews as prime candidates for experiencing outlaw emotions. He claims that, "the 'witch' has no masculine counterpart. The strong feminine tendency to indulge in detractive gossip is further evidence [that woman "is the weaker and therefore the more vindictive sex"]; it is a form of self cure" (*Ressentiment,* pp. 127–128). Scheler views gossip as Schopenhauer does *Schadenfreude*: both as a starting point and as a conclusive kind of evidence beyond which few questions can or need to be asked. Implicit in Scheler's analysis of gossip is the notion of cure or consolation that runs throughout my consideration of *Schadenfreude*.

In Scheler we find a link between gossip, envy, and *Schadenfreude*, each of which he considers feminine. According to Scheler, men do not need the consolation which gossip or *Schadenfreude* delivers. Remember that various thinkers (for example, Schopenhauer and Trench) have insisted that *Schadenfreude* exceeds envy in moral reprehensibility. How much worse for a man to be suspected of *Schadenfreude*, then, than of envy? One could hardly wonder at any manly denunciation of gossip; the narrator of "Billy Budd," Herman Melville's tale of justice on a British ship during the Napoleonic Wars, sums it up:

Well, though many an arraigned mortal has in hopes of mitigated penalty pleaded guilty to horrible actions, did ever anybody seriously confess to envy? Something there is in it universally felt to be more shameful than even felonious crime. And not only does everybody disown it, but the better sort are inclined to incredulity when it is in earnest imputed to an intelligent man.[18]

Much could be said about this conception of masculinity and its supposed ideological function, not least about the psychology on which it is based and the ontology that it presupposes. Because *Schadenfreude*, a weakness, is conceptually linked to envy (as its opposite but corollary), it is not surprising to find it identified as a *feminine* problem by men whose writing touched on it (Melville's juxtaposition of "mortal" with "man" raises some question as to how this remark is to be interpreted). Scheler defines masculinity by specifying its negative limits and in so doing reinforces the impotence of a class of persons to resist characteristics imputed to them.

Scheler regards women as generally passive; the passivity which defines *Schadenfreude* explains its association with women. Much feminist theory includes resistance to the identification of the feminine with the passive. The defining feature of feminist thought lies in a recognition and rejection of the ideological biases of patriarchy. Feminists oppose the traditional script of female passivity, dependence, and subordination. Feminist philosophers such as Cheshire Calhoun have linked gender bias to the social location of the male theorist and his audience as well as to the contours of the larger social world in which moral theories evolve. Without attending to the differences among human interests, temperaments, lifestyles, and commitments, as well as to how those interests may be malformed as a result of gender or power inequities, the egoism and group bias that the male theorist's focus on common humanity was designed to eliminate may slip in. So long as we avoid incorporating gender categories among the tools for theorizing or analyzing, Calhoun has argued in various places, we will continue running the risks of importing gender bias into our various theories and of creating an ideology of masculinity and femininity.

That ideology informs the work of the thinkers on whom I rely principally in this book. Claudia Card has noted that both Kant and Schopenhauer found virtues (and presumably vices as well) gender-related.[19] "The very thought of seeing women administer justice raises a laugh," says Schopenhauer in *On the Basis of Morality*. "They are far less capable than men of understanding and sticking to universal principles," although "they surpass men in the virtues of *philanthropy* and *lovingkindness*

[*Menschenliebe*], for the origin of this is . . . intuitive" (p. 151). Card observes that, at least with respect to women and principles, Schopenhauer followed Kant, who had exclaimed, "I hardly believe the fair sex is capable of principles," speculating that instead "Providence has put in their breast kind and benevolent sensations, a fine feeling for propriety, and a complaisant soul."[20] Within the terms of Kant's own moral theory, the implication was that women's virtues are not moral. This appears to have been his ideal for women, and, Card is correct in concluding, not something he saw as a problem.

Schopenhauer's vitriolic essay "On Women" mocks sexist ideals of female beauty: "Only the male intellect, clouded by the sexual impulse, could call the undersized, narrow-shouldered, broad-hipped, and short-legged sex the fair sex."[21] Despite the explicitly physical reference in this passage, we can generally read Schopenhauer's attacks on women as an indictment of femininity rather than of women, if we distinguish between gender concepts (femininity and masculinity) as social constructions and sex concepts (femaleness and maleness) as biological categories. Wanting to be masculine is understandable in a world such as Schopenhauer's: one wonders how he viewed masculine women. Men who exhibit feminine qualities might well be doubly despised by Schopenhauer, in part for having those qualities and in part for having betrayed their masculine gender privilege to do so. This supposition sits well with Bryan Magee's assessment of Schopenhauer's own erotic life, specifically the struggle to come to terms with his homosexual impulses.[22] Further, Schopenhauer's revulsion to men who have sex with one another may have something to do with his contempt for femininity.

Kant's misogyny, it should be pointed out in fairness to Schopenhauer, was no less pointed. At the age of forty, Kant took up the topic of women in a work seldom read by moral philosophers and in a chapter announcing itself as on "the interrelations of the sexes." "Women will avoid the wicked not because it is unright, but because it is ugly," he observes, after remarking that "the virtue of a woman is a *beautiful virtue*" and "that of the male sex should be a *noble virtue*" (*OFBS*, p. 81). Traits identified here as women's virtues were identified in the previous chapter of the same work as merely "adoptive virtues" and contrasted there with genuine virtues. "Adoptive virtues" are not based on principle, although they can lead to (outwardly) right actions. Kant's view was that someone with "adoptive virtues," such as sympathy and complaisance, is goodhearted, but that only someone who is virtuous on principle "is a righteous person" (*OFBS*, p. 61). Card asserts that Kant's ideals for women are those we might expect for domestic pets.

The misogyny of Nietzsche and Freud has received a great deal more attention than Kant's. The sad irony that emerges here is that the thinkers I credit for having been marvelously sensitive to the moral significance of human suffering were committed in some real sense to perpetuating the suffering of roughly half the human race. In the course of examining how women have learned to respond to powerlessness, recent scholarship has highlighted the conceptual similarity of women, Jews, and gay men — for example, Susan Sontag's classic essay on camp (linking the social status of gay men and Jews)[23] and Marjorie Garber's account of this conceptual identification in *Vested Interests*.[24] If there is, in fact, something dangerous or diabolical about outlaw emotions, it follows that we should watch women and Jews carefully, and gay men as well.

How bad are outlaw emotions? Not very, perhaps. Claudia Card asks, "Feminist thinkers are understandably reluctant to address publicly women's reputation for lying, cunning, deceit, and manipulation. But *are* these vices, one may ask, if they are needed for self-defense?" (*The Unnatural Lottery*, p. 53) Card, Calhoun, Jaggar, and others working in the field of feminist ethics challenge how and by whom the good gets defined. Their work can be seen as an illumination of the *ressentiment* at work in setting orthodox emotions off from outlaw ones. Women might reasonably find themselves bitter at a moral theory or system that describes deceitfulness and gossip in distaff terms. Lynne McFall has emphasized the rationality of bitterness, another outlaw emotion. McFall has argued that bitterness may be a justified response to harms and losses caused by human failings (wickedness, moral stupidity, weakness, or indifference) — what we think of as avoidable harms and losses, ones which are more bitter and therefore harder to bear. McFall's provocative essay makes the most sense in the context of a patriarchal system of domination of women (though she does not specify this context). McFall contends that one cannot "come to terms" with unrepentant brutality when there is no remorse. Acceptance of one's fate as a subjugated person is more than we can ask,

and forgiveness is inappropriate and self-destructive. As responses to undeserved suffering, forgiveness and active bitterness occupy opposite ends
of the continuum. Claiming that bitterness is a morally appropriate attitude is just as reasonable as claiming that it can be morally acceptable to
take pleasure in the injuries of other people.

What thinkers such as Jaggar, Card, and McFall help us to understand
is that the philosophical canon underlying our moral lives amounts to a
system of domination. This is not the sort of domination I referred to in my
discussion of suffering under rules; this is a kind of domination that denies
women their identities as full moral agents. Within a hierarchical society,
those norms and values which are taken to define what is characteristically
human tend to serve the interest of the dominant group. These dominant
values are implicit in responses taken to be precultural or so-called gut
responses. But people do not always experience conventionally acceptable
emotions: they may feel satisfaction rather than embarrassment when their
leaders make foolish mistakes; they may feel revulsion toward socially
sanctioned ways of privileging men. They may feel outlaw emotions.

Claiming or simply noting that an emotion is immoral can mislead us
into unreflective agreement. Male moralists have condemned *Schadenfreude* without commenting on the extent to which such condemnation is
supported or generally approved. Feminist ethicists have usefully reminded us that moral strictures do not fall from the sky, but are conceptu-
alized and articulated by living, breathing men. Many of these men have
acknowledged views of women which can hardly fail to strike contemporary readers as inaccurate or unfair.

Embedded in our judgments of emotions we can discern some of the
deepest dimensions of traditional gender differentiation in our culture.
Schadenfreude would be more readily tolerated in traditional moral philosophy if the emotions, like gossip, were taken as a masculine phenomenon. Misogyny, however covert, keeps feminist thinkers in business. The
many and varied achievements of women in the twentieth century remind
us that some powerful people (namely, misogynists) will maintain their
beliefs even when those beliefs have unfair and crippling consequences for
(even already disadvantaged) others.

On the Moral Impunity of Beliefs about Justice

It would be a gross misunderstanding of my analysis of *Schadenfreude* to conclude that we cannot blame others for their moral beliefs. What I have tried to do is highlight the plurality of moral beliefs about the good. Countless philosophers have pondered a point masterfully summed up by Shakespeare's Hamlet: "There is nothing either good or bad, but thinking makes it so" (2.2.249). My claim here is simply that we take what we believe to be true. Plenty of people really do believe that abortion and gay sex represent beastly crimes; they are not faking these beliefs, as some liberals have suggested. By the same token, plenty of people believe precisely the opposite about abortion and gay sex; those who morally defend these acts are not faking their beliefs either. Jaggar clarifies how systems of domination deny legitimacy to certain beliefs and emotions.

A plurality of beliefs makes for a good deal of moral trouble. Especially in this age of cultural pluralism and political correctness, we may wince at the thought of criticizing the beliefs of another tradition (for example, female circumcision in Muslim countries). Such criticism may seem deeply insensitive; however, it could easily be countered that we cannot respect or show sensitivity to beliefs that strike us as wholly unintelligible. Moreover, outsiders sometimes demonstrate an uncanny ability to see to the heart of a matter insiders cannot separate themselves from. This is certainly the case with psychoanalysis: it is no doubt the case with intercultural and interpersonal criticism as well.

A defense of *Schadenfreude* may seem to lead to a troubling endorsement of moral relativism. This would follow only if we could not argue with others about their moral beliefs. Some people who learned about the mass slaughter of Jews under the Nazis may have felt *Schadenfreude* (as opposed to malicious glee): that is to say that they may have felt justice had been done to Jews in concentration camps. They may think that, but we don't have to agree with them. What relativism aims at is an attitude by which one does not see another group's outlook or beliefs as wrong. This is not an attitude I advocate. Even toleration, which has traditionally been understood as an attitude one extends to views one considers wrong, may seem inappropriate in some circumstances.

What precisely the limits of toleration — both political and moral — should be continues to generate debate among political theorists. John Rawls considers political toleration one of the "settled convictions" of Western culture, which holds up the liberal notion of "justice as fairness."[25] This means that we have to tolerate politically people of whom we may disapprove morally. It is fair to say that the more undecided a person is, the less likely he or she is to experience *Schadenfreude*. But even toleration has its limits. The limits of toleration return us to the question of moral appropriateness. Political discussion of the extent to which we should tolerate the intolerant often involves drawing a line between those things the state can or should tolerate without repugnance and those things for which toleration should be viewed as inappropriate (*A Theory of Justice*, Section 35).

People sometimes hold beliefs we consider morally repugnant. Sincerity does not preempt rational discourse about those beliefs or moral blame for them, however. That misogynists and homophobes may consider themselves moral people does not mean that they are, only that they think they are (or that they may be in some aspects of their lives but not in others). Denying the conceptual possibility that others actually believe what they profess amounts to denying the very possibility of morally acceptable pleasure in the setbacks of others. For there could be no morally acceptable pleasure in the suffering of others if we did not take our beliefs to be true, just as they do theirs. Denying the sincerity of others involves intolerance on some fundamental level. And so we find ourselves in a world in which people disagree over *Schadenfreude*. Until the world around us agrees on whether I deserve my suffering today, there will be disagreement over whether to call your pleasure "*Schadenfreude*" or "malicious glee."

The question of impunity of moral beliefs arises within a social framework here, as *Schadenfreude* does. It might be thought that Nietzsche or Freud saw little benefit in public life, but this would be wrong. Although Freud criticized what he took to be the excessive constraints of civilization, he freely acknowledged the import of social justice in holding communities together. We keep the species going at a price, Freud saw, but we have to pay that price. Indeed, he affirmed in *Civilization and Its Discontents* that human life in common is only made possible when the power of the community is set up in opposition to the power of the individual.

Rousseau, Schopenhauer, and Nietzsche (among others) all reached this same conclusion before Freud. Social justice, arbitrary and unstable as it may seem, stands as a precondition of sorts even for having a personal life. Our private *Schadenfreude* can reveal something telling about the communities we inhabit. For our thoughts about social justice precede *Schadenfreude*.

I do not mean to suggest that since values collide there are no reasons for choosing one over another. There are doubtless better and worse reasons for espousing values. A real problem here is that religious believers insist on a kind of moral impunity for their beliefs in or about justice. The way in which Orthodox Jews, Roman Catholics, and Muslims treat women within their communities has enraged many, both from within these traditions and outside. (The treatment of women is only one case in point.) Plato's point in the *Crito* was that a community faces danger and decay when its members are no longer sensitive to the need to criticize and revise the community's form of life in the light of new experience and exigencies. That we do not include ourselves in a particular moral tradition should not in itself bar us from criticizing that tradition. I see nothing wrong with criticism, whether of our own communities or traditions or of others'.

Punishing an innocent person for a crime he or she did not commit is unjust even when those who punish believe in the person's guilt. If we may do an injustice to people merely by falsely believing they deserve a misfortune, then that injustice is caused by our belief. Our beliefs are in some frustrating way inadequate, for believing that we possess the truth is not enough to avoid injustice. We may believe, for instance, that the earth is flat and that those who disagree do not deserve research grants. Similarly, we may believe that it is immoral for a woman to leave her children in a daycare center while she pursues a career. Our moral beliefs can result in injustice to others.

Schadenfreude offers us a double lesson: people whom we take to be cruel or unjust may believe themselves righteous and just, and our moral assessment of ourselves as good may anger or amaze others.

Now, as ever, it is important to fight against systems of domination and repression. As Jaggar shows us, emotions can be an important instrument in this fight.

Knowing Limits

What separates Nietzsche from Alison Jaggar is not whether outlaw emotions, which are functions of disavowal, do or do not reveal hidden sources of morality (yes), but whether these hidden sources merit scrutiny. Through a discussion of two disavowal strategies, I have suggested that a (masculine) sense of cultural superiority, like an aversion to women, counts as a source of morality that holds significant explanatory power. Identifying this source of morality serves the same end as the repression of outlaw emotions: it exposes a moral theory's blind spot.

The position I impute to Jaggar involves two claims: that the *Schadenfreude* of women is largely justified and that an examination of the circumstances responsible for its generation can make morality less oppressive. Were Jaggar to praise social impotence as an outlaw emotion, Nietzsche would surely dismiss her ethics as an example of *ressentiment*, a baleful and originally religiously motivated inversion that he takes to corrupt Western morality. Jaggar makes no such recommendation, but she does claim the oppressed enjoy a certain "epistemological privilege." The question whether this privilege is one worth having is a moral one, for it plays off of the tendency to value something or someone in terms of how that person or thing is *known*. Nietzsche lacks what Alison Jaggar knows.

Conclusion

The Moral Problem of *Schadenfreude*

> For if justice goes, there is no longer any value to
> men's living on the earth.
> —Kant, *The Metaphysics of Morals*

> See how yond justice rails upon yond simple thief.
> Hark in thine ear: change places: and handy-dandy,
> which is the justice, which is the thief?
> —*King Lear* (4.6.156)

SOME PEOPLE HELP US; SOME PEOPLE HURT US. SOME PEOPLE ARE HELPED
by us; some people are harmed by us. That's life. There is no changing
this. We can, however, increase the store of happiness in our little worlds
by treating others well.

I have focused on misfortune and suffering in terms of what we believe
others deserve. We morally withhold some or all of our compassion for
those who suffer if we believe that they have brought their suffering upon
themselves. I have talked about harm in terms of judging others, not physically attacking them.

We are free to judge harshly people who suffer. However, we do well
to remember an ancient exhortation: judge as ye shall be judged. Mercy, I
am persuaded, unleashes a kind of satisfaction every bit as profound as revenge can.

I have presented *Schadenfreude*, the morally acceptable kind of pleasure in the setbacks of others, as an emotional corollary of justice. I have
contrasted *Schadenfreude* with *ressentiment*, which I take to be an in-
grained moral failing.

Foucault once remarked that all of Nietzsche's work was no more than "the exegesis of a few Greek words."[1] This study might be aptly described as the exegesis of a German word and a French one Germanicized by Nietzsche. I believe that one cannot properly understand Nietzsche's highly influential theory of *ressentiment* without understanding what is at stake in the moral problem of *Schadenfreude*. The moral problem of *Schadenfreude* is threefold. First, there is widespread confusion about the normative moral acceptability of taking pleasure in the suffering of a person whose *contretemps* is either trivial or a result of having trespassed justice. Second, this confusion over the normative status of *Schadenfreude* may give rise to self-deceitful attempts to persuade ourselves that we take pleasure in the knowledge that another suffers, as opposed to taking pleasure in the actual suffering itself. Third, this same confusion no doubt invites mental efforts to rationalize as justified the suffering we fear or otherwise cannot understand.

An examination of the pain and humiliation from which *Schadenfreude* blooms contributes to moral progress as it strains and clarifies conventional standards of justice and the appropriateness of suffering. The temptation to define *Schadenfreude* according to which instances of happiness in others' suffering we find acceptable provokes very difficult questions about justice and punishment. Feminist thinkers did not need Nietzsche to show them how easily and subtly justice degenerates into injustice, and how powerful groups assert the right to define what justice represents. Feminists already knew that powerful groups use notions of justice to disguise systems of domination. Many volumes of political philosophy have addressed the question of whether justice can be disinterested. The temptation to define *Schadenfreude* on the basis of suffering we consider justified leads to the old question of whether justice veils our self-interest. Through excerpts from the writings of mainstream religious thinkers, St. Thomas Aquinas and Bernard Häring, I have raised doubts about the possibility of our generating the kind of norms of justice that would or could satisfy a broad spectrum of people in a diverse society. That said, religious norms did not seem any more or less suspect than secular ones.

Nietzsche, of course, considered justice a rationalization for self-interest. This self-interest could create wide social ties, uniting entire groups (as for example, Jews, women, lesbian and gay people, even Nietzschean nobles). If justice could be shown as a kind of solidarity with others like ourselves, then my defense of *Schadenfreude* as an emotional corollary of (disinterested) justice would crumble. But my agreement with Nietzsche is not complete, for I want to hold on to the possibility of a purely punitive, non-retributivistic kind of justice.

Nietzsche's opposition to my position would not end here. He found the impulse to read wrongdoing into human suffering a silly superstition. The very idea of *Schadenfreude* as an emotional corollary of justice relies on the legitimacy of such a relation of cause and effect. Although I have labored to present *Schadenfreude* as a function of rationality, Nietzsche would insist that I have missed the point. One of Nietzsche's most famous passages (*GM* I, Section 13) challenges "the popular mind" to rethink lightning and its flash. Nietzsche insists that there is no "being" behind doing; "the doer" is merely a fiction added to the deed, he tells us, and the deed is everything. Whether we attribute the misfortunes of another to God, the invisible hand of justice, or whatever, we deceive ourselves. Misfortunes simply happen.

Schadenfreude is not so much a problem in and of itself on Nietzsche's terms, as a symptom of a much deeper problem, that of believing in the "fiction" of justice. There is no justice at work in suffering, Nietzsche says, which means that there is no justice at work in *Schadenfreude*. Although religious thinkers such as Maimonides and Rabbi Kushner have conceded the randomness of suffering, popular forms of religious belief continue to support causal links between human suffering and divine retribution.

Aside from the exception of trivial misfortunes, I have allowed this very link between "the doer" and the deed. I am willing to forbear "the popular mind" quite a bit more than Nietzsche is. Perhaps Nietzsche misses an important point, namely that people genuinely take their beliefs to be true. Whether or not God exists, people can believe in God. This means that people who attribute a neighbor's suffering to God can reasonably defend pleasure in what they take to be the spectacle of justice.

The moral problem of *Schadenfreude* raises a question about the sincerity of our beliefs. The problem leads us back to a long-standing debate between retributivist and utilitarian views of punishment. While allowing that pleasure in the suffering of others might stem from an objective concern for justice, I have expressed doubt about the frequency of that kind of morally acceptable pleasure. I have leaned on Nietzsche and Durkheim to question whether celebrating suffering differs fundamentally from exalting justice. If we agree with Nietzsche that justice amounts to revenge, then *Schadenfreude* as I have presented it here once again fails on its own terms. For if justice is simply revenge, then there can be nothing disinterested about *Schadenfreude*. Here again I part ways with Nietzsche: I am willing to believe in the possibility of disinterested justice, a response to wrongdoing that has nothing to do with revenge. That some people whose job it is to administer punishment (judges, prison officers, high school principals) may take sadistic pleasure in their professional work does not mean that all do. Nietzsche would say that my skepticism about disinterested justice does not reach far enough.

My measured faith in selfless justice gives way to ambivalence about the moral acceptability of *Schadenfreude*. I stand to the right of Nietzsche, but to the left of most moral philosophers (certainly far to the left of Schopenhauer). Though moral thinkers have deplored *Schadenfreude*, they have extolled the love of justice. An emotional schizophrenia of sorts results from this conceptual polarization, and the unspoken lesson we learn is that *Schadenfreude* is to be tamped down deep within the psyche, or at least deep enough not to threaten our reputations as good neighbors. Gossip and laughter are the precarious chinks in the armor of disguise; they stand as the chief behavioral manifestations of pleasure in the suffering of others.

A commitment to justice or a personal loyalty is not the only catalyst for *Schadenfreude* I have presented. The judgment of appropriate suffering may have less to do with justice than envy or malice. Unlike the *Schadenfreude* of justice, the pleasure in the suffering of others which is motivated by and constituted by malice must always be condemned (for the same reasons we condemn malice). I have suggested that this second kind of pleasure be referred to as "malicious glee." Though malicious glee remains unethical, the cognition of appropriateness (or triviality), together with the fact of passivity, may excuse *Schadenfreude* as morally acceptable. When it springs from an abhorrence of evil or injustice, *Schadenfreude* might even be considered exemplary.

Schadenfreude restricts its object to trivial or appropriate suffering. Despite the impossibility of definitively marking off trivial from non-trivial suffering, we may expect some consensus on what kinds of misfortune are serious enough to merit sympathy. *Schadenfreude,* which issues from an honest belief about trivial suffering, lies at the heart of laughter, and is recommended by Kant as a valuable asset that helps us get through life. *Schadenfreude* whose object is cognized as appropriate suffering may be a direct, though not necessary, result of caring about justice, and caring about justice remains a moral good (this formulation consciously combines both the "ethic of care" of feminism and the "ethic of justice" of Rawls). Part of the problem of *Schadenfreude* is that it has inaccurately been represented as aberrant and wicked. It is neither.

The vehemence with which thinkers, both religious and atheistic, have attacked *Schadenfreude* has exacerbated and clouded the moral question of appropriate suffering. And though moral censure of the emotion, or the expression of it, often takes forms sufficiently crude to be ignored, it is important to remember that the roots of *Schadenfreude*-fear are deep. Too deep, it seems, for exploration by those who, after their own fashion, equate hostility with the very idea of such pleasure. The vestiges of Jewish and Christian morality are especially apparent in secular reflection on compassion and human suffering.

Philosophically, the assumption that benevolence must aim at the *full* good of another works to collapse any distinction between *Schadenfreude* and malice. Religiously, the particular visions of appropriate suffering that various creeds generate blur the boundary between human satisfaction and divine *Schadenfreude*. What is most surprising is that our most conspicuous producers of codes of appropriate suffering should purport to be dead set against the idea that persons might take pleasure in the suffering of others.

Contrary to the view that *Schadenfreude* is diabolical, I advanced the notion that *Schadenfreude* is an ordinary object of rational assessment, not a knee-jerk reaction motivated by malice. Here is the pivotal question about the object of our pleasure: is it the actual suffering of another person or simply the fact that another person suffers? Kant, Aquinas, Bernard Häring, and many others have relied upon a distinction the legitimacy of which I question. I allow that pleasure in the injury of another person might not involve any benefit to ourselves whatsoever; however, I suspect that this purely non-selfish desire is quite rare. More often than not, pleasure surrounding the suffering of others probably involves both objects, namely *that* another suffers and his or her actual suffering. Beyond this, I have expressed skepticism about the ideas of hating the sin but not the sinner and laughing *with* someone, as opposed to laughing *at* someone. Mental gymnastics of this sort require such dedicated training that few ever master the routines expected of us.

The persistent theme running through this study is that emotional responses to suffering involve reason. The moral appropriateness of our emotional responses partly depends on their making sense within their respective contexts. There is more to know about *Schadenfreude* than this. It is a complex concept that feeds on conventional standards of morality — especially those of compassion, punishment, and equality — as well as personal ideals which may conflict with such standards. The morality we choose will color the world we inhabit. Our version of who the bad guys are and what people deserve will shape both our actions and our emotions.

Ultimately, we decide for ourselves what constitutes appropriate or trivial suffering. The possibility for self-deceit lurks here, as well as in the shame triggered by a realization that one cannot or does not feel compassion. Though *Schadenfreude* arises from the suffering of others, it may, when coupled with bad conscience, generate a new, internal pain of its own — what Nietzsche termed *ressentiment*. Nietzsche knew that suffering tends to bring out the worst in people and realized that we are most likely to relish the consolation others' suffering can provide when we are most vulnerable ourselves. We are least likely to give in to this pleasure when we feel ourselves to be least vulnerable. I have presented *Schadenfreude* not so much as a function of psychological extremes, though, as of a feeling that justice has been served or, following Nietzsche, as a revolt against the "spirit of gravity." To the extent that *Schadenfreude* centers on appropriate suffering, I have suggested that a theory of *Schadenfreude* might grow into a social or religious theory of misfortune.

It would be naive simply to say that Christians profess mercy and forgiveness toward all and that any *Schadenfreude* Christians feel would be hypocritical. Mercy and forgiveness can be ways of evading justice, and justice can hardly be separated from compassion in Jewish and Christian theology. Once we understand that mercy and forgiveness can be thought of as ways of tolerating or even encouraging wrongdoing, we see how important it is for Jews and Christians to expect punishment for wrongdoers. Forgiveness is consistent with punishment, for to ignore or dismiss the trespass against rules or beliefs which makes punishment appropriate may be taken to disrespect those rules or beliefs.

With so many different believers invoking God to justify their joy at others' suffering, it seems appropriate to present the invocation of God as among the most vexing of all those values which generate *Schadenfreude*.

Despite Kafka's careful use of the term in his *Brief an den Vater* and Peter Gay's purposeful choice in *My German Question*, I have resisted hanging too much on the German provenance of the word *Schadenfreude*. *Schadenfreude* did not enter the German language through the pen of Kant or Schopenhauer, nor exculpation of it from the works of Nietzsche. These influential thinkers were articulating a social phenomenon already a part of German culture just as much as they were contributing to moral assessment of that reaction. To view these Germans as serving both these ends is useful for two reasons: one, we refrain from thinking of them as utterly different from us; and two, we realize that the evaluation — and, by extension, the definition — of *Schadenfreude* is itself open to question.

I have agreed with Schopenhauer that *Schadenfreude* is a function of distance, that is, of the separateness between the *schadenfroh* person and the other whose suffering occasions pleasure. The greater the degree to which someone else resembles us, the greater the degree to which we will likely feel compassion for him or her. In everyday life some people adopt the perspective of a surgeon, a jailor, or a fanatical sports fan, habitually distancing themselves from others in order to finish a day's work. I have discussed the problem that separateness (as opposed to solidarity) poses and pointed out the difficulty of simply insisting that we empathize with others in order to overcome the manifest separateness of persons. It is the awareness of whether and how the sufferer agonizes that makes the cruel person cruel. Empathy may lead to cruelty as well as compassion.

Schadenfreude tells us something important about how a person views the world — what constitutes suffering and what counts as an appropriate response to it. Through examining *Schadenfreude*, we can better see genetic, psychological, and social assumptions which mold our characters. Understanding the evaluative premises inherent in *Schadenfreude* can increase our sensitivity to the particular details of the pain and humiliation of other, unfamiliar sorts of people. These evaluative assumptions enter into the vast majority of our common-sense judgments and opinions — we live by them. They evolve and we may hardly notice the change. Investigation of these assumptions and presuppositions can reveal what is unique in the outlook of a person or an age.

Because it does not fit received ideas, my normative defense of *Schadenfreude* can help us to see ourselves and others in new ways. Others may consider us to be acting cruelly though we ourselves do not. An increased sensitivity to pain and humiliation should strengthen our imaginative ability to think of strangers as fellow-sufferers and should prompt us to examine how we ourselves may perpetuate or exacerbate the suffering of others. As an explanatory category, *Schadenfreude* can inform ethical analysis in a way that studies of malice and hatred have not. And as an event that focuses our moral attention on another person, *Schadenfreude* can alert us to power structures and social forces through which our characters both take shape and shape the lives of those around us.

Although we stand alone, we live in communities. Our suffering involves other people. They are a part of many of the bad things that happen to us, just as we are a part of many of the bad things that happen to them. Distressing as it may initially sound, we naturally take pleasure in many of the misfortunes of others. Our moral beliefs and principles often lead us to conclude that others deserve their misfortunes. There is no point in torturing ourselves over the social inevitability of moral disagreement. We would do better to embrace moral conflict as a compelling reason to search our beliefs for evidence of oppression, abuse, or self-aggrandizement. More practically, we would do better to worry about how our communities can foster self-esteem in everyone. It would be foolish to conclude that people who like themselves harm others less, but it stands to reason that people who dislike themselves will find it hard to sympathize with others. Treating ourselves and others well animates and guides moral philosophy.

The introduction to this study took shape around a remark Kant makes in the *Critique of Practical Reason*, a remark which relies on an implicit notion of moral appropriateness. This appropriateness justifies our approving of the suffering of the guilty. How plausible is it psychologically to approve of the suffering of another without celebrating that suffering? This is a restatement, in the form of a question, of Augustine's exhortation to love the sinner but hate the sin. We may on occasion find it extremely difficult to hold our view of who someone is apart from our view of what he or she does.

Justice, like comedy, presupposes respect for the boundaries of personal dignity. In justice and comedy we stand united with others in common humanness. Revenge and malice separate us from them. The challenge we face is to distinguish justice from revenge on the one hand and comedy from malice on the other. This can be extremely difficult. It seems unlikely that someone will be cheered by the news that we are laughing with him (in comedy), not at him. It also seems unlikely that someone will be cheered by the idea that we approve of his prison sentence because of our love of justice, not because he will suffer terribly.

Ultimately, pleasure in others' misfortunes is as difficult to defend as it is to condemn. Both the identification and the appraisal of this outlaw emotion lead to moral and religious conflict.

The compassionate and long-suffering slave Baby Suggs, from Morrison's novel *Beloved*, came to believe shortly before her death that there was "no such thing as bad luck in the world, only white people." White people somehow caused all the bad things that happened to black people. Was Baby Suggs right? I have argued on the one hand that we ought not to view suffering as an effect of some hidden cause (and that Baby Suggs must be wrong) and on the other hand that the very principles by which we lead our lives harm others (and that Baby Suggs might be right). Few among us would now dispute that Baby Suggs was right in some way. The white people who enslaved and humiliated her no doubt acted kindly toward other (white) people. Baby Suggs grasped the dual roles most of us play in the world: we are ourselves the good things that happen to some people, and the bad things that happen to other people.

Notes

Introduction

1. Immanuel Kant, *Critique of Practical Reason*, trans. Lewis White Beck (Indianapolis: Bobbs-Merrill, 1956), p. 63.

2. C.D. Broad, "Emotion and Sentiment," in *Critical Essays in Moral Philosophy* (London: Allen and Unwin, 1971), p. 293.

3. Arlie Russell Hochschild, "Emotion Work, Feeling Rules, and Social Structure," in *American Journal of Sociology* 85 (1979): 572–573.

4. Richard Rorty, *Contingency, Irony, and Solidarity* (Cambridge: Cambridge University Press, 1989), p. 192.

Chapter One

1. Friedrich Nietzshe, *On the Genealogy of Morals*, trans. Walter Kaufmann (New York: Vintage, 1989), p. 57. Hereafter, *GM*.

2. Arthur Danto, *Nietzsche as Philosopher* (New York: Macmillan, 1965).

3. Arthur Schopenhauer, *The World as Will and Representation*, 2 vols., trans. E.F.J. Payne (New York: Dover Publications, 1969), vol. 2, pp. 171–172. Hereafter, *WWR*.

4. Franz Kafka, *Brief an den Vater* (Frankfurt: Fischer, 1992), p. 24. The translation is my own.

5. David Lodge, *Paradise News* (New York: Viking, 1992), p. 148.

6. H. Richard Niebuhr, *The Purpose of the Church and Its Ministry* (New York: Harper, 1956), p. 35.

7. Camille Paglia, "Junk Bonds and Corporate Raiders," in *Sex, Art, and American Culture* (New York: Vintage, 1992), p. 247.

8. C. Fred Alford, *What Evil Means to Us* (Ithaca: Cornell University Press, 1997), pp. 70–71.

9. Colin McGinn, *Ethics, Evil, and Fiction* (Oxford: Clarendon Press, 1996), p. 66.

10. Jon Elster, *The Cement of Society: A Study of Social Order* (Cambridge: Cambridge University Press, 1995), p. 256.

11. *Webster's New Collegiate Dictionary* defines "gloat" as "to observe or think about something with great and often greedy or malicious satisfaction, gratification, or delight." The lack of surprise is not explicit in this definition, and neither is the notion of misfortune.

12. Michel de Montaigne, "On Vanity," in *The Complete Essays of Montaigne*, trans. Donald Frame (Stanford: Stanford University Press, 1948), p. 729.

13. Robert Nozick, *Anarchy, State and Utopia* (New York: Basic Books, 1974), p. 239.

14. John Rawls, *A Theory of Justice* (Cambridge, Mass.: Harvard University Press, 1971), p. 532.

15. Melanie Klein, "Envy and Gratitude," in *"Envy and Gratitude" and Other Works*, vol. 3 of *The Writings of Melanie Klein*, ed. R.E. Money-Kyrle (New York: Free Press, 1975), p. 189.

16. Lucretius, *De Rerum Natura*, trans. Rolfe Humphries (Bloomington: Indiana University Press, 1969), p. 52.

17. Immanuel Kant, *Lectures on Ethics*, trans. Louis Infield (London: Methuen and Co., 1930), p. 219. Reprinted in *Vice and Virtue in Everyday Life*, ed. Christina Hoff Sommers (New York: Harcourt Brace Jovanovich, 1985), pp. 271–279. In the same passage Kant approves of gossip and taking pleasure in the fall of a rich man.

18. Iris Murdoch, *The Black Prince* (New York: Penguin, 1973), pp. 28–29. Vittorio Falsina kindly shared this passage with me.

19. Charles Dickens, *Great Expectations* (London: Oxford University Press, 1965), pp. 409–410.

20. Charles Dickens, *Our Mutual Friend* (New York: Random House, 1960), p. 132.

21. Richard Rorty, *Contingency, Irony, and Solidarity*, p. 189.

22. Judith Shklar, *Ordinary Vices* (Cambridge, Mass.: Harvard University Press, 1984), p. 8.

23. Judith Shklar, "The Liberalism of Fear," in Nancy Rosenblum's anthology *Liberalism and the Moral Life* (Cambridge, Mass.: Harvard University Press, 1989), p. 29.

24. Benedict de, *The Philosophy of Spinoza*, edited by Joseph Ratner (New York: The Modern Library, 1927), pp. 281–282.

Chapter Two

1. John Forrester, *Truth Games: Lies, Money, and Psychoanalysis* (Cambridge, Mass.: Harvard University Press, 1997), p. 171.

2. Richard McBrien, *Catholicism: Study Edition* (Minneapolis: Winston Press, 1981), pp. 151–162. Emphasis added.

3. Barbara Goodwin, *Justice By Lottery* (Chicago: University of Chicago Press, 1992), p. 144.

4. Paul Tournier, *Guilt and Grace: A Psychological Study*, trans. Arthur W. Heathcote (New York: Harper and Row, 1962), p. 174.

5. Karl Marx, *Early Writings*, trans. and ed. Rodney Livingstone and Gregor Benton (New York: Vintage, 1975), p. 201.

6. See *The Social Importance of Self-Esteem*, ed. Andrew M. Mecca, Neil J. Smelser, and John Vasconcellos (Berkeley: University of California Press, 1989).

7. *Francis Bacon: The Essays*, ed. John Pitcher (New York: Penguin, 1985), p. 85.

8. John Rawls, *A Theory of Justice* (Cambridge, Mass.: Harvard University Press, 1971), p. 440. Rawls argues that a well-ordered society is unlikely to give rise to feelings of envy because material inequalities are likely to be comparatively small (pp. 536–537) and because the worst off are more likely to accept them since they know they work to their advantage and are allowed to exist only because they work to their advantage (pp. 177–179, 496–499).

9. Both Nietzsche, the originator of the term, and Max Scheler, the principal phenomenologist of the reaction, used the French word *ressentiment*. It has become widely accepted within the German language. The English notion of resentment, indicating indignation or bitter feelings against some person or situation, is not equivalent in its impact or generality to the French notion of *ressentiment*. I will discuss the import of this distinction more fully in Chapter Seven.

10. Bernhard Schlink, *The Reader*, trans. Carol Brown Janeway (New York: Vintage, 1998), p. 157.

11. Sigmund Freud, *Group Psychology and the Analysis of the Ego*, trans. James Strachey (London: Hogarth Press, 1959), p. 51f. (As cited in Rawls, *A Theory of Justice*, p. 439.)

12. *Critical Inquiry* 20 (1994): 569. See also Wendy Kaminer's cover story "The Last Taboo" in *The New Republic*, 14 October 1996, pp. 24–32.

13. Charles Baudelaire, "On the Essence of Laughter," in *The Mirror of Art*, trans. and ed. Jonathan Mayne (New York: Phaidon Press Ltd., 1955), p. 135. French passages are taken from the Gallimard edition *Oeuvres complétes*, vol. 2..

14. *The Collected Dialogues of Plato*, ed. Edith Hamilton and Huntington Cairns (Princeton: Princeton University Press, 1980), 50d, p. 1132.

15. Sigmund Freud, *Jokes and Their Relation to the Unconscious* (Standard Edition), trans. James Strachey (New York: W.W. Norton, 1989), pp. 121–122.

Chapter Three

1. Mark Zborowski, "Cultural Components in Responses to Pain," in C. Clark and H. Robboy, eds., *Social Interaction* (New York: St. Martin's, 1992).

2. Marcel Proust, *Remembrance of Things Past,* trans. C.K. Scott Moncrieff and Terence Kilmartin, 3 vols. (New York: Vintage, 1982), vol. 3, p. 561.

3. Ludwig Wittgenstein, *Philosophical Investigations*, trans. G.E.M. Anscombe (Oxford: Basil Blackwell, 1953).

4. Tristram Engelhardt, *The Foundations of Bioethics* (New York: Oxford University Press, 1986), p. 113.

5. Richard Posner, *Overcoming Law* (Cambridge, Mass.: Harvard University Press, 1995), p. 448.

6. Fyodor Dostoyevsky, *Crime and Punishment*, trans. Richard Pevear and Larissa Volokhonsky (New York: Vintage, 1993), p. 180.

7. Peter Gay, *My German Question* (New Haven: Yale University Press, 1998), p. 83.

8. Thomas Hardy, *The Return of the Native* (New York: Oxford University Press, 1990), p. 206.

9. See Aaron Ben-Ze'ev, "Pleasure-in-Others'-Misfortune," in *Iyyun, The Jerusalem Philosophical Quarterly* 41 (1992): 41–61; "Another Look at Pleasure-in-Others'-Misfortune," *Iyyun, The Jersualem Philosophical Quarterly* 42 (July 1993): 431–440; and footnote number 19 in his "Envy and Inequality" in *Journal of Philosophy* 89 (1992): 551–581.

10. William Ian Miller, *The Anatomy of Disgust* (Cambridge, Mass.: Harvard University Press, 1997), p. 291 n. 25.

11. William Ian Miller, *Humiliation* (Ithaca: Cornell University Press, 1993), p. 207.

12. Judith Shklar, *The Faces of Injustice* (New Haven: Yale University Press, 1990), p. 55.

13. Melvin Lerner, *The Belief in a Just World: A Fundamental Delusion* (New York: Plenum, 1980).

14. William James, *The Varieties of Religious Experience* (New York: The Modern Library, 1958), p. 50.

15. See H. Richard Niebuhr, *The Responsible Self* (New York: Harper and Row, 1963), pp. 58–60.

16. Elisabeth Young-Bruehl, *The Anatomy of Prejudices* (Cambridge, Mass.: Harvard University Press, 1996), pp. 3–4.

17. *The Letters of Vita Sackville-West to Virginia Woolf*, ed. Louise De-Salva and Mitchell Leaska (London: Hutchinson, 1984), p. 110.

18. Hubert Dreyfus and Paul Rabinow, *Michel Foucault: Beyond Structuralism and Hermeneutics* (Chicago: University of Chicago Press, 1982), p. 212.

19. According to William Frankena, the love commandment is so ambiguous that everything "depends on how one interprets it." See his *Ethics* (Englewood Cliffs: Prentice-Hall, 1963), p. 42. Three major interpretations of the love commandment follow here.

First, love of neighbor is interpreted as the core of morality and follows from the modest use of it in Leviticus and those New Testament passages in which the love commandment is presented as a concise summary of the Mosaic or natural moral law. Charitable giving to others in need is required, as long as the cost to the agent is not excessive.

Second, love of neighbor is identified by some Christian theologians who insist on the purity of heart stressed in the Sermon on the Mount. What counts before God are not only deeds but also dispositions. The demand for love "goes all the way down," to use a phrase from Foucault. It is this interpretation that implicates *Schadenfreude* in blameworthiness.

Quoted in Ernest Wallwork, *Psychoanalysis and Ethics* (New Haven: Yale University Press, 1991), p. 194.

20. Carol Gilligan, *In a Different Voice: Psychological Theory and Women's Development* (Cambridge, Mass.: Harvard University Press, 1982).

21. *Psychoanalysis and Ethics*, Chapter Nine. I have greatly benefited from Wallwork's analysis.

22. Erving Goffman, "Fun in Games," in *Encounters* (Indianapolis: Bobbs-Merrill, 1961), p. 23.

23. Arlie Russell Hochschild, "Emotion Work, Feeling Rules, and Social Structure," in *American Journal of Sociology* 85 (1979): 551–575.

Chapter Four

1. Arthur Schopenhauer, *On the Basis of Morality,* trans. E.F.J. Payne (Indianapolis: Bobbs-Merrill, 1965), p. 135. Hereafter, *OBM*.

2. After Schopenhauer, Karl Marx was later to say, "There is only one antidote to mental suffering, and that is physical pain." In a similar vein, Oscar Wilde once quipped, "God spare me physical pain and I'll take care of the

moral pain myself." Quoted in Elaine Scarry, *The Body in Pain* (New York: Oxford University Press, 1985), p. 33.

3. Charles Baudelaire, "On the Essence of Laughter," in *The Mirror of Art*, trans. and ed. Jonathan Mayne (New York: Phaidon Press Ltd., 1955), p 135. French passages are taken from the Gallimard edition *Oeuvres complètes*, vol. 2.

4. Sigmund Freud, *Civilization and Its Discontents* (1930), trans. and ed. James Strachey (New York: W.W. Norton, 1961), p. 36.

5. Sigmund Freud, *The Future of an Illusion* (Standard Edition), trans. and ed. James Strachey (New York: W.W. Norton, 1961), p. 12.

6. Schopenhauer makes suffering a function of self-esteem. Similarly, William James in 1890 measures self-esteem according to the ratio of one's successes to one's pretensions. *The Principles of Psychology*, 2 vols. (New York: Dover Publications, 1950), vol. 1, p. 310.

7. Early in the *Nichomachean Ethics* Aristotle acknowledges that happiness depends at least modestly on the cooperation of "externals," such things as good birth, good health, and good looks.

8. Thomas Nagel, "Moral Luck," in *Mortal Questions* (Cambridge: Cambridge University Press, 1979), p. 28.

9. Immanuel Kant, *The Metaphysics of Morals,* trans. Mary Gregor (Cambridge: Cambridge University Press, 1966), p. 207. Hereafter, *MM*. This work of 1797 should not be confused with the *Groundwork of the Metaphysics of Morals* (1785), an earlier volume that is sometimes treated as the definitive statement of Kant's moral philosophy but which, in fact, merely lays the foundation for the longer work.

10. Alasdair MacIntyre, *A Short History of Ethics* (London: Routledge and Kegan Paul, 1968), p. 221.

11. John E. Atwell, *Schopenhauer on the Character of the World: The Metaphysics of Will* (Berkeley: University of California Press, 1995), pp. 16–17.

12. *The Journal of Religious Ethics* 20 (1992): 38. It is perhaps unfair to single out Roberts here, as there are so many other philosophers who walk around the problem I'm pointing to without noticing the distinction I'm trying to establish. See, for example, S.I. Benn, "Wickedness," *Ethics* 95 (1985): 795–810. Mention of *Schadenfreude* is strangely neglected in his discussion of "Wickedness and Moral Luck." It is also conspicuously absent from J.C.B. Gosling's *Pleasure and Desire* (Oxford: Clarendon, 1969), especially pp. 162–163.

13. Robert C. Roberts, "What is Wrong With Wicked Feelings?," in *American Philosophical Quarterly* 28 (1991): 13–24.

14. The self-righteous person delights in the moral failings of others. There may be a genuinely internal connection between self-righteousness and *Schadenfreude*, for a self-righteous person may perceive the moral weaknesses of others as misfortunes.

15. Robert Gordon, *The Structure of the Emotions* (Cambridge: Cambridge University Press, 1987), p. 25.

16. Adam Smith, *The Theory of Moral Sentiments*, ed. D.D. Raphael and A.L. Macfie (Oxford: Clarendon Press, 1976), p. 21.

17. Bernard Williams, "Persons, Character, and Morality," in *Moral Luck: Philosophical Papers 1973–1980* (Cambridge: Cambridge University Press, 1981), p. 3.

18. Joseph Fletcher, *Situation Ethics* (Philadelphia: The Westminster Press, 1964), p. 94.

19. Bernard Williams, *Ethics and the Limits of Philosophy* (Cambridge, Mass.: Harvard University Press, 1985), p. 88.

20. R.M. Hare, *Moral Thinking* (New York: Oxford University Press, 1981).

21. See Marcia Baron, "The Alleged Moral Repugnance of Acting from Duty," *Journal of Philosophy* 81 (1984): 197–220.

22. Nietzsche takes Schopenhauer to mean *"teuflisch"* in both the subjective and the objective sense. See *Human, All Too Human*, Section 103.

23. Nobel laureate in economics George Stigler emphasized the effects of greed. His contribution to "public choice theory" tries to explain political outcomes by assuming that people, including politicians, pursue selfish interests, often in well-organized private groups. Another Nobel laureate, James Buchanan, enhanced "public choice theory" by proposing institutions to help counteract the baleful tendencies of human nature.

24. Candace Clark, *Misery and Company: Sympathy in Everyday Life* (Chicago: University of Chicago Press, 1997).

25. M.F.K. Fisher, *Stay Me, Oh Comfort Me* (New York: Pantheon, 1993), pp. 222–223.

26. Max Scheler, *The Nature of Sympathy*, trans. P.L. Heath (London: Routledge and Kegan Paul, 1954), p. 138.

27. Friedrich Nietzsche, *The Will to Power*, trans. Walter Kaufmann and R.J. Hollingdale (New York: Vintage, 1968), Section 962. Hereafter, *WP*.

Chapter Five

1. Friedrich Nietzsche, *Human, All Too Human*, trans. R.J. Hollingdale (Cambridge: Cambridge University Press, 1986), p 314. Hereafter, *HH*.

2. Friedrich Nietzsche, *On the Genealogy of Morals*, trans. Walter Kaufmann (New York: Vintage, 1989), p. 192. Compare p. 207 of the 1974 Vintage edition of *The Gay Science*, trans. Walter Kaufmann. For the use of the phrase "with a good conscience," compare Section 58 of *Beyond Good and Evil*: ". . . a genuinely religious class requires a leisure class, or half-leisure — I mean leisure with a good conscience . . ." (p. 69, Kaufmann translation). And for Nietzsche's estimation of laughter, see Section 294 ("The Olympian vice") of *Beyond Good and Evil*, as well as Walter Kaufmann's helpful footnote to it, in which he suggests that Nietzsche benefited from Hobbes's conclusion in *Leviathan* (1651) that laughing at the infirmities of others manifests weakness on the laugher's part.

3. Cf. William James, *The Varieties of Religious Experience* (New York: The Modern Library, 1958), pp. 48–49, 76. James rejects Havelock Ellis's claim that laughter of any sort may be considered a religious exercise, because it bears witness to the soul's emancipation. According to James, any *persistent* enjoyment (which would exclude *Schadenfreude*) may produce the sort of religion which consists in a grateful admiration of the gift of so happy an existence.

4. Friedrich Nietzsche, *Twilight of the Idols/Anti-Christ* (1888), trans. R.J. Hollingdale (New York: Penguin, 1990), p. 71. Hereafter, *A*.

5. I have benefited from Alexander Nehamas's discussion of suffering in *Nietzsche: Life as Literature* (Cambridge, Mass.: Harvard University Press, 1985), pp. 123–127.

6. Lawrence Blum, "Compassion," in *Explaining Emotions*, ed. Amélie Rorty (Los Angeles: University of California Press, 1980), pp. 507–517.

7. Immanuel Kant, *Critique of Practical Reason*, trans. Lewis White Beck (Indianapolis: Bobbs-Merrill, 1956), p. 123.

8. See his "Kant, Schopenhauer, and Nietzsche on the Morality of Pity" in *The Journal of the History of Ideas* 45 (1984): 83–98. I have benefited from his lucid discussion.

9. *Thus Spake Zarathustra* in *The Portable Nietzsche*, trans. and ed. Walter Kaufmann (New York: Vintage, 1968), Part I, "On the Pitying," p. 200. Hereafter, *Z*.

10. Julian Young, *Nietzsche's Philosophy of Art* (Cambridge: Cambridge University Press, 1992), Chapter Two.

11. George Stauth and Bryan S. Turner, *Nietzsche's Dance: Resentment,*

Reciprocity and Resistance in Social Life (Oxford: Basil Blackwell, 1988), p. 69. It is puzzling, then, that the authors proceed to use the English "resentment." R. Jay Wallace has also pointed to the advisability of retaining the French *ressentiment*. See his *Responsibility and the Moral Sentiments* (Cambridge, Mass.: Harvard University Press, 1994), pp. 246–247.

12. Max Scheler, *Ressentiment*, trans. Lewis B. Coser and William W. Holdheim (Milwaukee: Marquette University Press, 1994), p. 25.

13. Fredric Jameson, *The Political Unconscious* (Ithaca: Cornell University Press, 1980), p. 201.

14. Walter Kaufmann, *Nietzsche: Philosopher, Psychologist, Antichrist* (Princeton: Princeton University Press, 1974), p. 371.

15. See Mary Midgley, "Brutality and Sentimentality," *Philosophy* 54 (1979): 385–389; Mark Jefferson, "What is Wrong with Sentimentality?," *Mind* 92 (1983): 519–529; and John Kekes, *Facing Evil* (Princeton: Princeton University Press, 1990).

16. See, for example, G.J. Barker-Benfield's *The Culture of Sensibility: Sex and Society in Eighteenth-Century Britain* (Chicago: University of Chicago Press, 1992). Barker-Benfield discusses the ease with which sentiment became the object of consumption and the lachrymose values that meant, in Rostrig's words, that "happiness is to experience another's woe."

Simon Schama's discussion of sensibility in France during this period fills out this notion nicely. In *Citizens: A Chronicle of the French Revolution* (New York: Knopf, 1989) he remarks: "Lavish use of words like *tendresse* (tenderness) and *âme* (soul) conferred immediate membership in the community of Sensibility; and words that had been used more casually, like *amitié* (friendship), were invested with feelings of intense intimacy. Verbs like *s'enivrer* (to become drunk) when coupled with *plaisir* or *passion* became attributes of a noble rather than a depraved character. The key word was *sensibilité*: the intuitive capacity for intense feeling. To possess *un coeur sensible* (a feeling heart) was the precondition for morality" (p. 149).

See also Ann Douglas's *The Feminization of American Culture* (New York: Knopf, 1977). Douglas argues that feminization means sentimentality and lies, the craven reaction of women (and some men) to a culture that has marginalized them.

Chapter Six

1. Michel Foucault, *Discipline and Punish: The Birth of the Prison*, trans. Alan Sheridan (New York: Vintage, 1979), pp. 16, 101. Antony Flew has ar-

gued that punishment must be an evil or unpleasantness but need not be physically painful. See "The Justification of Punishment" in *Philosophy* 29 (1954): 291–307.

2. W.D. Ross, *The Right and the Good* (Oxford: Clarendon Press, 1930), pp. 56–64.

3. C.L. Ten provides a clear and quite useful account of the various theories of punishment in *Crime, Guilt and Punishment: A Philosophical Introduction* (Oxford: Clarendon Press, 1987), which I follow here. Particularly interesting is the exposition and defense of the theory that punishment restores the just equilibrium of benefits and burdens which was disturbed by the wrongdoer's act, pp. 52–65. Mark Tunick's *Punishment: Theory and Practice* (Berkeley: University of California Press, 1992) has also been helpful.

4. Joel Feinberg, "The Expressive Function of Punishment," in *Doing and Deserving: Essays in the Theory of Responsibility* (Princeton: Princeton University Press, 1970), p. 100.

5. *Jewish Social Ethics* (New York: Oxford University Press, 1992), p. 170.

6. Edmund Burke, *A Philosophical Enquiry into the Origin of our Ideas of the Sublime*, ed. James T. Boulton (Oxford: Basil Blackwell, 1987), p. 47.

7. Pieter Spierenburg, *The Spectacle of Suffering: Executions and the Evolution of Repression* (Cambridge: Cambridge University Press, 1984).

8. David Garland, *Punishment and Society* (New York: Oxford University Press, 1990).

9. Emile Durkheim, *The Division of Labor in Society*, trans. W.D. Halls (New York: Free Press, 1984), p. 44.

Chapter Seven

1. Jack Miles, *God: A Biography* (New York: Knopf, 1995), p. 11.

2. David Leavitt, "The Term Paper Artist," in *Arkansas: Three Novellas* (New York: Houghton Mifflin, 1997), p. 56.

3. Harold Kushner, *When Bad Things Happen to Good People* (New York: Schocken Books, 1981), p. 4. The popularity of Kushner's book points up the overlap of Judaism and Christianity I have in mind here.

4. M. O'C. Drury, "Conversations with Wittgenstein," in *Ludwig Wittgenstein, Personal Recollections*, ed. Rush Rhees (Oxford: Blackwell, 1981), p. 129.

5. Norman Malcolm, *Wittgenstein: A Religious Point of View?* (Ithaca: Cornell University Press, 1994), p. 7.

6. Eugene O'Neill, *Long Day's Journey into Night* (New Haven: Yale University Press, 1989), p. 107.

7. Arthur Danto, *Analytical Philosophy of Action* (New York: Cambridge University Press, 1973), p. 147.

8. Most of these scriptural references are from various passages in the *New Catholic Encyclopedia,* ed. William J. McDonald (New York: McGraw Hill, 1967).

9. Aquinas states in the *Summa Contra Gentiles*: "There would be no everlasting punishment of the souls of the damned if they were able to change their will for a better will" (4.93.2). Aquinas views the everlasting suffering of the damned as a function of their everlasting refusal to repent. But the idea that one may change one's mind, as it were, after the final judgment would seem to subvert the very notion of eternity, which depends upon the stability of permanence.

10. Saadya Gaon, or Saadya ben Joseph, *The Book of Beliefs and Opinions*, trans. Samuel Rosenblatt (New Haven: Yale University Press, 1948), pp. 351–352.

11. Dante Alighieri, *The Divine Comedy*, trans. with a commentary by Charles S. Singleton (Princeton: Princeton University Press, 1975), *Paradiso*, 27.22–27, p. 303.

12. Richard P. McBrien, *Catholicism: Study Edition* (Minneapolis: Winston Press, 1981), pp. 1150–1152.

13. Moses Maimonides, *The Guide of the Perplexed*, trans. Shlomo Pines (Chicago: University of Chicago Press, 1963), p. 469.

14. See R.T. Kendall, *Calvin and English Calvinism to 1649* (Oxford: Oxford University Press, 1979), p. 52.

15. John Stachniewski, *The Persecutory Imagination: English Puritanism and the Literature of Religious Despair* (Oxford: Clarendon Press, 1991), pp. 22–23. Quotations from Calvin's *Institution* are taken from these pages.

16. Sherwin B. Nuland, *How We Die* (New York: Vintage, 1995), p. 167.

17. David Novak, *Jewish Social Ethics* (Oxford: Oxford University Press, 1992), p. 105.

18. Bernard Häring, *Free and Faithful in Christ: Moral Theology for Clergy and Laity,* (New York: Seabury Press, 1978), 3 vols., vol. III, p. 47.

19. Bernard Häring, *The Law of Christ*, 3 vols., trans. Edwin G. Kaiser (Westminster: Newman Press, 1966), vol. 3, p. 220. Originally, *Das Gesetz Christ,* (1954). Hereafter, *LC.*

20. Bernard Häring, *Christian Renewal in a Changing World,* trans. Sr. Lucidia Häring (New York: Desclee, 1964), pp. 143–144.

21. Bernard Häring, *The Christian Existentialist: The Philosophy and*

Theology of Self-Fulfillment in Modern Society, trans. Sr. Lucidia Häring (New York: New York University Press, 1968), p. 42. Hereafter, *CE.*

22. The question of whether pride or cruelty properly ought to dominate the pecking order of human wrongdoing has generated an interesting debate. See Judith Shklar, *Ordinary Vices,* p. 44, and Richard Rorty, *Contingency, Irony, and Solidarity,* p. 173. Claiming that "cruelty is not the worst vice for the Kantian, as it is for the Humean," Annette Baier has applauded Shklar and Rorty and credited them with having "the Humean moral judgment" ("Moralism and Cruelty," in *Ethics* 103 [1993]: 437). For a critical response to Shklar and Rorty, see Timothy Jackson, "The Disconsolation of Theology," in the *Journal of Religious Ethics,* 20 (1992): 1–35, and John Kekes, *Against Liberalism* (Ithaca: Cornell University Press, 1997), pp. 183–192.

23. John Mahoney, S.J., *The Making of Moral Theology: A Study of the Roman Catholic Tradition* (Oxford: Clarendon Press, 1987), p. xiv.

24. Bernard Lewis, *Islam and the West* (New York: Oxford University Press, 1993), p. 6.

Chapter Eight

1. Thomas Hardy, *The Return of the Native,* (New York: Oxford University Press), p. 279.

2. Simone de Beauvoir, *Memoirs of a Dutiful Daughter,* trans. James Kirkup (New York: Harper and Row, 1959), p. 95.

3. Alison Jaggar, "Love and Knowledge: Emotion in Feminist Epistemology," in S.R. Bordo and A. Jaggar, eds., *Gender/Body/Knowledge: Feminist Reconstruction of Being and Knowing* (New Brunswick: Rutgers University Press, 1989), p. 145.

4. See Lionel Trilling's *The Liberal Imagination: Essays on Literature and Society* (New York: Harcourt Brace Jovanovich, 1979). He argues that the aim of "adversary culture" is to perform a massive transvaluation of values, to insinuate that what Jews and Christians have for centuries called sin is naturally a high form of liberation. See also Michael Novak, *The Catholic Ethic and the Spirit of Capitalism* (New York: Free Press, 1993). Novak contends that the "adversary culture" now governs the mainstream in the universities, the magazines, movies, and television. According to Novak it celebrates anti-bourgeois virtues and defines itself against the common culture which it scorns.

5. John Boswell, *Christianity, Social Tolerance, and Homosexuality* (Chicago: University of Chicago Press, 1980), p. 28n.

6. Dorrit Cohn, *Transparent Minds* (Princeton: Princeton University Press, 1978), p. 88.

7. Nicholas Rescher, *Unselfishness: The Role of the Vicarious Affects in Moral Philosophy and Social Theory* (Pittsburgh: University of Pittsburgh Press, 1975), p. 16.

8. Friedrich Nietzsche, *On the Genealogy of Morals*, trans. Walter Kaufmann (New York: Vintage, 1989), p. 192. As I have noted, this edition includes excerpts from a number of Nietzsche's other works, among them *The Gay Science*. Compare p. 207 of the 1974 Vintage edition of *The Gay Science*, trans. Walter Kaufmann.

9. Dutch, another language greatly influenced by German, does have a one-word equivalent: *leedvermaak* (which is not, however, a "loan word").

10. In Italian, for example, *Schadenfreude* is italicized and used rarely. See Primo Levi's felicitous usage in *I sommersi e I salvati* (translated as *The Drowned and the Saved*, by Raymond Rosenthal), in the section entitled "*La violenza inutile*" ("Useless Violence"). Stefano Albertini brought this passage to my attention.

11. Alasdair MacIntyre, *Three Rival Versions of Moral Inquiry* (South Bend: University of Notre Dame Press, 1990), p. 191.

12. Theodor Adorno, "On the Question: 'What is German?'," trans. Thomas Y. Levin, in *New German Critique* 36 (1985): 121–131, 129.

13. Victor Farias, *Heidegger and Nazism*, ed. Joseph Margolis and Tom Rockmore (Philadelphia: Temple University Press, 1989).

14. Anthony Kenny, *Action, Emotion, and Will* (London: Routledge and Kegan Paul, 1963), p. 13.

15. See the brief children's play *Die Schadenfreude: ein Kleines Lustspiel für Kinder mit Liederchen* (Stuttgart: Reclam) by Christian Weisse (1726–1804). See also Leo Spitzer, "Schadenfreude," in *Essays in Historical Semantics* (New York: S.F. Vanni, 1948); and Lutz Röhrich, *Der Witz: Figuren, Formen, Funktionen* (Stuttgart: J.B. Metzler, 1977), pp. 140, 174, 184, 188, 215, 242, 268.

16. Klaus Scherer, Harold Wallbott, Angela Summerfield, eds., *Experiencing Emotion: A Cross-Cultural Study* (Cambridge: Cambridge University Press, 1986), p. 4.

17. Batja Mesquita and Nico H. Frijda, "Cultural Variations in Emotions: A Review," in *Psychological Bulletin* 112 (1992): pp. 170–204. See also K.R. Scherer, H.G. Wallbott, D. Matsumoto, and T. Kudoh, "Emotional Experience in Cultural Context: A Comparison Between Europe, Japan, and the

United States," in *Facets of the Emotions*, ed. K.R. Scherer (Hillsdale, N.J.: Erlbaum, 1988), pp. 5–30.

18. Herman Melville, "Billy Budd, Sailor," in *Billy Budd, Sailor & Other Stories* (New York: Penguin, 1983), p. 355.

19. Claudia Card, *The Unnatural Lottery: Character and Moral Luck* (Philadelphia: Temple University Press), pp. 56–57. I follow Card closely in the next few paragraphs; her view of Kant and Schopenhauer is well founded and clearly staked out.

20. Immanuel Kant, *Observations on the Feeling of the Beautiful and the Sublime*, trans. John T. Goldthwait (Berkeley: University of California Press, 1960), p. 81. Hereafter, *OFBS*.

21. Arthur Schopenhauer, "On Women," in *Parerga and Paralipomena*, trans. E.F.J. Payne, 2 vols. (Oxford: Clarendon Press, 1974), vol. 1, p. 619.

22. Bryan Magee, *The Philosophy of Schopenhauer* (Oxford: Clarendon Press, 1983), pp. 322–325.

23. Susan Sontag, "Notes on 'Camp'" (1964), in *Against Interpretation* (New York: Doubleday, 1990), pp. 275–292.

24. See Marjorie Garber, "Jew, Woman, Homosexual," in *Vested Interests* (New York: Routledge, 1992), pp. 224–233.

25. *The Unnatural Lottery*, p. 53.

25. John Rawls, *A Theory of Justice*, Chapter Four, Sections 33–35. See also John Rawls, "Justice as Fairness: Political Not Metaphysical," *Philosophy and Public Affairs* 14 (Summer 1985): 308–322.

Conclusion

1. Michel Foucault, *The Order of Things* (New York: Pantheon, 1970), p. 298.

Works Consulted

Adams, Marilyn McCord. "Hell and the Justice of God." *Religious Studies* I (1975): 433–447.

Adorno, Theodor. "On the Question: 'What is German?'" Translated by Thomas Y. Levin. *New German Critique* 36 (1985): 121–131.

Alford, C. Fred. *What Evil Means to Us*. Ithaca: Cornell University Press, 1997.

Alighieri, Dante. *The Divine Comedy*. Translated by Charles S. Singleton. Princeton: Princeton University Press, 1975.

Aquinas, Thomas. *Summa Contra Gentiles*. Translated by Fathers of the English Dominicans. London: Burns, Oates & Washbourne Ltd., 1924.

_____. *Summa Theologiae*. Translated by Fathers of the English Dominican Province. London: Encyclopedia Britannica, Inc., 1952.

Aristotle. *The Basic Works of Aristotle*. Edited by Richard McKeon. New York: Random House, 1941.

Atwell, John E. *Schopenhauer on the Character of the World: The Metaphysics of Will*. Berkeley: University of California Press, 1995.

Bacon, Francis. *The Essays*. Edited by John Pitcher. New York: Penguin, 1985.

Baier, Annette. *Postures of the Mind: Essays on Mind and Morals*. London: Methuen, 1985.

_____. "Moralism and Cruelty." *Ethics* (1993): 436–457.

_____. "What Do Women Want in a Moral Theory?" *Nous* 19 (1985): 53–63.

Barbour, John. "Religious *Ressentiment* and Public Virtues." *The Journal of Religious Ethics* 11 (1983): 264–279.

Barker-Benfield, G.J. *The Culture of Sensibility: Sex and Society in Eighteenth-Century Britian*. Chicago: University of Chicago Press, 1992.

Baron, Marcia. "The Alleged Moral Repugnance of Acting from Duty." *The Journal of Philosophy* 81 (1984): 197–220.

Baudelaire, Charles. "On the Essence of Laughter." In *The Mirror of Art*. Translated and edited by Jonathan Mayne. New York: Phaidon Press Ltd., 1955.

de Beauvoir, Simone. *Memoirs of a Dutiful Daughter*. Translated by James Kirkup. New York: Harper and Row, 1959.

Benn, S.I. "Wickedness." *Ethics* 95 (1985): 795–810.

Bernstein, Michael. *Bitter Carnival*. Princeton: Princeton University Press, 1992.

Ben-Ze'ev, Aaron. "Another Look at Pleasure-in-Other's-Misfortune." *Iyyun, The Jerusalem Philosophical Quarterly* 42 (1993): 431–581.

_____. "Envy and Inequality." *Journal of Philosophy* 89 (1992): 551–581.

_____. "Pleasure-in-Other's-Misfortune." *Iyyun, The Jerusalem Philosophical Quarterly* 41 (1992): 41–61.

Blum, Lawrence. "Compassion." In *Explaining Emotions*. Edited by Amélie Rorty. Los Angeles: University of California Press, 1980.

_____. "Kant's and Hegel's Moral Rationalism: A Feminist Perspective." *Canadian Journal of Philosophy* 12 (1982): 287–302.

Boswell, John. *Christianity, Social Tolerance, and Homosexuality*. Chicago: University of Chicago Press, 1980.

Broad, C.D. "Emotion and Sentiment." In *Critical Essays in Moral Philosophy*. London: Allen and Unwin, 1971.

Bultmann, Rudolf. *Die Geschichte der synoptishcen Tradition*. Göttingen: Vandenhoeck and Ruprecht, 1961.

Burgh, Richard W. "Do the Guilty Deserve Punishment?" *Journal of Philosophy* 79 (1982): 193–210.

Burke, Edmund. *A Philosophical Enquiry into the Origin of our Ideas of the Sublime and Beautiful*. Edited by James T. Boulton. Oxford: Basil Blackwell, 1987.

Burton, Robert. *The Anatomy of Melancholy: What it is, with all the kinds, causes, symptomes, prognostikes, and severall cures of it*. Edited by Flloyd Bell and Paul Jordan-Smith. New York: Tudor, 1938.

Calhoun, Cheshire. "Justice, Care, Gender Bias." *Journal of Philosophy* 85 (1988): 451–463.

Callan, Eamonn. "The Moral Status of Pity." *Canadian Journal of Philosophy* 18 (1988): 1–12.

Card, Claudia. *The Unnatural Lottery: Character and Moral Luck*. Philadelphia: Temple University Press, 1996.

Cartwright, David. "Kant, Schopenhauer, and Nietzsche on the Morality of Pity." *The Journal of the History of Ideas* 45 (1984): 83–98.

Casey, Edward S. "Imagining and Remembering." *Review of Metaphysics* 31 (1977): 187–209.

Clark, Candace. *Misery and Company: Sympathy in Everyday Life*. Chicago: University of Chicago Press, 1977.

Cohn, Dorrit. *Transparent Minds*. Princeton: Princeton University Press, 1978.

Danto, Arthur. *Analytical Philosophy of Action*. Cambridge: Cambridge University Press, 1973.

_____. *Nietzsche as Philosopher*. New York: Macmillan, 1965.

DeSalva, Louise, and Mitchell Leaska, editors. *The Letters of Vita Sackville-West to Virginia Woolf*. London: Hutchinson, 1984.

deSousa, Ronald. *The Rationality of Emotion*. Cambridge: MIT Press, 1987.

Dickens, Charles. *Great Expectations*. London: Oxford University Press, 1965.

_____. *Our Mutual Friend*. New York: Random House, 1960.

Donne, John. Devotions upon Emerged Occasions. Edited by Anthony Raspa. Montreal: McGill-Queen's University Press, 1975.

Dostoyevsky, Fyodor. *Crime and Punishment*. Translated by Richard Pevear and Larissa Volokhonsky. New York: Vintage, 1993.

Douglas, Ann. *The Feminization of American Culture*. New York: Knopf, 1977.

Dreyfus, Hubert, and Paul Rabinow. *Michel Foucault: Beyond Structuralism and Hermeneutics*. Chicago: University of Chicago Press, 1982.

Drury, M. O'C. "Conversations with Wittgenstein." In *Ludwig Wittgenstein: Personal Recollections*. Edited by Rush Rhees. Oxford: Blackwell, 1981.

Durkeim, Emile. *The Division of Labor in Society*. Translated by W.D. Halls. New York: Free Press, 1984.

Eco, Umberto, *The Name of the Rose*. Translated by William Weaver. San Diego: Harcourt Brace Jovanovich, 1983.

Elster, Jon. *The Cement of Society: A Study of Social Order*. Cambridge: Cambridge University Press, 1995.

Engelhardt, Tristram. *The Foundations of Bioethics*. New York: Oxford University Press, 1986.

Farrell, Daniel. "Jealousy." *Philosophical Review* 89 (1980): 527–559.

Feinberg, Joel. "The Expressive Function of Punishment." In *Doing and Deserving: Essays in the Theory of Responsibility*. Princeton: Princeton University Press, 1970.

Fisher, M.F.K. *Stay Me, Oh Comfort Me*. New York: Pantheon, 1993.

Flanagan, Owen. "Admirable Immorality and Admirable Imperfection." *Journal of Philosophy* 83 (1986): 41–60.

_____. *Varieties of Moral Personality*. Cambridge, Mass.: Harvard University Press, 1991.

Flanagan, Owen, and Kathryn Jackson. "Justice, Care, and Gender: The Kohlberg-Gilligan Debate Revisited." *Ethics* 97 (1987): 622–637.

Fletcher, Joseph. *Situation Ethics*. Philadelphia: The Westminster Press, 1964.

Flew, Antony. "The Justification of Punishment." *Philosophy* 29 (1954): 291–307.

Forrester, Duncan B. *Christian Justice and Public Policy*. Cambridge: Cambridge University Press, 1997.

Forrester, John. *Truth Games: Lies, Money, and Psychoanalysis*. Cambridge, Mass.: Harvard University Press, 1977.

Foucault, Michel. *Discipline and Punish: The Birth of the Prison*. Translated by Alan Sheridan. New York: Vintage, 1995.

_____. *The Order of Things*. New York: Pantheon, 1970.

Frankena, William. *Ethics*. Englewood Cliffs, N.J.: Prentice-Hall, 1963.

Freud, Sigmund. *Civilization and Its Discontents* (Standard Edition). Translated by James Strachey. New York: W.W. Norton, 1961.

_____. *Jokes and Their Relation to the Unconscious* (Standard Edition). Translated by James Strachey. New York: W.W. Norton, 1989.

_____. *Group Psychology and the Analysis of the Ego*. (Standard Edition). Translated by James Strachey. London: Hogarth Press, 1959.

_____. *The Future of an Illusion* (Standard Edition). Translated by James Strachey. New York: W.W. Norton, 1961.

Gaon, Saadya. *The Book of Beliefs and Opinions*. Translated by Samuel Rosenblatt. New Haven: Yale University Press, 1948.

Garber, Marjorie. *Vested Interests*. New York: Routledge, 1992.

Garland, David. *Punishment and Society*. Oxford: Oxford University Press, 1990.

Gaut, Berys. "Just Joking: The Ethics and Aesthetics of Humor." *Philosophy and Literature* 22 (1998): 51–68.

Gay, Peter. *My German Question*. New Haven: Yale University Press, 1998.

Gilligan, Carol. *In a Different Voice: Psychological Theory and Women's Development*. Cambridge, Mass.: Harvard University Press, 1982.

_____. "Moral Orientation and Moral Development." In *Women and Moral Theory*, Eva Feder Kittay and Diana T. Meyers, eds. Totowa, N.J.: Rowman & Littlefield, 1987.

Goffman, Erving. *Frame Analysis*. New York: Harper and Row, 1974.

_____. "Fun in Games." In *Encounters*. Indianapolis: Bobbs-Merrill, 1961.

Goodwin, Barbara. *Justice By Lottery*. Chicago: University of Chicago Press, 1992.

Gordon, Robert. *The Structure of the Emotions*. Cambridge: Cambridge University Press, 1987.

Gosling, J.C.B. *Pleasure and Desire.* Oxford: Clarendon, 1969.

Hardy, Thomas. *The Return of the Native.* New York: Oxford University Press, 1990.

Hare, R.M. *Moral Thinking.* New York: Oxford University Press, 1981.

Häring, Bernard. *The Christian Existentialist: The Philosophy and Theology of Self-Fulfillment in Modern Society* (1966). Translated by Sister Lucidia Häring. New York: New York University Press, 1968.

_____. *Christian Renewal in a Changing World* (1961). Translated by Sister Lucidia Häring. New York: Desclee Company, 1964.

_____. *Free and Faithful in Christ: Moral Theology for Clergy and Laity.* New York: Seabury Press, 1978.

_____. *The Law of Christ.* Translated by Edwin G. Kaiser. Westminster: Newman Press, 1966.

Hobbes, Thomas. *Leviathan.* Edited by Richard Tuck. Cambridge: Cambridge University Press.

Hochschild, Arlie Russell. "Emotion Work, Feeling Rules, and Social Structure." *American Journal of Sociology* 85 (1979): 551–75.

Hume, David. *Treatise of Human Nature.* Edited by L.A. Selby-Bigge. Oxford: Clarendon Press, 1989.

Jackson, Timothy. "The Disconsolation of Theology." *Journal of Religious Ethics* 20 (1992): 1–35.

Jacoby, Susan. *Wild Justice: The Evolution of Revenge.* New York: Harper and Row, 1984.

Jaggar, Alison. "Love and Knowledge: Emotion in Feminist Epistemology." In *Gender/ Body/ Knowledge: Feminist Reconstruction of Being and Knowing.* Edited by S.R. Bordo and A. Jaggar. New Brunswick, N.J.: Rutgers University Press, 1989.

James, William. *The Principles of Psychology.* New York: Dover Publications, 1950.

_____. *The Varieties of Religious Experience.* New York: The Modern Library, 1958.

Jameson, Fredric. *The Political Unconscious.* Ithaca: Cornell University Press, 1980.

Jefferson, Mark. "What Is Wrong with Sentimentality?" *Mind* 92 (1983): 519–529.

Kafka, Franz. *Brief an den Vater.* Frankfurt: Fischer, 1992.

Kaminer, Wendy. *It's All the Rage: Crime and Culture.* New York: Addison-Wesley, 1995.

_____. "The Last Taboo." In *The New Republic,* 14 October 1996: 24–32.

Kant, Immanuel. *Critique of Practical Reason.* Translated by Lewis White Beck. Indianapolis: Bobbs-Merrill, 1956.

_____. *Lectures on Ethics.* Translated by Louis Infield. London: Methuen and Co., 1930.

_____. *The Metaphysics of Morals.* Translated by Mary Gregor. Cambridge: Cambridge University Press, 1996.

_____. *The Metaphysical Principles of Virtue.* Translated by James Ellington. Indianapolis: Bobbs-Merrill, 1964.

_____. *Observations on the Feeling of the Beautiful and the Sublime.* Translated by John T. Goldthwait. Berkeley: University of California Press, 1960.

Kaufmann, Walter. *Nietzsche: Philosopher, Psychologist, Antichrist.* Princeton: Princeton University Press, 1974.

_____. *The Portable Nietzsche.* New York: Vintage, 1968.

Kekes, John. *Against Liberalism.* Ithaca: Cornell University Press, 1997.

_____. *Facing Evil.* Princeton: Princeton University Press, 1990.

_____. *Moral Wisdom and Good Lives.* Ithaca: Cornell University Press, 1995.

Kendall, R.T. *Calvin and English Calvinism to 1649.* Oxford: Oxford University Press, 1979.

Kenny, Anthony. *Action, Emotion, and Will.* London: Routledge and Kegan Paul, 1963.

Kierkegaard, Soren. *Works of Love.* Translaged and edited by Howard V. Hong and Edna H. Hong. Princeton: Princeton University Press, 1995.

Klein, Melanie. "Envy and Gratitude." In *"Envy and Gratitude" and Other Works,* vol. 3. of *The Writings of Melanie Klein.* Edited by R.E. Money-Kyrle. New York: Free Press, 1975.

Kushner, Harold. *When Bad Things Happen to Good People.* New York: Schocken Books, 1981.

La Rochefoucauld. *Maximes et réflexions diverses.* Edited by Jacques Truchet. Paris: Flammarion, 1977.

Leavitt, David. "The Term Paper Artist." In *Arkansas: Three Novellas.* New York: Houghton Mifflin, 1997.

Lerner, Melvin. *The Belief in a Just World: A Fundamental Delusion.* New York: Plenum, 1980.

Levi, Primo. *The Drowned and the Saved.* Translated by Raymond Rosenthal. New York: Summit, 1988.

Lewis, Bernard. *Islam and the West.* New York: Oxford University Press, 1993.

Lodge, David. *Paradise News.* New York: Viking, 1992.

Lucretius. *De Rerum Natura.* Translated by Rolfe Humphries. Bloomington: Indiana University Press, 1969.

Lyons, William. *Emotions.* New York: Cambridge University Press, 1980.

MacIntyre, Alasdair. *A Short History of Ethics.* London: Routledge and Kegan Paul, 1968.

_____. *Three Rival Versions of Moral Inquiry.* South Bend: University of Notre Dame Press, 1990.

Magee, Bryan. *The Philosophy of Schopenhauer.* Oxford: Clarendon Press, 1983.

Mahoney, John, S.J. *The Making of Moral Theology: A Study of the Roman Catholic Tradition.* Oxford: Clarendon Press, 1987.

Maimonides, Moses. *The Guide of the Perplexed.* Translated by Shlomo Pines. Chicago: University of Chicago Press, 1963.

Malcolm, Norman. *Wittgenstein: A Religious Point of View?* Ithaca: Cornell University Press, 1994.

Margolis, Joseph, and Tom Rockmore, editors. *Heidegger and Nazism.* Philadelphia: Temple University Press, 1989.

Marx, Karl. *Early Writings.* Translated and edited by Rodney Livingstone and Gregor Benton. New York: Vintage, 1975.

McBrien, Richard. *Catholicism: Study Edition.* Minneapolis: Winston Press, 1981.

McDonald, William J., et al. *New Catholic Encyclopedia.* New York: McGraw Hill, 1967.

McFall, Lynne. "What's Wrong with Bitterness?" In *Feminist Ethics.* Edited by Claudia Card. Lawrence: University Press of Kansas, 1991.

McGinn, Colin. *Ethics, Evil, and Fiction.* Oxford: Clarendon Press, 1997.

Mecca, Andrew M., Neil J. Smelser, and John Vasconcellos. *The Social Importance of Self-Esteem.* Berkeley: University of California Press, 1989.

Meltzer, Françoise and David Tracy. "Introduction to the Symposium on 'God.'" *Critical Inquiry* 20 (1994): 569–571.

Melville, Herman. "Billy Budd, Sailor." In *Billy Budd, Sailor & Other Stories.* New York: Penguin, 1983.

Mesquita, Batja, and Nico H. Frijda, "Cultural Variations in Emotions: A Review." *Psychological Bulletin* 112 (1992): 170–204.

Midgley, Mary. "Sentimentality and Brutality." *Philosophy* 54 (1979): 385–389.

Miles, Jack. *God: A Biography*. New York: Knopf, 1995.

Miller, William Ian. *The Anatomy of Disgust*. Cambridge, Mass.: Harvard University Press, 1997.

_____. *Humiliation*. Ithaca: Cornell University Press, 1993.

Montaigne, Michel de. *The Complete Essays of Montaigne*. Translated by Donald M. Frame. Stanford: Stanford University Press, 1958.

Moore, Michael. "The Moral Worth of Retribution." In *Responsibility, Character, and the Emotions*. Edited by Ferdinand Schoeman. Cambridge: Cambridge University Press, 1987.

Morris, David. *The Culture of Pain*. Berkeley: University of California Press, 1991.

Morrison, Toni. *Beloved*. New York: Knopf, 1987.

Murdoch, Iris. *The Black Prince*. New York: Penguin, 1973.

Nagel, Thomas. "Moral Luck." In *Mortal Questions*. Cambridge: Cambridge University Press, 1979.

Nehamas, Alexander. *The Art of Living: Socratic Reflections from Plato to Foucault*. Berkeley: University of California Press, 1997.

_____. *Nietzsche: Life as Literature*. Cambridge, Mass.: Harvard University Press, 1985.

Neu, Jerome. "Jealous Thoughts." In *Explaining Emotions*. Edited by Amélie O. Rorty. Berkeley: University of California Press, 1980.

Niebuhr, H. Richard. *The Purpose of the Church and Its Ministry*. New York: Harper, 1956.

_____. *The Responsible Self*. New York: Harper and Row, 1963.

Nietzsche, Friedrich. *Beyond Good and Evil*. Translated by Walter Kaufmann. New York: Vintage, 1966.

_____. *Ecce Homo*. Translated by Walter Kaufmann. New York: Vintage, 1989.

_____. *The Gay Science*. Translated by Walter Kaufmann. New York: Vintage, 1974.

_____. *Human, All Too Human*. Translated by R.J. Hollingdale. Cambridge: Cambridge University Press, 1986.

_____. *On the Genealogy of Morals*. Translated by Francis Golffing. New York: Doubleday, 1956.

_____. *On the Genealogy of Morals*. Translated by Walter Kaufmann and R.J. Hollindale. New York: Vintage, 1989.

_____. *Thus Spake Zarathustra*. Translated by Walter Kaufmann. New York: Vintage, 1968.

_____. *Twilight of the Idols/Anti-Christ*. Translated by R.J. Hollingdale. New York: Penguin, 1990.

_____. *The Will to Power*. Translated by Walter Kaufmann and R.J. Hollindale. New York: Vintage, 1968.

Novak, David. *Jewish Social Ethics*. New York: Oxford University Press, 1992.

Novak, Michael. *The Catholic Ethic and the Spirit of Capitalism*. New York: Free Press, 1993.

Nozick, Robert. *Anarchy, State, and Utopia*. New York: Basic Books, 1974.

Nuland, Sherwin. *How We Die*. New York: Vintage, 1995.

Oakley, Justin. *Morality and the Emotions*. London: Routledge, 1993.

Oldenquist, Andrew. "An Explanation of Retribution." *Journal of Philosophy* 85 (1988): 464–478

O'Neill, Eugene. *Long Day's Journey Into Night*. New Haven: Yale University Press, 1989.

Paglia, Camille. "Junk Bonds and Corporate Raiders." In *Sex, Art, and American Culture*. New York: Vintage, 1992.

Pascal, Blaise. *Pensées*. Edited by Francis Kaplan. Paris: Editions du Cerf, 1982.

Phillips, Adam. *On Flirtation: Psychoanalytic Essays on Uncommitted Life*. Cambridge, Mass.: Harvard University Press, 1994.

Pindar. *The Odes of Pindar*. Translated by Richard Lattimore. Chicago: University of Chicago Press, 1976.

Plato. *The Collected Dialogues of Plato*. Edited by Edith Hamilton and Huntingdon Cairns. Princeton: Princeton University Press, 1980.

Posner, Richard. *Overcoming Law*. Cambridge, Mass.: Harvard University Press, 1995.

Proust, Marcel. *Rememberance of Things Past*. Translated by C.K. Scott Moncrieff and Terence Kilmartin. New York: Vintage, 1982.

Rawls, John. "Justice as Fairness: Political Not Metaphysical." *Philosophy and Public Affairs* 14 (1985): 308–322.

_____. *A Theory of Justice*. Cambridge, Mass.: Harvard University Press, 1971.

Rescher, Nicholas. *Unselfishness: The Role of the Vicarious Affects in Moral Philosophy and Social Theory*. Pittsburgh: University of Pittsburgh Press, 1975.

Roberts, Robert C. "Emotions Among the Virtues in the Christian Life." *The Journal of Religious Ethics* 20 (1992): 37–68.

_____. "What Is Wrong with Wicked Feelings?" *American Philosophical Quarterly* 28 (1991): 13–24.

Röhrich, Lutz. *Der Witz: Figuren, Formen, Funktionen.* Stuttgart: J.B. Metzler, 1977.

Rorty, Amélie. "Explaining Emotions." In *Explaining Emotions.* Edited by Amélie Rorty. Berkeley: University of California Press, 1980.

Rorty, Richard. *Contingency, Irony, and Solidarity.* Cambridge: Cambridge University Press, 1989.

Ross, W.D. *The Right and the Good.* Oxford: Clarendon Press, 1930.

Russell, Jeffrey Burton. *A History of Heaven: The Singing Silence.* Princeton: Princeton University Press, 1997.

Sackwille-West, Vita. *The Letters of Vita Sackville-West to Virginia Woolf.* Edited by Louise DeSalva and Mitchell Leaska. London: Hutchinson, 1984.

Sandel, Michael. *Liberalism and the Limits of Justice.* Cambridge: Cambridge University Press, 1982.

Sankowski, Edward. "Responsibility of Persons for Their Emotions." *Canadian Journal of Philosophy* 7 (1977): 829–840.

Sartre, Jean-Paul. *Psychology of Imagination.* New York: Washington Square Press, 1966.

Scarry, Elaine. *The Body in Pain.* Oxford: Oxford University Press, 1985.

Schama, Simon. *Citizens: A Chronicle of the French Revolution.* New York: Knopf, 1989.

Scheler, Max. *The Nature of Sympathy.* Translated by P.L. Heath. London: Routledge and Kegan Paul, 1954.

_____. *Ressentiment.* Translated by Lewis B. Coser and William W. Holdheim. Milwaukee: Marquette University Press, 1994.

Scherer, Klaus, Harold Wallbott, and Angela Summerfield, eds. *Experiencing Emotions: A Cross-Cultural Study.* Cambridge: Cambridge University Press, 1986.

Scherer, K.R, H.G. Wallbott, D. Matsumoto, and T. Kudoh. "Emotional Experience in Cultural Context: A Comparison Between Europe, Japan, and the United States." In *Facets of the Emotions.* Edited by K.R. Scherer. Hillsdale: Erlbaum, 1988.

Schlink, Bernhard. *The Reader.* Translated by Carol Brown Janeway. New York: Vintage, 1998.

Schoeck, Helmut. *Envy: A Theory of Social Behaviour.* Translated by Michael Glenny and Betty Ross. New York: Harcourt, Brace and World, 1966.

Schopenhauer, Arthur. *On the Basis of Morality*. Translated by E.F.J. Payne. Indianapolis: Bobbs-Merrill, 1965.

_____. "On Women." *Parerga and Paralipomena*. Translated by E.F.J. Payne. Oxford: Clarendon Press, 1974.

_____. *The World As Will and Representation*. Translated by E.F.J. Payne. New York: Dover, 1969.

Scruton, Roger. "Laughter." In *The Philosophy of Laughter and Humor*. Edited by John Morreall. Albany: State University of New York Press, 1987.

Sher, George. *Desert*. Princeton: Princeton University Press, 1987.

Shklar, Judith. *The Faces of Injustice*. New Haven: Yale University Press, 1990.

_____. "The Liberalism of Fear." In *Liberalism and the Moral Life*. Edited by Nancy Rosenblum. Cambridge, Mass.: Harvard University Press, 1989.

_____. *Ordinary Vices*. Cambridge, Mass.: Harvard University Press, 1984.

Smith, Adam. *The Theory of Moral Sentiments*. Edited by D.D. Raphael and A.L. Macfie. Oxford: Clarendon Press, 1976.

Smith, Barbara Herrnstein. "Belief and Resistance: A Symmetrical Account." *Critical Inquiry* 18 (1991): 125–139.

Solomon, Robert C., and Cheshire Calhoun, editors. *What is an Emotion?* Oxford: Oxford University Press, 1984.

Sommers, Christina Hoff. *Vice and Virtue in Everyday Life*. New York: Harcourt, Brace, Jovanovich, 1985.

Sontag, Susan. "Notes on Camp." *Against Interpretation*. New York: Doubleday, 1990.

Sophocles. *Oedipus Rex*. Translated by David Grene. Chicago: University of Chicago Press, 1954.

Spinoza, Benedict de. *Ethics*. Translated by R.H.M. Elwes. New York: Dover, 1955.

_____. *The Philosophy of Spinoza*. Edited by Joseph Ratner. New York: The Modern Library, 1927.

Spierenburg, Pieter. *The Spectacle of Suffering: Executions and the Evolution of Repression*. Cambridge: Cambridge University Press, 1984.

Spitzer, Leo. "Schadenfreude." In *Essays in Historical Semantics*. New York: S.F. Vanni, 1948.

Stachniewski, John. *The Persecutory Imagination: English Puritanism and the Language of Religious Despair*. Oxford: Clarendon Press, 1991.

Stauth, George, and Bryan S. Turner. *Nietzsche's Dance: Resentment, Reciprocity and Resistance in Social Life*. Oxford: Basil Blackwell, 1988.

Stocker, Michael. "The Schizophrenia of Modern Ethical Theories." In *Journal of Philosophy* 73 (1976): 453–466.

_____. *Valuing Emotions.* Cambridge: Cambridge University Press, 1996.

Strawson, Sir Peter. "Freedom and Resentment." In *Freedom and Resentment.* London: Methuen, 1974.

Ten, C.L. *Crime, Guilt and Punishment: A Philosophical Introduction.* Oxford: Clarendon Press, 1987.

Thalberg, Irving. *Perception, Emotion, and Action.* New Haven: Yale University Press, 1977.

Tournier, Paul. *Guilt and Grace: A Psychological Study.* Translated by Arthur W. Heathcote. New York: Harper and Row, 1962.

Trench, Richard C. *The Study of Words.* New York: Macmillan, 1906.

Trigg, Robert. *Pain and Emotion.* Oxford: Clarendon Press, 1970.

Trilling, Lionel. *The Liberal Imagination: Essays on Literature and Society.* New York: Harcourt Brace Jovanovich, 1979.

Tunick, Mark. *Punishment: Theory and Practice.* Berkeley: University of California Press, 1992.

Vaillant, George. *The Wisdom of the Ego.* Cambridge, Mass.: Harvard University Press, 1993.

Wallace, R. Jay. *Responsibility and the Moral Sentiments.* Cambridge, Mass.: Harvard University Press, 1994.

Wallwork, Ernest. *Psychoanalysis and Ethics.* New Haven: Yale University Press, 1991.

Weber, Max. *The Sociology of Religion.* Translated by Ephraim Fischoff. Boston: Beacon Press, 1968.

Weisse, Christian. *Die Schadenfreude: ein Kleines Lustspiel für Kinder mit Liederchen.* Stuttgart: Reclam, 1900.

Williams, Bernard. *Ethics and the Limits of Philosophy.* Cambridge, Mass.: Harvard University Press, 1985.

_____. "Morality and the Emotions." In *Problems of the Self.* Cambridge: Cambridge University Press, 1974.

_____. "Moral Luck." In *Moral Luck: Philosophical Papers 1973–1980.* New York: Cambridge University Press, 1981.

_____. "Persons, Character, and Morality." In *Moral Luck.* Cambridge: Cambridge University Press, 1981.

_____. *Ethics and the Limits of Philosophy.* Cambridge, Mass.: Harvard University Press, 1985.

Wittgenstein, Ludwig. *Philosophical Investigations.* Translated by G.E.M. Anscombe. Oxford: Basil Blackwell, 1953.

Young, Julian. *Nietzsche's Philosophy of Art*. Cambridge: Cambridge University Press, 1992.

Young-Bruehl, Elisabeth. *The Anatomy of Prejudices*. Cambridge, Mass.: Harvard University Press, 1996.

Zbrowski, Mark. "Cultural Components in Responses to Pain." in *Social Interaction*. Edited by C. Clark and H. Robboy. New York: St. Martin's Press, 1992.

Index

DEMCO